VOICE
FROM THE
HILLS

PHILIP GREENSLADE

VOICE FROM THE HILLS

Costly grace | Crucial words

Sermon on the Mount | Words from the Cross

CWR

Published 2008 by CWR, Waverley Abbey House, Waverley Lane, Farnham, Surrey GU9 8EP, UK. Registered Charity No. 294387. Registered Limited Company No. 1990308.

See back of book for list of National Distributors.

Concept development, editing, design and production by CWR
Cover image: istockphoto.com/Celso Pupo Rodrigues
Printed in Finland by WS Bookwell
ISBN: 978-1-85345-469-1

CONTENTS

PREFACE

'Costly grace', the phrase used in the subtitle of this book, has been employed as Dietrich Bonhoeffer famously used it over seventy years ago. Writing in the shadow of the Nazis, Bonhoeffer protested against what he called 'cheap grace', and which he defined as 'grace without discipleship, grace without the cross, grace without the living, incarnate Jesus Christ'.

'Costly grace', by contrast, said Bonhoeffer, is 'the treasure in the field, for the sake of which people go and sell with joy everything they have'. This in no way suggests a legalistic attempt to earn salvation by one's own self-sacrifice. Quite the reverse. Rather, 'costly grace is the gospel which must be sought again and again, the gift which has to be asked for ...' So, maintains Bonhoeffer, 'it is costly because it calls to discipleship; it is grace, because it calls us to follow Jesus Christ ... Above all, grace is costly because it was costly to God, because it cost God the life of God's Son – and because nothing can be cheap to us which is costly to God.'[1]

The life of discipleship, then, is vitally connected to the dying of Jesus on the cross. This is the specific burden of my book.

Classic, conservative Evangelicalism, of which I am a product, clings to the 'old rugged cross' with a fierce attachment to substitutionary atonement. It seems less sure of its grasp on the teaching of Jesus with its radical demands.

Conversely, contemporary Evangelicalism seems more willing to get to grips with the radical Jesus of the Gospels while, at the same time, wanting to unravel the historic doctrines of cross.

But discipleship and cross go together.

It takes nothing less than the cross of God's Son to implement in us the Sermon on the Mount. The cost of discipleship (to us) reflects, however dimly, the cost of salvation (to God) paid at the cross. Discipleship and cross are inextricably connected, and what God has joined together let no one – Evangelical or otherwise – put asunder.

My thanks go as usual to all at CWR – especially Lynette Brooks, Mike Ashford, and Matt Taylor for commissioning and encouraging this book – and to those Bible Discoverers whose eagerness to hear the Word make my Bible Discovery Weekends at Waverley Abbey House so demanding and so enjoyable. I am particularly grateful to Greg Haslam, who by his appreciation for my work encourages me to believe that what goes on at the 'supply depot' is of use to those, like him, on the front line.

My friends Trevor Martin and Stuart Reid have again been staunch allies in the task of being human – an enterprise which both are rather good at. If a 'senior moment' is to ask an attractive woman at a party, 'Do I come here often?', then maturity is to have truthful friends around who will help you hilariously find out.

Above all, my wife Mary is God's gift to me for which I am continually thankful. She cheerfully and lovingly stays with me on the journey, even though I am a practising Christian – 'practising', that is, in the sense of repeatedly trying to get the hang of being a follower of Jesus.

Without claiming any special merit for this book, it is unusual, I believe, to combine a study of the Sermon on the Mount and one on the 'Words from the Cross', Jesus' cries from another hill. If this combination is in any way distinctive, I hope it serves my purpose as an urgent call to established and emerging Evangelicals both to hear and to practise the still largely untried and radical teaching of Jesus *and* – at the same time – to hold fast to the tried-and-tested and still radical theology of the cross. I myself need to do these two things at one and the same time. I need to hear the message of costly grace, to live *into* it, to live *up to* it, to live *out of* it. To that end, I invite you to listen with me once again to the utterly distinctive 'voice from the hills'.

Philip Greenslade
January 2008

CHECKPOINT
MOUNTAIN OF TESTING

checkpoint – scrutiny at frontier or border crossing to give proof of identity.

dictionary definition

Again, the devil took him to a very high mountain ...

Matthew 4:8

What price would you pay for the ultimate prize?

'Who would not sell his soul to the devil,' reflects sports journalist Simon Barnes, 'if only the prize was big enough? If the prize was, say, to be the fastest man in the world?' Barnes notes that of the past five Olympic 100 metre champions – from Ben Johnson to Warren Gatlin – three have been convicted of taking performance-enhancing drugs. This goes, too, for sprinters currently holding the women's world record. Did they regard the prize as worth the price they paid, ponders Barnes? Perhaps, even now in disgrace, Johnson thinks so. 'He knew, at least for a day, what it is to be king ... The devil came to collect his side of the deal and did so without compunction.' But perhaps, it was worth it to be 'the greatest of them all, the king of the world, the conqueror of conquerors ...'[1]

Why do they do it? Does the momentary fame of winning a race

1

and of standing on a podium three feet above mere mortals outweigh the ignominy and opprobrium of losing your name and foregoing a destiny?

At every level of human ambition, it is tempting to sell your soul to gain the whole world. But it was a temptation when presented in its ultimate guise – to be the king of the world – that Jesus firmly and decisively rejected. Why did He do so?

Jesus' confrontation with personified evil (Matt. 4:1–11) centres on the way in which God's appointed King should rule. Not by exploiting His power for selfish ends and turning stones into bread to feed Himself. Not by an act of self-promoting bravado in flinging Himself off the pinnacle of the Temple to prove His godliness. As Samuel Chadwick once said, 'No one honours God who flings himself off the pinnacle of the Temple when there are stairs.'

As the pressure reaches its climax, there is 'mounting tension'.[2] Having started at ground level, as it were – with stones at His feet – and having taken Him to the roof of the Temple – observable on the horizon – the temptation now lifts Jesus to an unimaginable vantage point – on the 'roof of the world'.

At every point Jesus rejects the temptation. Why? The primary answer is that Jesus is a *representative figure* who has come to succeed in faithful partnership with God where Israel and her kings have so conspicuously failed. This was why Jesus underwent a 'baptism for sinners' when by all accounts He was not one, for this further showed the extent to which He was identifying with Israel. Jesus did this both positively, in embracing Israel's vocation, and negatively, by being 'numbered with transgressors'. By such a baptism He intended to 'fulfil all righteousness' (Matt. 3:15), both in pursuing His own destiny and in demonstrating the covenant faithfulness of God acting to save, vindicate and restore Israel. This was what was being put to the test in the Judean wilderness.

Like David, as Israel's champion confronting Goliath, the newly anointed 'King in Waiting' strides out to meet the evil challenger to God's rule. His forty-day test re-enacts, as it were, the temptations Israel faced and failed to resist during forty years in the wilderness and thereafter in the Land. The three Deuteronomic references serve to confirm this. The contrast, however, is stark, for, as Ben Meyer puts it, 'whereas ancient Israel had collapsed under the test in the wilderness, the Israel of God of the last days, Jesus himself, emerged victorious from it'.[3]

Jesus has arrived at the frontier of His ministry, at the checkpoint between two worlds where He has to give proof of identity.

Here, Jesus is tested as 'the Son of God' (v.6). This may be a faint echo of the privileged calling of Adam himself. Luke implies as much by inserting the genealogy of Jesus between the Baptism and Temptations and tracing Jesus' roots back to 'Adam, the son of God' (Luke 3:38). As for Matthew, he seems primarily concerned to link Jesus with the covenantal sonship both of Israel's king (2 Sam. 7:14; Psa. 2:7) and of Israel herself, whom the king represented (Exod. 4:22–23; Hosea 11:1). Deuteronomy significantly describes the wilderness period as a 'test' for Israel, for Moses says, 'as a man disciplines his son, so the LORD your God disciplines you' (Deut. 8:5).

The first challenge Jesus faces is to pre-empt God's provision by turning stones into bread to meet His own needs. Like Israel before Him, Jesus is tempted to the sin of *unbelief*; tempted, that is, to live other than by faith in God's word of covenant promise.

Re-affirming Israel's covenant charter, Jesus replies with a quotation from Deuteronomy to the effect that 'Man does not live on bread alone, but on every word that comes from the mouth of God' (Matt. 4:4; Deut. 8:3).

Secondly, Jesus is urged to throw Himself from the pinnacle of the Temple while 'naming and claiming' Psalm 91 as His protection. Jesus resists what He sees as *presumption*, as putting God to the test, by again citing the Deuteronomy command: 'Do not put the Lord your God to the test' (Matt. 4:5–6; Deut. 6:16).

The climactic temptation comes when Jesus is invited to a 'very high mountain' and offered the kingdoms on condition that He bows down and worships Satan. Jesus, already reassured by Psalm 2, well knows from the same psalm that He only has to ask the Father for the nations as His inheritance. Thus emboldened, He repudiates the idea of *idolatry*, insisting, again in words from Deuteronomy: 'Worship the Lord your God, and serve him only' (Matt. 4:10; Deut. 6:13).

The thrust of the temptations is clear: *If* you are the true Israel, God's 'Son', *if* You are her representative King, God's 'Son', then go the way of Israel and her kings before You. But Jesus – 'savingly' – refuses to go that way. Unbelief, presumption, idolatry – these are the sins Israel continued to be bedevilled by throughout her life in the Land. But Jesus says, in effect, that where Israel had failed to rise to the covenant challenge and abide by the Deuteronomic vision, He will. 'On the shoulders of Jesus as the Son of God,' says Chris Wright, 'lay the responsibility of being the true son, succeeding where Israel had failed, submitting to God's will where they had rebelled, obeying where they had disobeyed.'[4]

The kingdoms of this world *are* destined for Israel's appointed king in Zion (Psa. 2:8; 72:8–11,19), but by divine donation not demonically-driven conquest. They will come to Him *in God's time and in God's way.* 'You shall have no other gods before me' translates into 'you shall have no other *goals* before me.'

Fortified by His moral victory in the desert, and with His course set, Jesus climbs a hill to announce the manifesto of that kingdom.

PART ONE

Costly Grace from
the Sermon on the Mount
Matthew 5–7

INTRODUCTION
AND OUTLINE

... when he [Jesus] saw the crowds, he went up on a mountainside ...
Matthew 5:1

The Sermon on the Mount is among the most familiar parts of Scripture and yet is often the most misunderstood and least practised. I profess to finding it a tough call, not merely because it stretches the mind – which assuredly it does – but because the more I do understand it the more challenging it becomes.

We call it 'the *Sermon* on the Mount' but it reads more like the revolutionary manifesto of a radical political party than a typical pastoral homily. We place it on 'the *Mount*' but we are not talking about the Himalayas here, and, in any event, Luke sets the sermon on the *plain*!

What are we to make of this?

Firstly, as to the 'mountain', Matthew is almost certainly using the term in a *typological sense* (as I am doing throughout this book) to highlight the theological significance of what is being said and done. In any case, Luke may not be contradicting Matthew, since a plateau among the Judean hills could well serve as a level place on the mount from which to address a gathered crowd.

Typology draws meaning from the correspondence between what are regarded as historical events. With this in mind, the phrase 'he went up on a mountainside' resonates with Old Testament significance. It echoes the giving of the Law at Mount Sinai and suggests Jesus is being portrayed by Matthew – at least in part – as a 'new Moses'.

7

The mountain imagery continues to be important to Matthew. As we shall see, it is on a 'high mountain' (Matt. 17:1) that Jesus is transfigured in glory, where He is joined by Moses and Elijah and where the voice from heaven directs us to 'Listen to him!', the Father's beloved Son, who encapsulates all that God has to say to us.

Perhaps there are also overtones in Matthew's narrative of Jesus being not only a new Moses but a new David, installed in the seat of authority on Mount Zion.

At His baptism, the Father in heaven says of Jesus, 'This is my Son, whom I love; with him I am well pleased' (Matt. 3:17). This declaration is a conflation of Psalm 2:6–8 and Isaiah 42:1. Psalm 2 is a coronation song for God's king installed on Mount Zion, who is designated God's 'son' (v.7) and who is promised all the nations of the earth as his inheritance and the ends of the earth as his possession. Isaiah 42:1 opens the first of the so-called Servant Songs, so that its use here alongside Psalm 2 means that we are being told unequivocally that *Jesus is the Servant King*.

It is this right to rule the world that, as we have noted, is put to the test in the third temptation, when the devil takes Jesus to a 'very high mountain' (Matt. 4:8) and offers Him all the kingdoms of the world at the price of worshipping him and thus avoiding the cross – an offer Jesus refuses.

Mountains, then, are symbolically significant; associated with revelation, covenant beginning, transcendent glory and royal authority.

As we shall also see, it is from the 'mountain where Jesus told them to go' (Matt. 28:16) that God's new Moses and new Davidic King issues His messianic commission. It is this message from the mountains – or, more modestly, this *voice from the hills* – that commands our attention.

Secondly, as to the *'sermon'* – what Matthew offers us is a summary of the teaching of Jesus on the impact and implications of the kingly rule of God experienced through Him.

The 'Sermon on the Mount' is the first of five blocks of teaching in Matthew which the evangelist has arranged perhaps to echo the five books of Moses which constitute the Law, each section of which ends with '... and when Jesus had finished ...':

- Chapters 5–7: kingdom discipleship
- Chapter 10: mission-orientated discipleship

- Chapter 13: subversive discipleship
- Chapter 18: community-shaped discipleship
- Chapters 23–25: expectant discipleship (including another 'Sermon on the Mount', 24:3)

The Sermon on the Mount has had a chequered history in Christian thinking. It has been treated in a number of ways:

- As outlining the entrance requirements for the kingdom of God. However, this produces only legalism and moralism, and seems quite out of line with Jesus' whole ministry.
- As deliberately too demanding – the classic Lutheran position – and meant to drive us to despair and then into grace. There is grain of truth in this, as we shall see, but it is surely altogether more positive than this.
- As an impossible ideal and not to be taken seriously. Even the Evangelical tradition – while never saying this – has come close to ignoring Jesus' plain words, preferring Paul instead. But the sermon is not idealism. As E. Stanley Jones puts it, 'Instead of it being an imposed idealism it is stark realism.'[1]
- As ethics for the elite – as in medieval Catholicism – as if it could be applied only to monks, nuns and other exceptionally pious people.
- As an ethic for any time but now! The sermon is then construed as either (a) an interim ethic for the first century – the assumption being that Jesus was expected to return within their lifetime – or as (b) applying only to the future millennial kingdom, though modern dispensationalism, which espouses this view (while correctly highlighting the future orientation of the rewards and inheritance aspects), has difficulty accommodating the persecution, evil and trouble confronted in the sermon.

None of the above options is satisfactory.

Granted the future references (as in 5:5,8,12), the sermon is nonetheless clearly intended to be lived out not in a future paradise or an ideal trouble-free realm, but in the real world where we need bread and face enemies. We may not be able to treat every facet of the sermon literalistically – as perhaps the Anabaptist tradition does – but we need to take it as practical and possible for the here and now – as the Anabaptist tradition has taught us.

Craig Keener surveys thirty-six ways of interpreting the sermon, reduces them to eight, and then suggests that the emergence of so many interpretations perhaps reflects a persistent desire to evade its plain truth! In order not to mitigate the challenge of the sermon, Keener argues, 'modern interpreters must let Jesus' radical demands confront us with all the unnerving ferocity with which they would have struck their first hearers'.[2]

As the American humorist, Garrison Keillor, quipped of believers, 'When will you stop being good Christians and start following Jesus!'

Two guidelines may be established which should be borne in mind as you study the sermon.

Firstly, *beware of idealism*. Idealism treats these words as hopelessly naïve and impractical, fit only for a fantasy world. But the teaching of Jesus is as down to earth as the mountain He was standing on to speak this sermon. If you are at any time tempted to treat it as *too idealistic* then you may be sure you have lost touch with the gospel, with the good news of the life-changing empowerment of God's kingdom.

Secondly, and equally, *beware of moralism*, which thinks that conforming behaviour to some outward rule constitutes holiness, which majors on minor issues (eg Matt. 23:23) and which, like its ally legalism, prefers short-term adherence to a list of dos and don'ts than to the long-term task of character formation. Moralism looks hard but is actually a soft option which baulks at the rebirth necessary to bring renovation of the heart, renewal of the mind and restoration to the soul. If, at any time, you are inclined to hear the sermon as *too moralistic*, then it is likely that once again you have severed the connection with the grace which comes with the invasion of God's kingly rule and which Matthew presupposes throughout.

It is to this theme of *the in-breaking kingdom of God* that we must turn if we are to understand the Sermon on the Mount correctly. We must link the sermon with what goes before – particularly as described in Matthew 4:13–25.

God's kingdom, in its final fullness and in its ultimate judgments, is indeed a future reality (Matt. 7:21). But, equally emphatically, the kingdom is present in its power and life-giving grace (Matt. 5:3,10; 6:33).

So, in E. Stanley Jones's words, 'as we approach the Sermon it is not with a bludgeon hanging over our heads but with a beckoning, a divine beckoning, an offer to us to partake in the most wonderful life imaginable, beyond our fondest dreams'.[3]

The most important point to grasp at the outset is this: *The Sermon on the Mount is an expansion of Jesus' essential preaching of the gospel – 'Repent, for the kingdom of heaven is near' (Matt. 4:17) – and the response it evokes (4:23–25). The sermon describes the kind of life to be lived by those participating in the reign of God.*

We can see this more clearly by noting *to whom the sermon is addressed*. It is addressed to *the disciples* (Matt. 5:1c) but with an eye to *the crowds* ('When he saw the crowds …' (cf. Matt. 9:36) – all of whom have been impacted by the preaching of the kingdom and have made some response to it. The crowds, *including the religious leaders,* overhear, as it were, the message to the disciples so that the message contains an implicit invitation to join them. Hence the crowds, having overheard all that is given to and expected of disciples, are astonished not least by the authority of Jesus (Matt. 7:28–29).

So, *the sermon must be taken totally seriously as describing the life of discipleship that God is now creating among the followers of Jesus as they embrace God's kingdom rule and blessing.* In Matthew 5–7, Jesus is describing what happens when His gospel of the in-breaking and saving rule of God grabs hold of individuals and a community. In this 'sermon', Jesus is describing kingdom people, 'gospelised humanity', to use Darrell Johnson's telling phrase. Every line expresses a radical discipleship which lives out the reality of the kingdom of God in an invariably hostile world. The Sermon on the Mount establishes the whole of Matthew's Gospel as a 'manual of discipleship'.

Even more important, of course, than the question, 'Who is being addressed?' is the question of *'Who is speaking?'* How has Matthew introduced Him at this point? Jesus is the One whom Matthew presents as the climax of the long covenantal history of Israel, whose origins are in Abraham's call and commission.

Jesus is the Saviour of Israel, Emmanuel – 'God with us', the Lord acclaimed by heaven's praise and acknowledged by the best that Eastern wisdom has to offer.

Jesus is the One who has pledged His life to 'fulfil all righteousness'–

both negatively by immersing Himself in the task of saving sinners and positively by proving to be God's faithful covenant partner – this committed Jesus defies demonic temptation and is confirmed as God's true Son and messianic King. In Charles Talbert's sober assessment: 'When Matthew's auditors heard that Jesus fulfilled all righteousness before he spoke to his disciples about seeking a righteousness that surpassed other models, they would have inferred the legitimacy of Jesus' teaching and would have accorded the authority due a true teacher.'[4]

It is this Jesus whom Matthew shows us standing on a hillside and giving us 'Part One' of His 'manual of discipleship' with the '… authority and attractiveness to gather disciples'.[5]

OUTLINE OF THE SERMON ON THE MOUNT (MATT. 5–7)

1. Surprising reversals – Beatitude people

5:2–16   The kingdom character of disciples, spelt out in eight third-person beatitudes and one second-person beatitude.
(vv.13–16 The kingdom community as 'salt' and 'light'.)

2. Surpassing righteousness – the Law fulfilled

5:17–20   The sermon's relation to the Old Testament as interpreted and fulfilled by Jesus: 'Do not think that I have come to abolish the Law or the Prophets; I have not come to abolish them but to fulfil them' (cf. inclusio with 7:12).

5:21–48   The 'surpassing righteousness' as the deepening and intensifying of the Law, illustrated by six 'antitheses' or 'fulfillers' – '… but I tell you …':
  • anger (5:21–26)
  • lust (5:27–30)
  • divorce (5:31–32)
  • oaths (5:33–37)
  • retaliation (5:38–42)
  • loving enemies (5:43–48)

3. Surpassing righteousness – spiritual disciplines

6:1–18   The 'surpassing righteousness' in the spiritual disciplines, or practices of piety, the first two being:
- giving (6:1–4)
- prayer (6:5–8)

4. The Lord's Prayer – the heart of the sermon

6:9–15   The Lord's Prayer – the heart of the sermon
And the third spiritual discipline:
- fasting (6:16–18)

5. Surpassing righteousness – priorities and necessities

6:19–24   The surpassing righteousness in trusting the Father of the kingdom: getting *priorities* right and trusting for *necessities*:
- treasure: two investments? (6:19–21)
- vision: two eyes? (6:22–23)
- serving: two masters? (6:24)

6:25–34   Therefore … 'do not be anxious':
- take lessons from the logic of creation (6:26–30)
- take note of the lifestyle of the pagans (6:32)
- take heart from the love of the Father (6:32)
- take life a day at a time (6:34)
- above all … revalue your investment, refocus your vision, renew your allegiance (6:33)

6. Surpassing righteousness – relationships

7:1–12   The surpassing righteousness in relationships – a dynamic balance:
- *against* 'judging' in the sense of condemning others by one who has not judged him/herself (7:1–5)
- *for* 'judging' in the sense of moral and spiritual discernment by one who asks God for wisdom and applies the 'Golden Rule' (7:6–12)

7. The call for commitment

7:13–29   Call for commitment

- two gates/ways – fatal for many, life-giving for few (7:13–14)
- two trees: bad fruit from false prophets, good fruit from genuine prophets (7:15–20)
- two foundations: stupidity and subsidence, sagacity and storm-proof living! (7:24–28)

Effects of Jesus' teaching:

- astonishment
- authority

SURPRISING REVERSALS
BEATITUDE PEOPLE (MATT. 5:1–16)

The Beatitudes (Matt. 5:1–12)

'The counterintuitive paradoxes of the Beatitudes alert us to the fact that Jesus' new community is a contrast society, out of synch with the "normal" order of the world.'[1] This statement of Richard Hays sums up the great 'reversal of values' announced by Jesus. He continues, 'The Beatitudes [describe] an upside-down reality, or – more precisely – they define reality in such a way that the usual order of things is seen to be upside-down in the eyes of God.'[2]

Firstly, let me make a number of reflections.

1. The much loved words of Jesus in this passage are called the 'Beatitudes' because each begins with the Greek word *makarioi*, translated into Latin as 'beatus' – hence the 'Beatitudes'. The term carries the connotation of 'happy, blessed, joyful ...' Some modern English translations opt for 'happy', but this is misleading, I think, especially in our touchy-feely culture concerned for personal feelings of wellbeing. Are the mournful 'happy'? Yes, but only in a very deep sense; it hardly helps to suggest 'happy are the unhappy'.

   Two other directions in which we can take this term are more accurate. We might read *makarioi* as signifying God's approval and pleasure and might, therefore, translate the word as 'fortunate are ...' or 'congratulations'. Certainly, as E. Stanley Jones suggested, the Beatitudes are no funeral dirge, more the sound of wedding bells! But better still is the translation 'blessed ...'

   'Blessing' in the Old Testament is a performative word not just a descriptive word; it bestows and conveys favour and blessing on another in a transforming way. Furthermore, 'blessing' is a covenantal category – the announcement of a bestowal of blessing – whose opposite is 'woe' – the invoking of a curse (cf. Deut. 27:14ff; 28:3ff – note 30:1: matter of life or death, 30:15). Luke highlights this in his version of the sermon where 'blessed ...' and 'woe ...' are matched (Luke 6:20–26). As for Matthew, the Beatitudes in the first block of Jesus' teaching are mirrored by the 'Woes' in the fifth block of teaching (Matt. 23) – as if Matthew is a new Deuteronomy.

What is happening here in the message and ministry of Jesus is the dawning of the kingdom and the inauguration of the new covenant relationship between God and His people as promised by the prophets (notably Jeremiah and Ezekiel). As we shall see later, their prophetic vision about the kingdom and how God's royal law works within God's renewed people is precisely what Jesus has come to fulfil (Matt. 5:17–20).

2. So the Beatitudes are not only about what disciples *do*, but also, and more fundamentally, about what they *are*.

The Beatitudes – and the sermon as a whole – are concerned with what Charles Talbert terms 'character formation', the shaping of the mindset and heart of a disciple. The Beatitudes are, therefore, to be construed not as describing eight different types of people but as depicting one. Characteristics flow from character – or, as E. Stanley Jones typically puts it: 'The *be*-attitudes precede the *do*-attitudes.'

3. Following on from my previous reflection, the Beatitudes are, therefore, emphatically *not* natural attitudes or dispositions or actions which are being commended. It is not as though we cast around for any who are poor in spirit or meek and say to them that they are the really fortunate ones and that, without their knowing it, the kingdom of God is there. This is about the blessing of participating in the rule and reign of God – which comes into our lives as we respond with repentance and belief to Jesus – and will one day come in its fullness.

4. The Beatitudes declare that the prophetic announcement of the dawning of God's kingdom rule and salvation is now being fulfilled. A comparison of Matthew 4:13–17 and verses 23–24 with Isaiah 6:1–11 shows this:

- Preach good news to the poor (Isa. 61:1), that is, the good news of the kingdom of God (Isa. 52:7) – so Matthew 5:3: 'poor' or 'poor in spirit, for theirs is the kingdom of heaven'.
- Comfort for mourners (Isa. 61:2) – so Matthew 5:4: 'Blessed are those who mourn, for they will be comforted'.
- Honour for the disinherited (Isa. 61:1,7) – so Matthew 5:5: 'Blessed are the meek, for they will inherit the earth'.
- Righteousness (Isa. 61:3,8,11) – so Matthew 5:6: 'Blessed are those who hunger and thirst for righteousness, for they will be filled'.
- Pardon, liberty (Isa. 61:1) – so Matthew 5:7: 'Blessed are the merciful, for they will be shown mercy'.
- Heal the broken-hearted (Isa. 61:1) – so Matthew 5:8: 'Blessed are the pure in heart, for they will see God'.
- Joy over righteousness (Isa. 61:10–11) – so Matthew 5:10–12: 'Blessed are those who are persecuted … because great is your reward in heaven'.

The reality which this comparison shows and which Matthew depicts *has nothing to do with earning the favour of God and everything to do with enjoying the life and blessedness of participating in the kingdom of God.* There is all the difference in the world, then, between these two statements:

- Blessed are the poor in spirit *because* being poor in spirit makes them virtuous and qualifies them to merit and deserve the kingdom's blessing

and:

- Blessed are the poor in spirit *because God is gracious and His kingly rule is now acting to save and deliver precisely those whose poverty of spirit is exposed by its impact.*

Jesus has not come looking for a beatitude people – they don't exist; He has come to create such a community. The first four Beatitudes, in Warren Carter's words, 'describe not personal qualities but oppressive situations of distress or bad fortune, which are honoured or esteemed *because God's reign reverses them*'.[3] The other four Beatitudes are the blessings pronounced over those whose responses are evoked by the proclamation of the kingdom – blessings on attitudes and actions '*inspired by the experience of God's reign*'.[4]

In short, the Beatitudes describe the character and actions of radical disciples who are – to use Hays' phrase – 'out of synch with the world'. They announce what it means to be 'in synch' with God's kingdom.

Let us now look at each Beatitude in more detail.

'Blessed are the poor in spirit, for theirs is the kingdom of heaven' (Matt. 5:3)

The 'poor in spirit' are 'those who embrace the poverty of their condition by trusting God rather than favors from the powerful for their deliverance'.[5]

God's blessing does not rest on poverty *per se* but on those who, perhaps because they are financially deprived or exploited, are 'poor in spirit' and so are utterly dependent on God. If the rich embrace the kingdom, they too become 'poor in spirit'. If the rich are often sent 'empty away', it is because their hands are clenched tight and not open to receive the kingdom as a gift.

Material prosperity is good and God normally wills it for us – but it is not the gospel, despite what the wealth-and-prosperity teachers tell us. In fact, prosperity can make us forget God (Deut. 8:12–14a; Hosea 2:8 and cf. Hosea 13:6: '... they were satisfied; when they were satisfied, they became proud ...').

Poverty is not good; no one benefits from it, there is no virtue in it and Jesus is not advocating it. But riches are not meant to fill the human heart as only God can. In Don Carson's words, 'Poverty of spirit then is the personal acknowledgement of spiritual bankruptcy.'[6] If the actual poor are often the quickest to realise this it is because they are at the end of their resources and God is all they have. The poor are more than ready for any startling reversal of fortunes which the kingdom brings in its wake. The 'poor in spirit' are not self-sufficient, not 'full of themselves' (unlike the self-deceived Laodiceans [Rev. 3:17]) but humbly and boldly God-dependent. As David Gill says, 'Only those who are empty have room to receive what God has to give.'[7] Perhaps only the 'empty' know it.

Whether one has become poor through being a victim of economic oppression or as the outcome of making wrong choices, or – a very real prospect when Jesus spoke – as a result of renouncing all things for the sake of the kingdom, the way one comes to embrace the kingdom settles the way one is then called to continue. Being 'poor in spirit' is the definitive starting-point of kingdom character renewal and, paradoxically, of a refusal to be defined only by poverty. 'Gospelised' by the impact of Jesus and the kingdom of God, 'we face up to our condition. We recognise it as our truth and reality, but do not remain there. We bring it to God. We cling to Jesus in our emptiness. And he fills us with his kingly presence'.[8]

This is fleshed out later in the sermon in practices which befit the kingdom. So the 'poor in spirit' are free to express their dependence on God rather than their own resources precisely by freely giving to others (5:42; 6:1–4), by prayer and the pursuit of God (5:44–48; 6:5–13; 6:7–11) and by fasting (6:16ff).

Bonhoeffer said of kingdom people who are 'poor in spirit': 'they have no security, no property to call their own … no earthly community to which they might fully belong. But they also have neither spiritual power of their own, nor experience or knowledge they can refer to and which could comfort them … They have their treasure well hidden, they have it in the cross.'[9]

In David Gill's words, 'the "poor in spirit" are people who have learned that they don't know everything [and, I would add, don't need to know everything] and don't have everything'.[10] Nothing that is, except the secret of the kingdom which enables them to live the dynamic but mysterious and paradoxical life of the kingdom in the ambiguous here and now (eg 2 Cor. 6:4–10).

So, in one sense, this Beatitude is the key to all the rest. To renounce self-sufficiency is to be poor in spirit; to renounce indifference and Olympian detachment is to mourn; to renounce a self-assertive claim to our rights is to be meek; to renounce our own self-righteousness is to hunger and thirst for God's; to renounce victimisation is to accept mercy and to give it; to renounce our own goodness is to be pure in heart; to renounce violence is to be a peacemaker. As Dale Bruner puts it, 'The purpose of every Command in the Sermon on the Mount is to drive its hearers back to this First Beatitude.'[11]

'Blessed are those who mourn, for they will be comforted' (Matt. 5:4)

Of all the Beatitudes, this one most closely echoes Isaiah's prophetic vision of the anointed messenger of God and the blessings He brings.

> *The Spirit of the Sovereign* LORD *is on me,*
> *because the* LORD *has anointed me*
> *to preach good news to the poor.*
> *He has sent me to bind up the broken-hearted …*
> *to comfort all who mourn,*
> *and provide for those who grieve in Zion –*
> *to bestow on them a crown of beauty*
> *instead of ashes,*
> *the oil of gladness*
> *instead of mourning,*
> *and a garment of praise*
> *instead of a spirit of despair.*
> Isaiah 61:1–3

This Old Testament connection gives us a clue as to the primary meaning of this Beatitude. It is not first and foremost addressing the pain of bereavement; it is not principally about the grief we feel at the loss of a loved one – although who would want to exclude this from its scope. But, as in Isaiah's day, the condition being addressed is *primarily that of the people of God who are grief-stricken and heart-broken over the sins that have cast them into exile.* Jesus exemplified such grief when He wept over Jerusalem (Luke 19:41); He did not weep for His own fate but at the terrible fate about to overwhelm the city (Luke 23:28).

This Beatitude speaks to those who are awakened by the good news of the kingdom to mourn for their own sins and for the sins of God's people and – by extension – for the state of God's world. Whichever way you look at it, things are not what they were supposed to be. It's enough to make you weep. The invasion of the kingdom of God throws up the disparity as never before and those who sense this are brought to mourning over the way our world is, misruled by the devil's agents.[12] But the good news is: it is precisely those who mourn in this way over whom God pronounces 'blessings on you'. 'You shall be comforted', for the kingdom is now at work among you.

Intriguingly, when Luke reports this Beatitude he offsets the grief with laughter (Luke 6:25b). Now, genuine laughter, too, is a sign of the kingdom, one of the key 'signals of transcendence'.[13] In our day, humour – even irony and satire – is a needful protest against self-important secularism and overbearing power. But the reducing of everything – serious matters and all – to flippancy and coarse jokes, is a sign of the feckless fool (Prov. 10:23; Eccl. 7:6; cf. James 4:8–10). In such a climate – both outside the Church and increasingly within it where celebrity wit is prized over saintly wisdom – truth is trivialised and the good news watered down to 'gospel lite'. Against all such trends, says Os Guinness, 'the holy fools stand as a weeping road block'.[14]

There is a marvellous passage, among so many, in Bonhoeffer on 'Blessed are those who mourn ...' that I cannot forbear from quoting at length:

> [By] mourning, Jesus means ... refusing to be in tune with the world or to accommodate oneself to its standards. Such men mourn for the world, for its guilt, its fate and its fortune. While the world keeps holiday, they stand aside, and while the world sings, 'Gather ye rose buds while ye may ...' they mourn.
>
> They see that for all the jollity on board, the ship is beginning to sink ... And so the disciples are strangers to the world, unwelcome guests and disturbers of the peace ... Nobody loves his fellowmen better than the disciple, nobody understands his fellowmen better than the Christian fellowship, and that very love impels them to stand aside and mourn ... The disciple-community does not shake off sorrow as though it were no concern of its own, but willingly bears it ... Sorrow cannot tire them or wear them down, it cannot embitter them or cause them to break down under the strain; far from it, for they bear their sorrow in the strength of him who bears them up, who bore the whole suffering of the world upon the cross. They stand as the bearers of sorrow in the fellowship of the Crucified: they stand as strangers in the world in the power of him who was such a stranger to the world that it crucified him. This is their comfort, or better still, this *Man* is their comfort, the Comforter (cf Luke 2:25). The community of strangers find their comfort in the cross, they are comforted by being cast upon the place where the Comforter of Israel awaits them. Thus do they find their true home with their crucified Lord, both here and in eternity ...[15]

Of course, in the end, we mourn too over the ravages caused by death. Even as we grieve differently to the pagans because we have the hope of resurrection, we remain deeply moved – even roused to anger, as Jesus was at the grave of His friend Lazarus (John 11:38). We are angered at the spoiling of God's good creation.

Inspired by the Spirit's own groans, we groan with a groaning world that longs for its release from bondage to decay and death into the full freedom of the sons of God (Rom. 8:22–23). We have tasted of God's good and life-giving rule, and so we share the divine discontent that, as yet, God's kingdom has not fully come, God's will is not perfectly done. We are in denial if we do not mourn this fact.

And yet, because the kingdom of God has come, we lament that it has not yet *finally* come, and pray to that end even through our tears.

'Blessed are the meek, for they will inherit the earth' (Matt. 5:5)

To 'inherit land', or at least to have a portion of the earth that can be called one's own, is the dream and demand of every one of us. For the poor and dispossessed – then as now – the possession or repossession of land becomes almost an obsession. No doubt, among the first hearers of these startling words of Jesus, were poor peasant farmers whose fields had been stolen from them by bullying and arrogant landlords who had crushed them out of existence by extortionate rents and taxes.

All who heard Jesus teach lived in an occupied land where Roman imperial rule, though mostly unobtrusive, was close at hand and ready to enforce its occupation rights. It is not difficult to imagine how angry and bitter the dispossessed and disenfranchised might become, nor how ready they were to hear the seductive voices of the burgeoning revolutionary movements urging violent repossession of their lost property. Now along comes this strange and fascinating preacher offering good news of another kind of kingdom than Rome's – the long-awaited kingly rule of God. And what He tells them is strange and provocative and tough: 'Blessed are the *meek*, for you shall inherit the earth' (my italics).

'Meek' is not the note we expect Jesus to strike in such circumstances. It sounds as if He is endorsing being weak and wimpish, or advocating being a doormat for every one to walk over. Quite the opposite.

Only two people in the Bible are described as 'meek'. One is Moses (Num. 12:3, ESV – 'humble' in the NIV), and you would hardly say Moses was wimpish or lacking in boldness and courage. The other, of course, is Jesus, who describes Himself as 'gentle [or 'meek'] and lowly in heart' (Matt. 11:27–30, ESV – in NIV, 'gentle and humble in heart'). Yet He rode bravely and boldly into the eye of the storm, but on a donkey (Matt. 21:5) to show that though He was the King, He was a King coming in meekness; a King who would win back His throne not by inflicting suffering but by enduring it.

Psalm 37, which is echoed in Jesus' Beatitude, is perhaps the best commentary on it. The psalm concerns those who are fit to 'inherit the land' by displaying certain characteristics (Psa. 37:9,11,22,29,34b – note especially vv.11–12).

Firstly, meekness has to do with *one's attitude to oneself*. Here, being meek is offset against 'fretting' and 'anger' (Psa. 37:1,7–8). Meekness is about self-control. In my case, it means refusing to allow myself to be eaten up by what others have done or are doing. I can all too easily be consumed either by envy (v.1) or by anger (v.8). To fret is to be vexed, irritated to such a degree that I lose my composure and peace. To be meek is to be willing to 'let go', to stop being worked up into a lather over things I cannot control.

Secondly, the secret of meekness lies in *our relationship with God*. As the psalmist puts it, meekness means to 'trust in the LORD' (Psa. 37:3). It means to 'commit your way to the LORD' (v.5) rather than to your own emotionally conceived course of action. It means finding joy in the Lord even in the tough times (v.4), as you risk entrusting your deepest desires to God to work out. To be meek is to 'be still' (v.7); it is about calming down and letting God work, and about being prepared to 'wait' for Him to do so (vv.7,34).

Now the revelation given to the psalmist has been intensified and focused in the grace and truth of the kingly rule of God in Jesus. The 'gospelised', says Jesus, those being changed by the transforming power of the kingdom of God, are enrolled in the school of long-suffering, enlisted in the tough academy of fortitude and are being trained in endurance … but blessed are the meek for they shall inherit the land! 'Do not be afraid, little flock, for your Father has been pleased to give you the kingdom' (Luke 12:32). Of this band of disciples, Bonhoeffer says: 'They show by every word and gesture that they do not belong to this earth. Leave heaven to them, says the world in its pity, that is where they belong. But, says Jesus, "they shall inherit the earth". To these, the powerless and the disenfranchised, the very earth belongs ...'[16]

Bonhoeffer goes on:

The powerless have here and now received a plot of earth, for they have the Church and its fellowship, its goods, its brothers and sisters, in the midst of persecution even to the lengths of the cross. The renewal of the earth begins at Golgotha, where the meek One died, and from thence it will spread. When the kingdom comes, the meek shall possess the earth.[17]

Meekness, then, is a tough stance because it is willing to let go, to forego aggression and high-handedness, and to risk a gentle response and reaction. To be meek involves surrender to the will of God. The 'meek' are those who are so impacted by His in-breaking kingdom that they forego asserting their rights and instead submit to the will of God.

'Blessed are you meek' – especially if you feel powerless and put upon because the gospel empowers you to realise you have nothing to lose and everything to gain by coming under Jesus' lordship and so make the tough call to let go of your justified anger and let God decide your destiny.

Being meek is about as far removed as you can imagine from being a docile doormat.

In Douglas Webster's words, meekness 'is a bold humility, an aggressive patience. It is the spiritual discipline that overcomes the world'.[18]

'Blessed are those who hunger and thirst for righteousness, for they will be filled' (Matt. 5:6)

The immediate point at issue here is what Jesus meant by 'righteousness'. 'Righteousness' is certainly central to the Beatitudes (Matt. 5:10) as it is to the whole sermon (5:20; 6:33). Yet here again, we need to hear the sermon as a counter-cultural message. In the modern, post-Enlightenment Western world, it is customary to understand 'righteousness' – if at all – in individual terms. As Christians we tend to construe it either as individual morality or, in Pauline terms, as to do with the justification of the individual sinner. But Jesus' usage, as always, has deep Old Testament roots.

In the Old Testament, the concept of 'righteousness' emerges as a way of describing an activity of God as well as an attribute of God.

'Righteousness', of course, represents God's covenant integrity, but it comes to convey, too, the notion of this righteousness and covenant faithfulness actively going forth to save and renew His people. So, for example, Psalm 98:2: 'The LORD has made his salvation known and revealed his righteousness to the nations.' In the prophets, too, God's 'righteousness' is virtually synonymous with His 'salvation'. So God says through Isaiah, 'My righteousness draws near speedily, my salvation is on the way ...' (Isa. 51:5). Once again we see that Isaiah 61 may well be the seed from which the Beatitudes are developed (see Luke 4:16ff). In the prophet's description of the anointed servant of God declaring 'good news to the poor', 'righteousness' features strongly (Isa. 61:3,10–11). The result of such a God's saving righteousness is, of course, that God's people are 're-righteoused' or vindicated (Isa. 61:10) and a community characterised by righteousness springs up (Isa. 61:11).

Glen Stassen is correct then, I think, to translate 'righteousness' as 'delivering justice' or 'restorative justice', by which is meant that righteous action of God which rescues and releases the oppressed. By implication, as Stassen correctly emphasises, this is a 'community restoring justice'.[19] Psalm 37 – which is echoed in the previous Beatitude – also confirms this: 'He will make your righteousness shine like the dawn, the justice of your cause like the noonday sun (Psa. 37:6; cf. vv.39–40).

The proclamation was that such a move of God was now happening in Jesus. God was putting things right – socially as well as spiritually – through His Son, and by coming to Him you could taste the presence and power of the kingdom – this was truly good news.

And tasting the presence of the kingdom of saving justice stirs up a whirlwind of desire for God's new order of things, an aching appetite for God's empire of freedom rather than Rome's empire of oppression, a craving for a compassionate justice that restores God's true covenant community among us. Who is there who has tasted the grace and power of God's gracious kingdom who does not look out on our fractured and dysfunctional world and not 'hunger and thirst' for such righteousness? Blessed are those who do so. Blessed are those who 'do not believe they can live until they find or see righteousness. They long for what is right, they crave justice, they cannot live without God's victory prevailing; for them right relations in the world are not just a luxury or a mere hope but an absolute necessity if they are to live at all ...'[20]

And '*... they will be filled*'.

Such assuaging will come only as the final settlement of their deepest prayer: 'your kingdom come ... on earth as it is in heaven.' Any satisfaction we feel now, as Dale Bruner points out, is a mere drop in the ocean compared to the satisfaction of seeing the new world order when Jesus returns and God's kingdom finally and fully comes. But 'the marvellous consolation of the world to come is promised not to those mildly uncomfortable with the present world who seek refuge in a dream, but to people who suffer, weep, and sigh. "God shall wipe away every tear from their eyes" (Rev. 7:17).'[21]

Even now, as those justified by faith, we are blessed to be swept up as His 'righteous ones' in the saving and restorative justice of God. Disciples are those who long for God to be all in all, who pray for God's heavenly will to be done on earth's stage, who are learning to want what God wants, even to see a little of what God sees and to feel what God feels. Followers of Jesus are those whose deepest hunger and thirst can never be satisfied by anything less than God's kingdom because they have read the menu, tasted the hors d'oeuvres and now long for the final feast.

'Blessed are the merciful, for they will be shown mercy' (Matt. 5:7)

The Sermon on the Mount, it is worth repeating, is dealing in reality not fantasy. Jesus is very realistic about the imperfections, brokenness and failure that mar God's world, and about our contribution to that brokenness. As a consequence, everyone stands in need of mercy. Mercy is giving what is not deserved. Mercy is not merit; mercy is unmerited favour.

Let me again make several reflections to clarify my thinking on this point.

Firstly, let us look at what this Beatitude reveals about *the character of God in His kingdom*.

'Blessed are the merciful, for they will be shown mercy' *because mercy is just the way the kingdom of God works*. This must be the starting-point, and for a very good reason which I mentioned earlier but I cannot repeat too often. The Beatitudes are not describing *natural* qualities but attitudes inspired by the presence of Jesus as He proclaims and embodies the kingly rule of God. Mercy is the beating heart of the One Creator God as He revealed Himself to Israel and is characteristic of the way He runs His kingdom. When God displayed His essential glory as He passed by the rock in which Moses hid, that glory turned out to be a revelation of a God who is *'merciful* and gracious, slow to anger, and abounding in steadfast love ...' (Exod. 34:6, ESV, my italics). Now this divine mercy is embodied in Jesus and enacted in His ministry, and evokes the response it deserves.

Where would any of us be without this mercy?

In Jesus' parable of the tax collector and the Pharisee (Luke 18:9–14), it was the tax collector who went home justified, because he prayed: 'God, have mercy on me, a sinner' (v.13). Like him, we ask for mercy because mercy is the only thing we dare ask for! Without mercy we would be, literally, 'no-people', non-recognised, non-covenant pagans. But the gospel has made all the difference and created a new covenant community. 'Once you were not a people, but now you are the people of God; once you had not received mercy, but now you have received mercy' (1 Pet. 2:9–10). What a difference mercy makes.[22]

So, later in the sermon, when Jesus urges His disciples to 'Be perfect, therefore, as your heavenly Father is perfect' (Matt. 5:48), it is just this quality of mercy in God that He wants us to emulate. Luke leaves us in no doubt by spelling it out for us: 'Be merciful, just as your Father is merciful' (Luke 6:36). We who are in receipt of God's royal mercy are to mete out mercy to others. The sequence must never be reversed. Being merciful does not earn God's grace, but it should be an inevitable outcome.

The second reflection concerns the need to position this Beatitude in the setting of *Jesus' conflict with the Pharisees.*

This Beatitude comes across with particular force when we bear in mind that Jesus is undoubtedly pronouncing these 'blessings' in a particular context: His conflict with the religious leaders, the scribes and Pharisees.

When defending Himself against Pharisaic criticism of His habit of eating with sinners, Jesus cites the prophet Hosea and bluntly tells His critics: 'It is not the healthy who need a doctor, but the sick. But go and learn what this means: "I desire *mercy,* not sacrifice"' (Matt. 9:12–13, my italics).

In His pronouncement of the 'woes' of covenantal judgment – which match the announcement of God's kingdom 'blessings' – Jesus says this: 'Woe to you, teachers of the law and Pharisees, you hypocrites! You give a tenth of your spices – mint, dill and cumin. But you have neglected *the more important matters of the law – justice, mercy and faithfulness.* You should have practised the latter, without neglecting the former' (Matt. 23:23–24, my italics).

The religious leaders – albeit often for sincere reasons – were fastidious about imposing the surface details of the Law's demands but were failing to express the Law's overarching intention. The scrupulous details should not be heedlessly set aside, says Jesus, but preoccupation with the minutiae can so easily crowd out the larger interests of justice and mercy which are dear to God's heart. What is created are fussy, lightweight legalists. God's Law was never meant to produce a strict religious observance society or a punctilious legal adherence company. Rather it was intended to create God's free and righteous covenant community. Jesus is bitingly ironic on the religious leader's failure at this point: You are concerned by what animals are unclean so you strain your wine to get rid of a tiny insect while at the same time swallowing the largest animal in the land, a camel![23]

So 'Blessed are the merciful ...' is a provocative challenge to the Judaism of Jesus' day, and a perennial challenge to those who have been impacted by the merciful kingdom to practise what they have received in their dealings with others. We receive mercy from God, and as we show mercy to others, we *go on* receiving mercy from God. An unmerciful heart blocks the flow of God's mercy into our hearts and makes it less likely that we will receive mercy from others (cf. the 'Golden Rule' works well here – Matt. 7:12).

Being merciful is one of the key ways in which 'gospelised' followers can display a righteousness that *surpasses* that of the scribes and Pharisees (cf. 5:20). Being *merciful* means practising mercy by being generous in doing deeds of kindness and deliverance. So the parable of the Good Samaritan ends with the punch line: '"Which of these three do you think was a neighbour to the man who fell into the hands of robbers?" The expert in the Law replied: "The one who had *mercy* on him." Jesus told him, "Go and do likewise"' (Luke 10:36–37, my italics).

Lastly, we may reflect on how well this Beatitude goes with the previous one. Being merciful surely follows hard on the heels of having a hunger and thirst for justice. Anyone who cares passionately about justice and righteousness will soon find much to hurt and wound their spirit. The temptation at this point will be to harden up and to demand – automatically and without distinction – pitiless punishment or strict sanctions.

It is here that justice and mercy need each other.

A craving for justice without mercy can become cold and harsh; a concern for mercy without justice can become slushy and a sentimental cover-up of what needs to be put right. David Gill spells out the balance well: 'Righteousness without mercy leads only to judgment and death; but mercy without righteousness sells out the high calling of God for some insipid lower standard.'[24]

So those with merciful and compassionate hearts, softened by the grace of the kingdom, will long for justice in a way that reflects God's merciful heart. Shown mercy, and showing mercy, they attract mercy – and that is a true blessing!

'Blessed are the pure in heart, for they will see God' (Matt. 5:8)

To come to this Beatitude is in a real sense to come to the 'heart' of the matter. In order to hear Jesus at this point it is worth recalling what the Bible usually intends us to understand by 'heart'.

We often use the term 'heart' very loosely and unbiblically to refer to our feelings, our emotional take on life. In this sense, we often contrast 'heart' with 'head', as if one were emotional and the other merely cerebral. But this will not do when we come to the Bible.

Apart from the obvious reference to the heart as the physical organ of the body, the biblical writers almost invariably use 'heart' in its metaphorical sense to refer to the whole human personality. Biblically, the 'heart' includes feelings and emotions, but also willing and thinking – so that heart, will and mind are all covered by the term 'heart'. It represents the deepest core of our personality. To use Darrell Johnson's military analogy, the 'heart' is the 'control and command centre' of our lives. The 'heart' is at the heart of being human.

'Purity of heart' – as with poverty of spirit or meekness – is not a *naturally occurring* phenomenon in those whose hearts are deceitful and unclean. The power for 'purity of heart' is generated by the in-breaking kingdom of God as it is proclaimed and embodied in Jesus. It is these hearts which Jesus is blessing.

So, what are the characteristic features of a 'pure heart'?

First of all, *purity*! We scarcely need educating, do we, about the uncleanness of the human heart? From Noah's day (Gen. 6:5–6) to Paul's day, such is the reality of our condition (Eph. 4:17ff). Jesus diagnoses the human condition for His disciples in contrast to those who safeguarded spiritual soundness by ritualised regulation of consumption. 'What goes into a man's mouth does not make him "unclean" ... For out of the heart come evil thoughts ...' (Matt. 15:11,19).

Spurred more by spiritual longing than by intellectual speculation, the psalmist had once pondered: 'Who may ascend the hill of the LORD? Who may stand in his holy place? He who has clean hands and a *pure heart* ...' (Psa. 24:3–4, my italics). Now, with this Beatitude, spoken not from the 'hill of the LORD', which is Jerusalem, but from the hill on which the Lord teaches, the psalmist's aspiration is set to be met.

In deep contrition, David had prayed fervently, 'Hide your face from my sins, and blot out all my iniquity. Create in me a *pure heart*, O God, and renew a steadfast spirit within me' (Psa. 51:9–10, my italics). With the in-breaking of the kingly rule of God, David's prayer is set to be fulfilled.

Secondly, a pure heart signifies *transparency*. This is not easy or natural. Whether deeply wounded or not, we all develop a well-practised instinct for self-protection. We have been taken advantage of too often by politicians, manipulated by clever persuaders, damaged by family feuds or hurt by friends who have betrayed our confidence, that we set up elaborate self-defence mechanisms. Most of us learn to conceal our mixed motives and hidden agendas behind a smokescreen of social rituals.

Jesus is not saying we should have no private thoughts or that we should bare our souls to all and sundry, but what the kingdom evokes is a genuine openness, an openness that respects others and listens to them. A pure heart is one which engages with another without guile or deceit or ulterior motive. Only the power of the kingdom of God can purge our hearts of deviousness and defensiveness; only the power of the kingdom can keep out hearts pure from suspicion or cynicism or bitterness.

And those with 'purified hearts' are truly blessed.

Thirdly, a pure heart denotes *integrity*.

This was at issue in Jesus' clash with the Pharisees – already referred to – over what defiles a person: is it what goes into our physical bodies or what comes out of our hearts that defiles us (Matt. 15:10–20)? '... out of the heart come evil thoughts ... These are what make a man "unclean" ...' (vv.19–20).

Here the dispute is not so much about inner holiness being better than outer holiness, but rather it is about the matching up of the two. It will not do for the Pharisees to advocate external conformity to the Law, in this case to the laws concerning unclean food, while ignoring the corruption at the command centre of the personality. Conversely, if the heart is right, what happens externally should match up to it. In the psalmist's language, 'clean hands' (holy actions) should result from a 'pure heart' (a holy disposition). This is integrity, and when the gospel of the kingdom evokes it, Jesus pronounces it 'blessed'.

Fourthly, pure in heart signifies *singleness of heart*.

'… give me an undivided heart that I may fear your name' (Psa. 86:11). How often are we distracted, torn apart by competing loyalties, our hearts fragmented by being pulled in too many directions. We more often speak of 'single-mindedness' than 'an undivided heart', but the meaning is the same. James – who so often faithfully recalls and applies his Lord and Brother's teaching – confirms this linkage by combining the two: 'Wash your hands, you sinners, and purify your hearts, you double-minded' (James 4:8). Søren Kierkegaard – that strange but insightful nineteenth-century Danish Christian – once encapsulated this perfectly when he said: 'purity of heart is to will one thing …' And what, asks Kierkegaard, is that one thing? 'That one thing', he replies, 'is God who is the good'.

In this Beatitude Jesus anticipates His later challenge in the sermon which probes whether His disciples can possibly cherish two treasures or one, see with two eyes or one, owe allegiance to two masters or one (Matt. 6:19–24). Purity of heart settles the issue: purity of heart is to be focused on God, concentrated on doing His will. Out of a concentrated heart Paul could say 'one thing I do' (Phil. 3:13). As E. Stanley Jones wryly commented: 'Where Paul said this one thing I do, we are more likely to say, "these forty things I dabble in".' And, he added, those who are 'pure in their ends' are also 'pure in their means to get those ends'.[25]

The blessedness attending a pure heart is evoked by the kingdom and sustained by pursuing the kingdom of God as our exclusive priority (Matt. 6:33). As we allow the in-breaking kingly rule of God in the lordship of Jesus lovingly to take over the control and command centre of our lives, our hearts are made and kept 'pure' and we enjoy His blessing. The 'pure in heart' shall *'see God'*!

This is the ultimate eschatological hope – heralded by John on Patmos

– who says of the saints that 'They will see his [God's] face' (Rev. 22:4). This prospect which was denied to the Old Testament saints, became for the Christian mystics the ultimate prize, the 'beatific vision'. 'Blessed are the pure in heart, for they will see God.'

And in the meantime, to see God is to:

- know Him as Father and to appreciate His Fatherly care, and also to enjoy His Fatherly favour and approval – this is the blessed life.
- see Him in His handiwork all around us in creation, so that, as Jesus goes on to say, it makes sense to observe the flowers of the field and to watch what birds do (6:26ff) in order to see some of the Father Creator's loving care and provision.
- see God in Jesus, who is Emmanuel – 'God with us'. Matthew records for us, '… no-one knows the Father except the Son and those to whom the Son chooses to reveal him. Come to me, all you who are weary and burdened, and I will give you rest. Take my yoke upon you and learn from me, for I am gentle and humble in heart, and you will find rest for your souls. For my yoke is easy and my burden is light' (Matt. 11:27–30).

Blessed indeed are the pure in heart, for they will see God.

'Blessed are the peacemakers, for they will be called sons of God' (Matt. 5:9)

Jesus spoke these words in a highly charged atmosphere. The land was under Roman Imperial occupation. Rome's domination of its conquered territories, though discreet, was all-pervasive and ruthless when necessary. It kept the peace in these lands by the threat of military action and levied heavy taxes for the privilege of garrisoning their troops on foreign soil to keep that peace. It was called the *pax Romana* ('Roman peace') – a term no doubt conjured up by the spin-doctors in Rome for what was in effect a glorified protection racket.

Jesus spoke at a time of mounting tensions with incipient Jewish revolutionary groups lurking in the very hills where He was standing. These precursors of the zealots were already fomenting trouble, storing up swords and talking up violence as the only way to rid God's land of the pagans.

Talking of peace then, as now, must have seemed like a pipe dream. It does today, as our world groans under the weight of terrorism, military conflicts, drug-wars, ghetto violence and strife-torn communities and families. Added to which, as David Gill notes, are facile provocateurs in TV studios and Hollywood movie sets, who pander to anger, hatred, vengeance and bloodshed.

And where are Evangelical Christians in all this? Too often either wrapping themselves in the flag and calling down fire on the enemies of Western democracy, or retreating to the privacy of personal therapies and spiritual self-fulfilment.

Where on earth then is true peace to be found?

Biblically, 'peace' is not simply the cessation or absence of hostilities – though heaven knows that is welcome enough! Biblically, 'peace' is *shalom* – a rich concept which carries with it notions of wholeness, wellbeing, social harmony, the flourishing of potential into prosperous community.

Such 'peace' is a fruit of the kingdom of God breaking into human affairs – a vision for which we are again indebted to the prophet Isaiah: 'How beautiful on the mountains are the feet of those who bring good news, who proclaim peace, who bring good tidings, who proclaim salvation, who say to Zion, "Your God reigns!"' (Isa. 52:7). This, say the evangelists, is just what is now happening with Jesus. His advent is the arrival of 'the Prince of Peace', which heralds a change of government to a benevolent rule whose expansion and peace are unlimited (Isa. 9:7; Matt. 4:14–16).

First, of course, comes *peace with God*. Estrangement from God is our worst-case scenario, and it has happened. Reconciliation to God is our first priority, and it is offered in the gospel. Such peace comes as a gift of the kingdom: 'Therefore, since we have been justified through faith, we have *peace with God through our Lord Jesus Christ* ...' (Rom. 5:1, my italics). Reconciled to God we are reconnected with the source of peace and we can face the challenge of making peace with others in our fractured world.

Secondly, we practise this peace *in the Church*. In the New Testament Church, the greatest division and potential point of contention was between Jewish and Gentile Christians, who each brought to their new-found faith in Christ their own cultural habits and rituals. How they could live together in harmony taxed the wisdom of the apostles and called for the Holy Spirit's constant renewal of their God-given peace forged at the cross and sustained in the unity of the Spirit. Contrary to much received wisdom, Paul actually wrote the Letter to the Romans to achieve this very pastoral goal. The gospel is the power to save both Jew and Greek (Rom. 1:16) for all have sinned (Rom. 2:9; 3:23) and all have been saved by the one God in Christ, therefore don't divide the Church over different eating habits! 'For the kingdom of God is not a matter of eating and drinking, but of righteousness, peace and joy in the Holy Spirit … Let us therefore make every effort to do what leads to peace and to mutual edification' (Rom. 14:17,19). In the creation – or re-creation – of an intentional cross-cultural community, the Roman church would be a proving ground for the grace of the kingdom and would serve both as a showcase of the gospel of reconciliation and an authentic springboard for taking that same gospel to the 'foreign' regions of Spain. All such apostolic exhortation to peace in the church reads as a virtual commentary on the Beatitudes (eg James 3:16–18).

Then, thirdly, we can be the community that *seeks to make peace in the world*. The blessing of the kingdom empowers believers to take to heart Paul's words to the Romans, 'If it is possible, as far as it depends on you, live at peace with everyone …' (Rom. 12:18), and, where possible, energises them to heed the words of the writer of Hebrews to actively 'Strive for peace with everyone' (Heb. 12:14, ESV).

The *pax Romana* was a spurious peace, an enforced placebo, that healed the torn wounds of the world lightly. But blessed are the real empire-builders of peace, the peacemakers of the Prince of Peace Himself. David Gill summarises things neatly: 'In a world of tribalism and self-assertion, we want to promote a healthy diversity in unity. In a world of conflict, we want to promote co-operation. In a world of competition, we want to promote teamwork …'[26]

Two streams of biblical thought converge here. Jesus stands apart from us as the unique Son of the Father by eternal generation; we are God's children derivatively by adoption. But, we share the same family likeness. So it is in being peacemakers that we are most distinctively *the sons and daughters of God*.

Furthermore, being a peacemaker is invariably costly, almost always painful. The only Son of the Father, Jesus, made peace, but only by the blood of His cross (Eph. 2:14–17). Likewise, says, Bonhoeffer, 'The peacemakers will carry the cross with their Lord, for it was on the cross that peace was made.'[27]

Not surprisingly, then, being sons of God is invariably linked to suffering. As the children of Israel were first called 'the sons of God' so we, as inheritors of their calling and as part of the renewed 'Israel of God', make our way across the groaning wilderness of our present world on the way to the promised new world (Rom. 8:14–17). By our willingness to suffer in the cause of making peace, we prove ourselves to be truly the sons of God and the co-heirs of the suffering Son of God who made peace by the blood of His cross!

Here we see again how the Beatitudes hang together. If you want to make *peace*, you will need a *pure heart* which is free from guile and self-interest and manipulation; if you want to make *peace*, you will need a *meek* spirit, lest you contradict you aim by trying to make peace violently and answer strife with strife; and if you want to make *peace*, you will need to *hunger and thirst for God's justice* to prevail, for peace is not worth the paper the peace-treaty is written on unless injustices are dealt with and truth and reconciliation established.

But of such is the kingdom of heaven ... and by such peacemaking are the sons of God distinguished and blessed.

'Blessed are those who are persecuted because of righteousness, for theirs is the kingdom of heaven. Blessed are you when people insult you, persecute you and falsely say all kinds of evil against you because of me. Rejoice and be glad, because great is your reward in heaven, for in the same way they persecuted the prophets who were before you' (Matt. 5:10–11)

It is a sobering fact, but historians estimate that more Christians were killed for their faith in the twentieth century than at any time before. And the killing is still going on in one form or another – ranging from outright murder down the scale to social marginalisation, insults and sneering.[28]

Persecution comes on the followers of Jesus for two interconnected reasons:

1. On account of *a great cause* – God's righteousness and justice (v.10)

2. On account of *a great name* – Jesus (v.11 cf. John 15:21)

'The gospel,' said Lesslie Newbiggin, 'is a *name* and a *fact*' – the fact is that the kingdom of God is breaking into human affairs both to save and to transform; the name is Jesus through whom this is happening. The invasion of the kingly rule of God is a threat to all other claimants to human allegiance and terrifies the powers-that-be.

No wonder Jesus was crucified and the first disciples were persecuted. They were persecuted:

- *by the Roman authorities* for pursuing God's justice – because the kingdom of God undermines all Rome's Imperial claims and exposes the *pax Romana* as a hollow sham. They confess Jesus not Caesar is 'Lord' (*kurios*) and 'Saviour' (*sôter*)
- *by the religious authorities* for practising God's 'higher righteousness'. The Sermon on the Mount was a direct challenge to the Israel of Jesus' day and to the religious leaders in particular.

As N.T. Wright challenges us:

> *Do you long for the kingdom? – it belongs to the poor in spirit!*
> *Are you looking for the consolation of Israel? – it is given to the mourners!*
> *Do you seek to inherit the earth and reclaim God's promised land from the pagans? – it is reserved for the meek – not the revolutionaries.*
> *Do you thirst for justice to be done? – are you sure your thirst is deep enough and is a thirst for God's true justice which does not come by force of arms?*
> *Are you proud to be known as the sons of God? – but God's sons are known for being peacemakers like the Father!*[29]

Jesus' challenge was to a new way of being Israel, to *His* way of being Israel, and this Jesus-way of being Israel aroused strong hostility among those who thought they knew which way God's people should be going.

Disciples are fortified to endure suffering by:

- *inspiration from the past* – the precedent of the persecuted Old

Testament prophets (Matt. 5:12). Jesus was very conscious of this as He recognised what lay ahead for Himself as a prophet of God to His people (Luke 13:33–34). And it formed another aspect of His critique of the religious leaders of His day (Matt. 23:29–31).

- *incentive in the future* – the promise of 'reward' in heaven (Matt. 5:12). 'Well done, good and faithful servant! … Come and share your master's happiness' (Matt. 25:21).
- *invigoration now* by the presence and power of the kingdom (Matt. 5:10 – 'theirs *is* the kingdom of heaven' [my italics])

One great sign of this is the astonishing *hopefulness* of the early disciples and in particular their amazing ability to 'rejoice and be glad' in such circumstances. This is no doubt the fruit of the Spirit in them (cf. Rom. 15:13; 1 Pet. 4:13). Hope is born because Jesus comes to meet us from the future. Joy arises from His companionship so that we trust and travel – and suffer too if need be – with what David Gill calls 'the lightness and release of the spirit within us … with that deep mirth that bubbles up as we see everything in the light of eternity and thus do not take others or ourselves *too* seriously …'[30]

Disciples are urged by the first apostolic followers of Jesus as they walk this road:

- Don't be surprised by pressure and opposition (1 Pet. 2:21–25; 4:12–19).
- Don't forget to identify with the Persecuted Church around the world (1 Pet. 5:9–11).
- Don't underestimate what a character formed by the Beatitudes and filled with hope and joy by the Holy Spirit can endure (cf. Rom. 5:2–5).

THE SALT AND LIGHT AND CITY COMPANY (MATT. 5:13–16)

'The community's vocation to be "salt" and "light" for the world is to be fulfilled precisely as Jesus' followers embody God's alternative reality through the character qualities marked by the Beatitudes.'[31] Richard Hays captures well the continuing inter-connectedness which can be detected in the sermon.

In particular, two features of truth are linked here:

1. *Identity* – as delineated in the Beatitudes to form *kingdom character*.
2. *Influence* – as depicted in the metaphors 'salt' and 'light' which define *kingdom vocation*.

In this vivid way, Jesus again throws down the gauntlet to His contemporaries. Is Israel not the salt of the earth? Has she lost her distinctive flavour? Was Israel not called to be the 'light to the nations'? Has she now surrounded herself with mirrors rather than being a lighthouse? Were not God's people meant to be a city set on a hill – as in Isaiah 2 – to whom the Gentile nations would gravitate for God's truth and salvation like moths to a flame? Hasn't Israel's role been obscured, her magnetism lost? Israel's God, it seems, is still looking for and is now creating a true salt and light community.

Salt

Jesus' statement in verse 13 follows a simple outline:

- A description: 'You are …'
- A question: '… if salt loses its saltiness …?'
- An answer: 'It is no longer good for anything …'

Without over-pressing the metaphor, we may reflect on salt's influence.

- Salt *preserves from decay.* We bemoan the Church's lack of impact but who knows how much worse the world would be without the Church's witness. Salt sealed a covenant (see 2 Chron. 13:5), so we should be seeking to preserve and strengthen bonds of commitment wherever we can in marriage, family, friendship and community (cf. Mark 9:50).

- Salt *fertilises the ground*. On this score, our influence should be to foster growth and further the potential of everyone we work with, tending especially to the frail and vulnerable.
- Salt *flavours food*. Christians should be against blandness in every conceivable way, and for colour and diversity, richness and rainbows.
- Salt *creates thirst*. Should not our presence make people ask for our secret – and maybe – just maybe – long for something better, even for God Himself?

For salt to work two things are vital. On the one hand, *it must get out of the saltshaker*. It's not only that we need Christians out there in the marketplace and opinion-forming centres, as journalists, businessmen and women, politicians, media pundits, artists and so on, but we need them to act as Christians when they get there!

And, on the other hand, *salt must not assimilate with culture and lose its savour*. As George Bernanos once said: 'we need to be the salt not the honey of the world.'

Christians are too often perceived as those who pour sloppy sentimentality over every problem. Salt, however, is 'tangy'; it bites and adds zest to life. It offers difference as standard (see Rom. 12:1ff). Its default position is distinctive: 'Let your conversation be always full of grace, seasoned with salt, so that you may know how to answer everyone' (Col. 4:6).

Light
Jesus' words in verses 14–16 also form a neatly framed statement:

- A description: 'You are the light of the world' (Matt. 5:14).
  - Illustration one: 'A city on a hill cannot be hidden'.
  - Illustration two: 'A lamp' is not 'put under a bowl'.
- An exhortation: 'In the same way, let your light shine before men, that they may see your good deeds and praise your Father in heaven' (5:16).

There are three important points to consider in relation to this statement. Firstly, we note what an amazing description this is. Christians are ordinary people who make extraordinary claims about Jesus, and, at the same time, Jesus makes extraordinary claims about ordinary people, inviting them to share in His own exclusive role as 'the light of the world' (John 8:12).

As for light's influence, the metaphor is capable of many applications. Light certainly dispels the darkness, *illuminating and exposing, guiding and showing the way*. This much is true, although in the passage on which we are focusing Jesus applies the term in a particular way, as He shortly makes clear.

Secondly, 'city' implies a community, the children of the light whose relational bonds are evident so that the pagans say, 'see how they love one another'. Jesus elaborates on this in the so-called 'High Priestly Prayer' recorded by John, where He emphasises the vital witness of the Church's unity. This 'oneness' among Christians is created by their participation in the mutual indwelling of the Father and the Son. When love is practised among Christians the mysterious divine unity-in-Trinity is made known to the world (John 17:21–23)!

Thirdly, Jesus says if you have the light, *don't obscure it*. This sounds obvious. But His words had a special resonance with His Jewish audience whose historic destiny was to be a 'light to the gentiles'. Jesus' re-affirmation of this national vocation to His own disciples was thus no doubt an implied criticism of the self-protective official Judaism of His day which led the way in turning the windows into mirrors.

But, the primary thrust of this metaphor as applied to the Christian community is in the exhortation Jesus gives: 'In the same way, let your light shine before men, that they may *see your good deeds* and *praise your Father* in heaven' (Matt. 5:16, my italics). The light within the kingdom people becomes visible in *good deeds*. The word 'good' here is *kala* (not *agathos*) which often adds to the idea of practical deeds of kindness the idea of 'beauty' or 'attractiveness'. It is not only in *what* we do but *in the way* we do it, that the light shines. 'You know … how God anointed Jesus of Nazareth with the Holy Spirit and power, and how he went around *doing good* and healing all who were under the power of the devil, because God was with him' (Acts 10:37–38, my italics). This is the only Jesus-way to be 'high-profile'.

No one doubts that the Church frequently seems to need a makeover. Outsiders have a negative impression of us – and often with some justification. Dark passages of Church history, intemperate dogmatism,

internecine strife, irreconcilable disunity, majoring on minor issues …
it is not difficult to find fault with the way the Church washes its dirty
linen in public.

On the other hand, not least in the modern world, Christians can
become over-obsessed with the way they are perceived by unbelievers,
too concerned to keep up appearances. Perhaps we concede too much
to an image-conscious culture as we strain to present the Church in a
positive light. Jesus warns us against valuing society's approval above
heaven's applause (cf. Matt. 6:1–6). Society's esteem is no guarantee of our
authenticity: 'Woe to you when all men speak well of you, for that is how
their fathers treated the false prophets' (Luke 6:26). Jesus' exhortation
bears on our current pre-occupation with making the Church 'relevant'.
Only God can make us effective. Over-anxious attempts to re-brand the
Church, however well-meaning, risk doing God's work for Him. *But just
as the Father rewards personal devotion in secret, so He rewards corporate
faithfulness by making the Church relevant in the public arena.*

If we ask what kind of 'good deeds' Jesus has in mind, He soon tells us:
foregoing anger, persistently seeking reconciliation, ruthlessly avoiding
lust, treating divorce as the sad last resort, speaking the truth when it
costs us, refusing to retaliate but going the extra mile, and – above all
– loving our enemies!

In the period immediately after the death of the apostles, the Early
Church grew exponentially at a faster rate than at any time since. But
it did so without overt evangelism (which was often too dangerous) or
even seeker-friendly worship (worship was opened only to committed
disciples). The Church grew largely because of the unusual 'good deeds'
it practised, often doing the 'dirty jobs' – caring for the lepers, laying out
the dead and so on, which pagans were increasingly refusing to do, seeing
these tasks as too demeaning.

Going the extra mile in these ways, lets the light shine and causes the
inquisitive now, as then, to ask, 'Why do you do that?' Contrary to our
perceived notions of influence and visibility, it may be that the more
'low-profile' disciples are, the more the world will seek after God and
may come to glorify Him.

There is, I suggest, an intimate connection between being 'salt' and
being 'light'. As if Jesus is saying: 'Dare to be *distinctive* (salt) and I will
make you *effective* (light).'

SURPASSING RIGHTEOUSNESS
The Law Fulfilled (Matt. 5:17–48)

The Sermon's relation to the Old Testament as interpreted and fulfilled by Jesus (Matt. 5:17–20)

'Do not think that I have come to abolish the Law or the Prophets; I have not come to abolish them but to fulfil them.'

Matthew 5:17

Now we come to the theological and Christological crux of the whole of the Sermon on the Mount. It establishes Jesus' unique authority as the true and final interpreter of God's Law.

1. Jesus has not come to abolish the Law and the Prophets
The phrase 'the Law and the Prophets' may well signify the whole of the Old Testament Scriptures (cf. Luke 24:27).

Allow me to make two general points first of all. Firstly, we must state emphatically that *Jesus has not come to abolish or dispense with or cancel the Old Testament.* From the time of Marcion (AD 80–160) in the Early Church until today, there have always been those Christians who have wanted to jettison the Old Testament as outmoded revelation, no longer important or in any way authoritative as God's Word.

Jesus specifically contradicts this tendency. Everywhere He endorses the abiding validity and authority of Israel's Scriptures (cf. Matt. 5:18), which were, after all, the only Bible the first Christians had. This is significant at a very basic level. Without Jesus we cannot understand the

43

Old Testament properly but equally, we cannot understand Jesus *without* the Old Testament or hear His witness clearly and completely (so Matt. 1:1–17).

Secondly, however, *Jesus has come to fulfil the Old Testament Scriptures*. More will be said about this in a moment, but at a very basic level this must be said about the opposite mistake to Marcion's. You cannot take a stand on the Old Testament alone without passing it through Jesus. You cannot extract truth from the Old Testament without taking into account the impact of Jesus. There is a strain of Evangelicalism – perhaps represented by certain teaching about Israel or certain kinds of prosperity teaching – that lifts texts straight from the Old Testament and treats them as if Jesus had never happened. But you cannot go straight from Old Testament revelation to today and bypass Jesus as irrelevant to the way such revelation works. Like light put through a prism, something happens to the Old Testament revelation when it is channelled through Jesus.

Is God's will today expressed in the Old Testament, asks John Piper? 'Yes' and 'no' is his qualified answer. 'Yes', provided that the Law is filtered through the sieve of all the changes brought by Jesus, who is the goal and fulfilment of the law.[1] God's previous revelation is not abolished – put like that, how could it be – but fulfilment in Christ transforms it. We are in a different relation to the Old Testament now that Jesus has come.

2. Jesus 'fills-full' the prophetic expectations of the Old Testament

The word 'fulfil' means more than rubber stamp or endorsement without alteration; it means to endorse by taking to a new level. It means to 'fill-full' with meaning and actuality what was true and good but incomplete and partial.

In particular, Jesus 'fills-full' the prophetic hopes of what God promises to do, which had been laid down in the Law and the Prophets. The trajectory which began with God's blessing of Abraham that was meant to bring blessing to all nations, now converges on Jesus (Matt. 1:1ff), and Matthew ends his Gospel by showing the nations on the verge of receiving it (Matt. 28:18–20).

The saving movement which began with the Exodus, and the making of covenant with Israel through Moses, now reaches its climax here in the new Exodus of Jesus' death which inaugurates the new covenant promised by the prophets, Jeremiah and Ezekiel.

The dreams of messianic kingship fostered since David's day of a true king to rule the world (Psa. 2) are now being concentrated in Jesus – royal Son of God by birth. By testing, He will enter David's city of Jerusalem and achieve all authority over the nations by His resurrection.

Jesus 'fills-full' the significance of all Israel's God-given feasts and institutions. So, for example, the Temple, which was the place of God's focused presence and where sins were atoned for, is fulfilled in Jesus, who is Emmanuel, God with us, and who takes away sins by His sacrificial death. And everywhere in his Gospel, Matthew notes that this or that happened in the ministry of Jesus to 'fulfil' what was spoken by the prophets, not least Isaiah (see Matt. 4:12–17).

3. Jesus fulfils all the expectations not only of what God will do but what Israel is expected to do as God's faithful covenant partner

Jesus submits to baptism because He says 'it is proper … to do this to fulfil all righteousness' (Matt. 3:15). Jesus fulfils all righteousness in this act both from God's side – by fulfilling all the covenant faithfulness and promises of God – and from Israel's side – by immersing Himself totally in fulfilling all the obligations of covenant loyalty through obedience to the Father.

So, in His temptations (4:1–11) – as we have seen – He is tested as to His royal Sonship and, unlike Israel in the wilderness, He succeeds by obedience where Israel failed. In other words, Jesus perfectly embodies the righteousness of the Law.

All that we have said so far is crucial then to the whole sermon and can be summarised thus: *The ways in which Jesus 'fills-full' the Scriptures establishes Jesus' unique authority as the true and final interpreter of God's Law.*

4. Jesus exposes the deepest intention of the Law

Jesus completes and brings to full expression the deepest intention of the Law. As His fellow Jew Martin Buber put it: 'He sought to pierce the clouds above Sinai.' The prophets themselves had begun this process by pressing beyond the external compliance with the Law to God's deeper aims for the human heart (see Hosea 6:6; Matt. 9:13; cf. Psalm 40).

So Jeremiah and Ezekiel had been entrusted with the new covenant which did not promise a new law but a different way of operating the Law by writing it on the renewed human heart.

Now, in the time of fulfilment, *Jesus perceives the direction God intended the Law to take and pushes it beyond how its current interpreters treated it.* Jesus does not abolish the Law nor even relax the Law by making it a 'softer touch' (cf. Matt. 5:19). Rather, *Jesus deepens and intensifies the meaning and purpose of the Law.*

The immediate consequences for teachers and disciples is clear:

- As for *teachers*, their status in the kingdom rests on the integrity of Scripture of which they cannot pick and choose (Matt. 5:19).
- As for *disciples*, they are called to practise a 'surpassing righteousness' (v.20).

So radically does Jesus 'fill-full' the Law and the Prophets, He can demand of His disciples a righteousness that *surpasses* that practised by the scribes and Pharisees (v.20).

What this 'surpassing righteousness' looks like is now spelt out in six sample cases …

THE 'SURPASSING RIGHTEOUSNESS' AS ILLUSTRATED BY SIX 'ANTITHESES' OR 'FULFILLERS' (MATT. 5:21–48)

Glen Stassen and David Gushee have helpfully pointed out the 'triadic pattern' employed here.[2]

- Traditional (mis?)interpretation: 'You have heard that it was said …'
- Diagnosis of vicious circle: 'But I tell you …' – with regard to anger … lust … adultery … swearing falsely … retaliation … hating enemies
- Transforming initiative: 'be reconciled … gouge it out …', etc

Notice first of all that the wording is probably significant. Jesus never contradicts 'what is written' (cf. Matt. 4:4f) but only what is 'said'. That is, in all likelihood, He is correcting traditional or mistaken interpretations of the Law of God and, at the same time, extracting the true meaning and significance of the Law.

In these six areas addressed by Jesus in this part of the sermon – anger, lust, adultery, swearing falsely, retaliation and hating enemies – we can see how He completes and brings to full expression the deepest intention of the Law. Now, in the time of fulfilment, Jesus pushes the Law deeper and further in the direction God intended the Law to take.

In the first example, the movement is *from murder to dealing with anger* (Matt. 5:21–26). Note the 'triadic pattern':

- Traditional interpretation: 'You have heard that it was said ...'
- Diagnosis of vicious circle: 'But I tell you ...' Here Jesus exposes an increasing intensity which was especially serious in an honour–shame society:
  - *anger* ... incurs judgment
  - *insults* ... incur answering to the Sanhedrin
  - *'You fool'* ... incurs hell fire!

But He offers a ...

- Transforming initiative: '... leave your gift ... First go and be reconciled ...'

Even if there is a measure of hyperbole here (after all, it would be physically difficult to go back and forth from Jerusalem to Galilee during a religious feast – vv.23–24), Jesus' teaching ought to be taken more not less seriously.

No one can be in relationship with God and not be concerned about relationships with other people. Being reconciled to God forces us to seek reconciliation with others. Jesus deepens and intensifies the Law.

So, Jesus is not saying it is never right to get angry (after all, He did). But it is never right to 'go on being angry', either by harbouring longstanding resentment or entertaining murderous intentions, and then to glibly come to worship God. Jesus is not putting anger on the same level as murder. He is, however, getting to the root of what makes us rage against people – whether it stays at road-rage or not.

Jesus pushes the Law deeper and further in the direction God intended the Law to take in a further instance. In the second example, the movement is *from adultery to acknowledging lust* (5:27–30).

Note again the 'triadic pattern':

- Traditional interpretation: 'You have heard that it was said ...'
- Diagnosis of vicious circle: 'But I tell you' – 'anyone who looks at a woman lustfully has already committed adultery with her in his heart.'
- Transforming initiative: 'gouge out' your eye ... 'cut off your hand'

Jesus is surely not condemning the appreciation of female beauty, nor is He crushing the glance or greeting which thinks or says, 'You really look good'. He is, however, rebuking the gazing at someone across a crowded room or at a dinner party which begins to conjure up mental images of undressing and sex (and no doubt He would say the same to the many men drawn to or even addicted to pornography). To go on looking at another woman 'with lustful intent' (as the ESV has it) is tantamount to adultery because it is the deliberate nurture of desire for an illicit relationship.

These two initiatives are hyperbole – deliberate exaggerations, but nonetheless they tell us that tough choices need to be made; we need to deal radically and ruthlessly with our lust. Do something about it, Jesus says. 'Make a covenant with your eyes'; turn the TV off, don't rent or buy that video; don't tune in to that channel when in a lonely hotel bedroom; don't read that article or magazine left lying in the canteen or the restroom at work; don't go to that newsagents; don't go to see that movie; don't read those books ...

This is not some new rigid law – *Jesus is about forming Beatitude people; Jesus is about character formation; Jesus wants kingdom disciples!*

Jesus pushes the Law deeper and further in the direction God intended the Law to take.

In the third example the move is *from divorce to practising faithfulness* (Matt. 5:31–32). Just two verses, but what millions of words of controversy and study and debate they have stirred up! Especially in our day when divorce is so frequent both outside and inside the Church and when it presents itself to us a pastoral issue as well as a personal issue, we need wisdom and sensitivity and courage to follow through on what Jesus says here.

Needless to say, devout Evangelicals differ on what the New Testament teaches about divorce and remarriage – and indeed over what Jesus means here – and what I say may not satisfy everyone. But in the end, after prayerful study, everyone has to make a judgment on this issue which one's conscience can live with. So, rather than offering lengthy arguments I refer you to the relevant literature and simply seek to state my current viewpoint in ten statements.

1. Jesus was probably speaking in the context of a dispute between two schools of rabbinic thinking arguing over the divorce concession of Deuteronomy 24:1f.

    Rabbi Shammai took a strict line – seeing 'unchastity' as the only ground for divorce; Rabbi Hillel took a lenient line allowing for what some scholars call 'any-matter-divorce'. The suggestion is that the lenient view of divorce was prevalent, with women being given certificates of divorce for trivial reasons – like burning the toast! It is against this backdrop that Jesus – mirroring the Shammai school – teaches a much tighter interpretation of the Law.

2. Jesus presses to the deep intention of the Law by reiterating that divorce is not God's original creation intention: 'But it was not this way from the beginning' (Matt. 19:8c).

    God's intentional creation order – not followed in early Israel it seems – was one flesh union between, we might add, a man and a woman, a union which God may separate but not man.

3. God made provision for divorce in the Law but as a *permission*, not a command. It was a concession, a concession to what Jesus calls 'hardness of heart'. This is not 'incompatibility', which is the usual catch-all nowadays, but an inveterate unresponsiveness which destroys the relationship.

4. Jesus endorses the stricter view of the Law by limiting the grounds for divorce to *porneia*. Now *porneia* is not the usual word for adultery, and perhaps includes any sexual deviancy or unfaithfulness! Paul seems to extend this further to include 'desertion' by an unbelieving spouse (1 Cor. 7:15).

    In his recent research, David Instone-Brewer points to 1 Corinthians 7:3, which forbids refusal of conjugal rights and, noting that it depends on Exodus 21:10, argues from this last text that material and emotional neglect and abuse might then be included in biblical grounds for divorce – making four in all. I am persuaded by his arguments but others are not. John Piper for example resists this in his usual pungent way.[3]

5. God works wonders through Jesus and the Holy Spirit to change the 'hearts hardened' by sin and rebellion to the demands of the old covenant and to create a new covenant people with soft and responsive hearts. Given the vision in the sermon of 'gospelised' humanity, the greatest tragedy is that – in the US for example – the divorce percentage is the same *inside* Evangelical churches as it is outside, and this is scandalous. We should not give up too soon but believe in the power of the gospel to change people's hearts and therefore their marriages.

6. Jesus certainly sets Himself against quick and easy and trivial divorces. In actual experience, few divorces are pain-free – most are anguished affairs for one or more of the spouses involved, and particularly for the children.

7. In Jesus' day, re-marriage was assumed to be the norm – after a biblical divorce had taken place (cf. 1 Cor. 7:15). Piper for one disagrees with this but many Evangelical scholars agree.

8. Divorce, even where sinful, is not the unforgivable sin, and should evoke repentance, renewal and recommitment.

9. Jesus' restrictive words here were almost certainly aimed at protecting women who might otherwise find themselves dismissed from marriage and home for trivial reasons on the whim of their husbands.

10. Jesus is here challenging His disciples to 'surpass' the Pharisees in practising a righteousness which eschews easy divorce and even goes beyond the Mosaic Law to embrace the deeper faithfulness and commitments God intends.

Jesus pushes the Law deeper and further in the direction God intended the Law to take, and in this fourth example the movement is from *oathtaking to truthful speech* (Matt. 5:33–37). Note the 'triadic pattern':

- Traditional interpretation: 'You have heard that it was said …'
- Diagnosis of vicious circle: 'But I tell you …' – 'do not take an oath …' (ESV)
- Transforming initiative: 'Simply let your "Yes" be "Yes", and your "No, "No" …'

According to Craig Keener, at this point 'Jesus addresses a popular abuse of oaths in his day'.[4] Refusing to swear by God's name, religious faddists conjured up all kinds of circumlocutions (cf. Matt. 5:34–35). This led to ridiculous hair-splitting and convoluted pedantry on an almost bureaucratic scale. Furthermore, such trivialising of oathtaking inevitably masked duplicity and deception. Adjudication had then to be made as to which oaths were binding and which were not (cf. Matt. 23:16–22).

All this is nonsense, says Jesus. You should not need oaths at all to verify the seriousness of what you are saying or to guarantee its truthfulness. Let your 'Yes' mean 'Yes' and your 'No' mean 'No' – anything else springs from an evil intent of the heart and opens the way for the evil one to work mischief and to poison communication. Rather, your righteousness should 'surpass' the scribes and Pharisees in this regard; make a habit of being truthful at all times. Speak so that your words do not need buttressing with affirmations at all. Guard against the devaluation of truthfulness and integrity.

Some Christian traditions, notably the Anabaptists, have taken this with total literalism and therefore banned taking oaths in court or when joining the military or the police. Others have argued that accepting or taking an oath asked for by others was acceptable, but making an oath was not!

Whatever the rights and wrongs of this in exegetical terms, it raises an important question: *Where does our ultimate allegiance lie?*

If we can, in all good conscience as kingdom people, sign over our rights and lives to the state, then we must be very clear-eyed about it and realise that it is not a light thing we are doing. The Law's true intention needs to be recognised – the protection of speech from corruption and falsehood and manipulation. As Dale Bruner points out, 'All swearing is invoking God's name and "Jesus'" prohibition … placed disciples in a tense relationship with the secular powers. The state has never historically enjoyed being told "no".'[5]

By *not* taking the Lord's name in vain, by *not* bearing false witness, we love God and our neighbour by our speech.

Dale Bruner summarises: 'In a certain sense all four of Jesus' social commands so far are united by a desire *for good faith towards people*: by avoiding that which hurts them (unbridled anger); toys with them (unbridled lust); sits loose to them (infidelity in marriage), or fails to speak trustworthily (by undisciplined speech)'.[6]

Jesus pushes the Law deeper and further in the direction God intended the Law to take, and in this fifth example the movement is from *retaliation to taking positive initiatives* (5:38–42). Note yet once more the 'triadic pattern':

- Traditional interpretation: 'You have heard that it was said ...'
- Diagnosis of vicious circle: 'But I tell you ...' – 'Do not resist an evil person.'
- Transforming initiative: 'If ...' by which Jesus offers three extreme cases to illustrate His point.

'Do not resist ...' is tough talk. Of course, this does not cover every situation in which *someone else* is being attacked, but it urges us not to let our emotional energy be generated by evil or channelled by evil or dragged down to its level.

In the cultural context of the sermon, the three cases make sense.

1. To be slapped on the right cheek (with the back of the hand) was a humiliating insult.
2. Letting someone have your inner garment as well as outer is obvious hyperbole because otherwise all Jesus' followers would go around naked!
3. Roman soldiers had the right to commandeer you and force you to carry their burden or pack for a mile (cf. Simon of Cyrene carrying Jesus' cross in Matt. 27:32).

None of the three examples, it is worth noting, is totally *passive*. Jesus does *not* say, if someone slaps you on the right cheek, let him slap you on the other also, but, rather, 'Turn to him the other.' That is, even in this moment of crisis, refuse to cede control of the situation.

Jesus does *not* say that if some one sues you for your tunic you should let him sue you for you cloak as well; but let him have your cloak also. Again, take a positive step.

Jesus does *not* say if a soldier forces you go one mile let him force you to go two. No, offer the extra mile free! Since Roman soldiers could be disciplined for over-using this right, you might even embarrass the soldier and in so doing take back control of the situation in some small way.

Jesus did *not* say if someone asks you, give whatever it is and whenever they ask, but give to them, whether beggar or borrower (perhaps even before they ask).[7]

Everything here, in other words, must be taken seriously if not literally. Jesus cites extreme cases but they establish a pattern of conduct for the way 'Beatitude people' look at things in the light of God's in-breaking kingdom. And if every word is to be taken seriously then a risk of faith is required of the disciples. *'Jesus does not say that if we turn our cheek we will not be hit. He just reassures us that if we live as He lived we shall be living the way God rules the world'.*[8]

Jesus pushes the Law deeper and further in the direction God intended the Law to take and in this sixth example the movement is *from limited love to loving enemies* (Matt. 5:43–48). Note, for the final time, the 'triadic pattern':

- Traditional interpretation: 'You have heard that it was said …'
- Diagnosis of vicious circle: 'But I tell you …', which is followed by a series of rhetorical questions to press home the point: 'For if …!' (vv.46–47).
- Transforming initiative: 'But … love … pray … (bless; Luke 6:28) …'

Several reflections come to mind at this point. Firstly, strictly speaking the Old Testament does not have a command to 'hate your enemy'. The Old Testament certainly urged neighbour-love but did not go this far.

Secondly, recognise that you will have enemies. This is not what a greetings-card view of the sermon might lead you to expect; after all, if the sermon is about being nice to everyone, why would it ever arouse hostility?

But building an alternative kingdom community threatens worldly vested interests. Perhaps it is a shock to realise it, but not everyone liked Jesus.

Thirdly, recognise the need to break the vicious circle of violence and recrimination and counter-violence, if only to prevent it poisoning your own soul.

Fourthly, take an initiative in the spiritual realm: *'pray for those who persecute you'* (Matt. 5:44b). Bonhoeffer bravely said: 'Through the medium of prayer we go to our enemy, stand by his side, and plead for him to God ... We are doing vicariously for them what they cannot do for themselves.'[9] The psalmist complains to God about his enemies and calls down curses on them. And maybe we have to do this – to get this passion out of our system by pouring it out to God – before we can then pray for our enemies to be blessed.

What kind of love is this?

It is not the urge to protectiveness we feel towards family members so that we instinctively want to cherish, nourish and care for them; love is all this but goes further ... 'For if you love those who love you ...'

It is not the love that is evoked by what we admire or are attracted to, that is called forth by what is beautiful or beloved, drawn from us by what is desirable or lovely. You can't help that kind of loving, but enemies are not loveable. You tend not to 'fall in love' with those who are hurting you.

It is not the love that is based on shared interests or mutual respect (as between friends) but such love falters when the relationship is poisoned by mistrust or misunderstanding or betrayal.

No, this love goes further; it is a surpassing righteousness.

This is the love that wills the good and seeks the best for the enemy, that refuses to yield control of the situation to the enemy by retaliating in kind or seeking revenge. This is the love that seeks to find – however bad the situation – a transforming initiative – however tiny – that will heap coals of fire on the enemy's head by positive acts of kindness. Bless your enemies, pray for them, do good to them – once again apostolic injunctions faithfully reflect the Master's teaching (eg Rom. 12:14–21).

Thankfully, there are the heroes of faith like Martin Luther King who lived out the sermon by following Jesus whatever the cost.

To our most bitter opponents we say: 'we shall match your capacity to inflict suffering by our capacity to endure suffering. We shall meet your physical force with our soul force. Do to us what you will, and we shall continue to love you. We cannot in all good conscience obey your unjust laws, because non-cooperation with evil is as much a moral obligation as is co-operation with good. Throw us in jail, and we shall still love you. Send your hooded perpetrators of violence into our community at the midnight hour and beat us and leave us half dead and we shall still love you. But be assured that we will wear you down with our capacity to suffer. One day we shall win freedom, but not only for ourselves. We shall so appeal to your heart and conscience that we shall win *you* in the process and our victory will be a double victory'.[10]

And if we ask Jesus 'What kind of love is this?' He will answer: this is the *Father's love* in action (Matt. 5:45). We who are His disciples need to live out who we are by loving in this way. We are 'sons of God', 'children of the Father' and we are 'gospelised' in order that we may grow into the likeness of the Father. We must refuse to let the Enemy define who we are; we must let the Father define who we are. In His Fatherliness, God Himself is not defined by the response He gets or lack of it; He does not wait to be appreciated or thanked but releases sun and rain on the just and unjust alike. His is an indiscriminate love. And we are challenged in our turn to give expecting nothing in return (Luke 6:35) because that is what God the Father is like and we are His children.

The growth goal that Jesus has in mind for followers is: Be like the Father (Matt. 5:48). Be complete, be perfect – not in the sense of moral perfection but in the sense of maturity. Be mature as your heavenly Father is mature when it comes to loving. What do you want to be when you grow up? Our answer should be, *'To be fully grown-up as our Father is fully grown-up.'*

Very significantly, Luke's version of the words of Jesus reads: 'Be merciful, just as your Father is merciful' (Luke 6:36). This was a striking expansion of Israel's covenant charter, which called her to 'be holy as I am holy'. As members of a holiness movement, the Pharisees were defining that holiness in tighter and tighter ways, restricting the circle of covenant participation to an increasingly exclusive group. Jesus goes in precisely the opposite direction, enlarging the circle on the more inclusive grounds of showing mercy to sinners.[11]

Here we glimpse the goal of the character-formation of the Sermon on the Mount. This is the aim of 'surpassing righteousness' – to reflect God's loving character in the world as salt and light. Here is a love which reaches further than family or friends, nice people or neighbours and embraces enemies. We ask: What kind of love is this? The New Testament answers: *This is the love of Jesus that took the Preacher on the mount to the hill of sacrifice.*

Here is the kind of love which when commandeered to carry a soldier's pack one mile, ends up willingly carrying the whole world's cross the full nine yards to Calvary.

Legalism freezes the Law and does exactly and only what it has to do, to the letter and no more, and so prides itself on getting it right.

Antinominianism flouts the Law in the name of being under grace, and seeks to get away with as little as it can and still think itself godly.

Only *love* fulfils the Law; only *love* is surpassing righteousness.

Bonhoeffer, as ever, memorably states the case: 'What makes Christians different from others is the *"peculiar"*, the *"περισσον"*, the "extraordinary", the "unusual", that which is not "a matter of course" … The "natural" is *τό αὐτό* (one and the same) for heathens and Christians' – that which Jesus said even the pagans do instinctively out of self-interest (Matt. 5:46–47).

But the keynote of kingdom character, says Bonhoeffer, is the 'more', the 'beyond-all-that': 'The cross is the differential of the Christian religion, the power which enables the Christian to transcend the world and to win the victory. The *passio* in the love of the crucified is the supreme expression of the "extraordinary quality" of the Christian life.'[12]

Summary of Matthew 5:21–48

If we were to risk putting this section of Jesus' sermon into aphorisms, it might mean 'looking at every person we meet and saying, at least once, "I will never, God helping me, do anything to hurt you"; neither by angrily lashing out at you, lustfully sidling up to you, faithlessly slipping away from you, verbally oiling you up, protectively hitting you back, or even justifiably disliking you'.[13]

- To see into the divine will and intention is to fulfil the Law and the Prophets (v.17).
- To fulfil the Law and the Prophets is to practise a 'surpassing, higher righteousness' (v.20).

Character formed this way creates 'Beatitude people' and means:

- being a person who neither needlessly breaks nor fails to attempt to restore relationships (5:21–26)
- being a person who does not violate another's marriage partner either by act or thought (5:27–30)
- being a person who does not violate the indissoluble marriage bond (5:31–32)
- being a truthful person (5:33–37)
- being a non-retaliatory, non-vindictive person (5:38–42)
- being a person who does not exclude enemies from the love shown to friends (5:43–48)

SURPASSING RIGHTEOUSNESS
SPIRITUAL DISCIPLINES (MATT. 6:1–18)

The spiritual disciplines Jesus' promotes in this passage are:

- giving to the needy (6:1–4)
- prayer (6:5–8)
- fasting (6:16–18)

In reflecting on these texts, a number of considerations spring to mind.

1. *We are actors in a great drama.* Interestingly, the words used in this section of Matthew 6 are theatrical terms.

   The word 'seen' (v.1) is the word *theathēnai* – from which the word 'theatre' is derived.

   Jesus criticises those who are parading their piety by wanting to be seen by men. They may be doing this by ostentatious almsgiving (v.2), by praying showily on street corners (v.5) or by making it obvious that they are holy people much given to fasting by smearing their faces – perhaps with sackcloth and ashes (v.16).

   Jesus deplores this tendency to make a performance out of their religion – what Oswald Chambers once called 'going into the show business'. Now, as actors in a great drama, we are all play-acting, but are we playing ourselves in our own part or pretending to be what we are not and playing another part?

   This is the meaning of 'hypocrites' (Matt. 6:2,5,16). The *hupŏkritēs* were actors who donned a mask in order to impersonate another person.

Given that fasting is a biblically approved spiritual discipline, don't try to show it off by disfiguring your face – with ashes or anything else – but anoint your head and wash your face and appear normal.

2. *Jesus is probing our motives at a deep level.* Jesus is protecting the spiritual disciplines from becoming corrupted. Religion can be the last refuge which conceals our inveterate self-centredness; we appear godly but our religious practices are a cloak for our self-interest or even our vanity. 'Beware,' says Jesus, be on your guard. Don't become neurotically self-absorbed as if you had to monitor yourself every moment in an introspective way. But certainly examine yourself from time to time.

In this light, I wonder what Jesus would make of our obsession with public testimonies which, with the best will in the world, often come out sounding self-serving by showing just what spiritual people we are.

3. *We all want to be seen, noticed, admired and applauded – it's part of our psychological make-up.* Children say 'Notice me, Mummy' or 'Daddy, look at me ...' It is psychologically damaging to grow up without such approval or with constant discouragement and criticism. But if we never grow out of such attention-seeking, then we are also in trouble.

Too many leaders – I know from firsthand experience – are emotionally insecure and want to be loved by the people we serve so much that we milk the adulation and feed on the approval of the congregation. Even when we give to others, our left hand should not know what the right hand is doing so that we are not giving alms because we crave to hear the blowing of the internal trumpets of self-applause.

What is the antidote to all this?

4. *We must seek affirmation elsewhere – namely in the Father's approval of us and of what we do.* Act for the benefit of 'your Father, who sees what is done in secret ...' When we give or pray or fast, we are performing to an audience of One – the Father who sees and knows (Matt. 6:4,6,8,18).

As a consequence, 'your Father will reward you' (Matt. 6:4b,6b,18b). Those who relish public affirmation will get their reward in the here and now – the reward of being 'honoured by men' (Matt. 6:2b). If you crave Christian celebrity status you can have it right now; if you want to make an impression, an impression is what you will make right now, but that is all you will get. Plaudits and honours are yours if that's what you want. But among the Beatitude people, the 'Salt and Light Company' which Jesus is creating, different dynamics are at work. Here we are 'performing' for the hidden reward of the Father's good pleasure not the obvious reward of the praise of men.

But what of this matter of 'reward'? Some Christians struggle when Jesus talks of rewards. However, there is a rightness in the way that some actions lead to certain results. If a man marries a woman for her money then he is a mercenary, but if he marries for love, the marriage is the reward of his love.

The reward Jesus speaks of is not money or prosperity or fame but the approval of the Father who sees all and looks on the heart. 'The aim of Matthew 6:1–18 is not the privatisation of piety but the purification of motives in our relating to God. Piety may be public but when it is, it should be for God's sake.'[1]

I love my Emerging Church friends, and admire their passion, innovative and creative thinking and willingness to take risks. However, I have one chief worry for them and for others like them: it is that they seem almost *too* concerned that the Church does not appear to the world in a negative light. So anxious do they seem to be to counter negative images of the Church with positive ones, that 'keeping up an appearance' seems to rank too high on their agenda. The impression which is conveyed is: Does the world like us and like what it sees when it looks at us? Jesus specifically warned: 'Woe to you when all men speak well of you ...' (Luke 6:26). These words of Jesus call us back to our true focus; to where our reward is. They remind us – as Max Lucado puts it – that what matters most is the 'applause of heaven'.

THE LORD'S PRAYER
THE HEART OF THE SERMON
(MATT. 6:9–15)

What might there be to say about this prayer; it is holy ground trampled on by finer spirits than mine. I can only offer my reflections, beginning by way of introduction with a number of points.

1. Note the *contrast* in the context in which Matthew sets the prayer. The Lord's Prayer is offset against both possible *Jewish ostentation* while praying (6:5–6) and *Gentile long-windedness* in prayer (Matt. 6:7).

   In contrast, prayer should be neither *ostentatiously visible* (with a view to impressing others) nor *pretentiously verbose* (in order to impress God – which pagan prayers tended to do by piling up names for God). Public displays of piety have no effect on God who 'sees what is done in secret' and therefore what is really going on in the heart of the worshipper (Matt. 6:6c). Prolonged prayers to gain His attention or inform Him in detail are futile because as our Father He already knows what we need before we ask Him (Matt. 6:8).

2. The Lord's Prayer is a *gift*. Jesus offers an alternative way of praying which is effective: 'This, then, is how you should pray ...' (6:9). Luke pictures the disciples observing Jesus at prayer and asking to be taught to pray: 'Lord, teach us to pray ...' (Luke 11:1) with the implication 'Teach us to pray like that' ... 'Teach us to pray the way You do.' As Willimon and Hauerwas have it: 'We don't choose this prayer; it chooses us. It reaches out to us, forms us, invites us into the adventure called discipleship.'[1]

63

3. The *scope* of the prayer could not be wider. It covers every need from the physical (bread) through the social and relational ('Forgive …') to spiritual warfare ('… lead us not …').

   As for the *time-frame*, the prayer covers past, present and future: the past (forgiveness), the present (daily bread), the future (guidance and the coming kingdom). This truly is what Helmut Thielicke called 'The prayer that spans the world'.

4. The *order* of the prayer is deliberate and important. As *first priority* the prayer has three 'your' clauses: your name, your kingdom, your will. Then, and only then, the 'we' and 'us' clauses: pleading 'our' provision, 'our' pardon, 'our' protection.

   This is a crucial learning curve. True prayer – prayer the Jesus way – starts with God's agenda and glory; not with 'give me …' but with 'Father … hallowed be your name …' In fact, if we could learn to pray this way, we would rise from prayer with our burdens lifted and our hearts lighter (cf. Phil. 4:6–7).

5. Note the *direction* of the prayer – *from heaven to earth*. 'On earth as it is in heaven' should probably be attached to all three previous clauses – name, kingdom and will.

   God's passion is to bring the blessed reality of heaven to earth. Isn't this why Jesus came? In heaven the Father's name is honoured and feted; His kingdom is uncontested and serenely established; His will is perfectly embraced and His pleasure perfectly enjoyed. *So we pray that these heavenly realities may come here on earth to us, to our family and friends, to our cities and nations.* The causality of prayer does not work in straight lines and is part of the mysterious way in which God sovereignly rules the world. But through prayer we are invited to share in the implementing of His kingly rule.

   An old Jewish tradition suggested that during the day God silences the angels in order to hear the prayers of Israel. The apostle John sees something similar going on around the heavenly throne (Rev. 8:1–5). As the seals are broken and the scroll of history unfolds, there is silence for half an hour, as the prayers of the saints rise like incense to the golden altar before God. George Beasley-Murray comments: '… it would seem that God has willed that the prayers of his people should be part of the process by which the kingdom comes.'[2]

6. The prayer is marked by a studied *urgency*. Though carefully structured the prayer is at the same time *fervent not formal*. This shows that heartfelt prayer need not be spontaneous or innovative but can utilise set forms without becoming formal.

The verbs used are direct and forceful not hesitant and vague. This is because Jesus is teaching us to pray in ways which line up with God's revealed will. When we know God has said or promised something, we can humbly but boldly 'hold God to His Word', as it were (cf. 2 Sam. 7:25–29). In prayer we need not work up an artificial head of steam; but neither should we be tentative or formal but fervent and urgent.

7. The prayer conveys a spirit of *intimacy*. It breathes an atmosphere of close relationship with God, exemplified by addressing God as *abba*. But this is not at the expense of reverence. We must not trade off God's terrifyingly holy otherness for His cuddly closeness. Even when close up, perhaps especially when He draws near, we sense God's holy majesty and realise that we must never get over-familiar with Him. In this way, the invitation to intimacy does not become an overfamiliarity that breeds contempt. Rather, everything else in the prayer is drawn close to God's heart.

If we were to see the prayer as suggesting various relational images, we might perhaps see it as an address of a bride to her husband (hallowed ...), as a subject to a king (your kingdom come ...), as a servant to a master (your will be done), as a soldier to a commander (give me my daily rations), as a sinner to a saviour (forgive ...), and as a pilgrim to a guide (lead ... protect ...). But all these images would need to be subsumed under the intimate image of child to its parent.

8. Obviously, we may pray this prayer when we are alone. In spite of this, however, the prayer is never a prayer prayed apart from others. It always evokes *the community of fellow disciples* – so that 'we' and 'our' come naturally to us and therefore, even in solitary prayer, each of us prays '*Our Father ...*'

9. We should note that Matthew sets the prayer in the context of the

sermon so that the prayer is a key section in the manual of discipleship and a key stage in our training.

The Lord's Prayer is an *education of our desires*.[3] This insight is strongly reinforced if we look at the chiastic structure of the sermon and notice that the Lord's Prayer is the organising centre of it (see chart below). It suggests that praying like this, the Jesus-taught way, is the beating heart of being a disciple and absolutely essential if we are to live out the Sermon on the Mount.

5:1–16 Foundations: character and vocation

   5:17–20 Jesus: Law and Prophets

      5:21–48 Surpassing righteousness in action: six antitheses

        6:1–4 Righteous piety

        ➤ **6:5–15** The Lord's Prayer

        6:16–18 Righteous piety

      6:19–34 Surpassing righteousness in action: four considerations

   7:1–12 Judging – Law and Prophets

7:13–28 Foundations: choices and destiny

FATHER – 'ABBA'

In seeking to make this astonishing prayer our own in the modern world and to dare to call God 'Father' in our generation, we may need to re-establish some basic truth.

We should note that to call God 'Father' is metaphorical in a profoundly true sense. It is important – not least in our present climate – to remind ourselves that biblically-speaking, God transcends sexuality (God is

Spirit) and gender.

All the more, therefore, is it vital to emphasise that the revelation of God as Father is just that – *revelation*. To address God as Father is not a projection upwards of a once patriarchal society so that 'fatherhood' is a category that can now be jettisoned in the wake of cultural changes.

In the Old Testament, God is spoken of in parental terms but with some subtlety. God is said to act like a mother (which is a simile) and is addressed as Father (which is a metaphor). God is never addressed as 'Mother'.

If masculine terms are used for God it is because of a decisive break with 'goddess' concepts in paganism. Biblical revelation stands in complete contradiction to sexuality in divinity – whether between the gods (eg Baal and Ashteroth in Canaanite religion) or between the gods and the world. It offers a revealed alternative to female deity systems where the female deity produces creation by a birthing process so that the world is an extension of the divine (which is pantheism). God as Father preserves the qualitative difference between Creator and creature, while at the same time preserving personality in God and relationship with us.

So this revelation of God as Father stands *over against modern feminist theology*. Feminist theology prefers a trinity of Creator, Redeemer and Sustainer. But this at one stroke depersonalises God, confuses the persons of the Trinity – to each of whom the three epithets could apply – and severs the unique relationship of Jesus to God. Biblical revelation stands contrary to this.

The revelation of God's fatherhood also stands *over against Islam* which persists in misunderstanding the Trinity in sexual and reproductive terms. In so stressing monotheism, it serves to distance God from close relationship and to deny the divinity of Jesus.

What is conclusive for Christians is that Jesus addressed God as 'Father', though significantly, never as '*our* Father', always as '*my* Father'. Direct address to God as 'Father' was, if not unique, very rare in Judaism, and so the use of the intimate term for that filial relationship *abba* is very striking.

So, what does it mean for us to be taught to pray '*Abba*, Father'?

For us it means *growing in the security of sonship*

Jesus enjoyed a unique relationship as Son of God; He now invites us to share in that sonship: '… no-one knows the Father except the Son and those to whom the Son chooses to reveal him' (Matt. 11:27b). This invitation is made good by our adoption into God's family through new birth and the work of the Holy Spirit (Gal. 4:4–6). As the Spirit moves within us, He witnesses with our spirits that we are children of God and we find, welling up from the depths in us, a cry – expressed in a strong word – a cry of '*abba*'.

'Abba' is the Christian's 'primal scream' which blurts out our identity. 'Abba' is a way a child addresses his or her father. It implies intimacy and the warmth of a secure relationship. But this is often popularly misunderstood. In contradiction to a lot of sermons and seminars 'Abba' does not mean 'Dada' or 'Daddy'. It is not a baby's word for 'Father', but one which continues to be used throughout one's adult life. It is best translated as 'dear Father'.

Praying to God as *abba* is for us to utter *a cry of freedom and hope for our inheritance*

Here we need to recall the origins of 'sonship' language in Israel's calling to represent God on earth as His people (Exod. 4:22–23). It was in this confidence that Israel was challenged to cherish her salvation and to live as the 'exodus people' – dependent on God in trust and obedience on the journey through the wilderness.

The 'sons of God' at this point are those who are have been freed from oppression and bondage to follow God in His great adventure.

So, as Tom Wright says, the very first word of the prayer, 'Father', implies 'not just intimacy, but revolution. Not just familiarity; hope'.[4] When we pray this prayer then, we do so as God's new Exodus people, calling on *Abba* to sustain us in our new found freedom and on our hopeful pilgrimage through a groaning wilderness. Our pilgrimage is to the promised new world that is coming, which is our inheritance as joint-heirs with Christ (Rom. 8:14–25).

It is a cry for times of *crisis* and *suffering*

The Aramaic word itself – *abba* – was treasured in the Early Church even beyond the Aramaic speaking world, no doubt because of its association with Jesus. Significantly, it was in Gethsemane that Jesus entreated His Father most intimately and urgently as *Abba*. As the Beatitudes made clear, the vocation of sonship seldom avoids the valley of suffering

(Matt. 5:9–10).

It is at such times of affliction and trials, when our senses are numbed, our faith tested, and we least know what to pray for, that the cry of *Abba* most spontaneously erupts from the pressured heart (cf. again Rom. 8:15–30).

There can be no circumstances – however extreme – where you cannot pray the Lord's Prayer.

'HALLOWED BE YOUR NAME'

God's name stands for *God's self-revelation*. This originates in God's disclosure to Moses at the burning bush that 'Yahweh' is His name (Exod. 3). So sacred was this revealed name that Jews would not utter it, using instead *adonai* (Lord). In our English versions of the Bible, the occurrence of 'Yahweh' in the text is conveyed by printing 'LORD' with capital and small capital letters.

Because it enshrines His self-disclosure, God's 'name' is highly significant in the Old Testament story. God's name speaks of His *presence* and the manifestation of His glory (Deut. 12:5,21) as in the Temple (1 Kings 8:20,29; 9:3).

God's name stands for God's *reputation*. Deeds were done 'for his name's sake ...' with the hope that God's reputation would be furthered not diminished. Judah's final exile to Babylon was God's judgment on her sin and is summed up by the prophets as 'profaning God's name' (Ezek. 36:20). Persistent unfaithfulness to the covenant on the part of God's people dishonoured God, and dragged His name down in the eyes of the pagans.

Jesus Himself is the first answer to this prayer. He came to do what God's people had failed to do. Jesus made it His own priority to bring Israel out of spiritual exile and to save her from her sins by hallowing the Father's name. 'Now my heart is troubled, and what shall I say? "Father, save me from this hour?" No, it was for this very reason I came to this hour. Father, *glorify your name!*' (John 12:27–28, my italics).

In His great high-priestly prayer on the eve of His death, Jesus was able to testify with confidence: 'I made known to them your name, and I will continue to make it known ...' (John 17:26, ESV).

The great Swiss preacher Walter Luthi, preaching on the Lord's Prayer immediately after World War II, said that God put 'his name into circulation among us ... here on earth ...'. Like a signature on a cheque or banknote, or the image on a coin, God has put His name into circulation and in so doing risked the misuse of the promise or the defacing of the image. And, says Luthi, 'what a worn coin the name of God has become among us religious people'. Hence the need to pray 'Hallowed be your name' with real intent.

But, Luthi goes on,

> God himself answered this prayer by sending the One who is the great exception. The name of God entered through his ear into his holy heart and crossed his pure lips; dirtied and debased as it was when he found it on earth, he took it upon himself. He withdrew all the worn and forged coins, melted them down and minted them anew. There on the cross he bore all the misuse of the name of God and also suffered all the punishment for it. On the cross and there alone God's name is hallowed.[5]

Jesus could achieve this because He revealed the character and nature of God as never before, and because He uniquely embodied the power and presence of God. By His living and His dying, Jesus restores the lustre to the name of God, and – to use Luthi's analogy – puts it back into circulation among us. Jesus enhances God's glory and establishes God's reputation for faithfulness and mercy (John 17:1–5; cf. Rom. 15:8–9).

It is not surprising, then, to find that Jesus teaches us that *our first priority in prayer is to pray that God's name be hallowed*. Our prayer for God's revelation and reputation to be made known is in essence a prayer for both ethics and mission. To pray this way reflects a concern for *ethics* – that God would hallow His name by raising up a people who would worship and praise, live and behave, in ways that glorify His name and enhance His reputation in the sight of all the world. It is to pray that God would establish a people in holiness and love, whose light would shine in the darkness and whose good deeds would be so unmistakably the work of God that men would see them and glorify our Father in heaven (Matt. 5:16).

And that in itself is a part of what makes this a *missional* prayer. To ask God to hallow His name is surely to ask that the revelation of God in Jesus will be established as the final definition and vision of God; that God's presence and power in Jesus might be felt and experienced everywhere; and that the reputation of God as Father and Saviour be acknowledged everywhere, replacing all idols and the false gods of power and violence with the true knowledge of a God of sacrificial love and mercy.

'YOUR KINGDOM COME'

As we approach this second petition, it is worth recalling that the concept of 'the kingdom of God' as used in the Gospels refers primarily to God's *kingly rule* in powerful operation, rather than simply to the territory or realm over which He rules. So in the Old Testament, God's kingship is *acknowledged as over all creation* – again not as a mere domain, over which God presides as the rightful but distant landlord, but as God's dominion activity in which He exercises lordly and creative powers in regularly creative ways (cf. Matt 6:26–30).

Even more particularly, as we have seen in the prophetic vision, God's kingdom comes to stand in a dynamic sense for the *hoped-for coming salvation*. 'Your God reigns' is the good news announced by Isaiah's herald. And God 'reigns' not merely in the sense of His continuous providential superintendence of affairs but also in terms of the invasive demonstration of His covenant love in winning victories over His enemies and saving His people (Isa. 52:7ff). The Isaianic vision, in particular, is especially crucial in shaping our understanding of all that Jesus has come to achieve – and most likely Jesus' own self-understanding of His identity and mission. It is the kingdom of God in this dynamic and saving sense that is celebrated as having been *inaugurated and present in Jesus* (Matt. 4:12–25).

At the same time, what Jesus embodies and enacts is the model of what is yet to come in its entirety and completeness. And because the kingdom of God in its final consummation and fullness is still to come, Jesus teaches us to pray: 'Your kingdom come …' Furthermore, since the future of the kingdom is as material and down-to-earth as its inauguration in Jesus, we are taught to pray, 'Your kingdom come … *on earth* as it is in heaven.'

Let us be clear what it is we are hoping and waiting and praying for. What we await is the coming of God Himself – a final advent in the coming of Jesus. Let us pray for that.

We await the future with hope – not as the prospect of going to heaven when we die (true though that it is for those who die 'in Christ') but in the expectation of *heaven coming here*. Let us pray for that.

We await the final consummation of the kingdom. 'Then I saw a new heaven and a new earth …' (Rev. 21:1) – John envisages the ultimate answer to the prayer we are praying when God's kingly rule in heaven fully comes to earth. As George Eldon Ladd conspicuously reminded Evangelicals a generation ago, '… a redeemed earth is the scene of the future kingdom of God.'[6] It is for this we pray when we say, '… your kingdom come on earth as it is heaven …'

To pray for the kingdom to come is not, therefore, to engage in some escapist enterprise but to deal in stark and well-founded realism. And none of us should pray this prayer for God's future to come without realising that in doing so we are aligning ourselves in the here-and-now with Jesus' radical kingdom movement.

So we pray for the Father's 'kingdom to come', that the full impact of Christ's death and victory might be seen in the world.

We pray that the powerful signs of the kingdom – the powers of the age to come – might be demonstrated among us in healing the sick, in delivering the oppressed and above all in giving new birth to those dead in sin.

We pray for the Holy Spirit to invade our lives and churches with the kingly power of God to display His fruits and gifts.

We pray that Jesus will be Lord in our work and families and leisure, so that we will be seen to be 'kingdom-people', radical disciples of the kingdom as followers of Jesus.

Let your kingdom of justice, mercy and peace come, Father – and come quickly – to our fractured, tormented world.

We are not called to control how history pans out – and we should be thankful we are not, but we are given this prayer as one of the ways in which we may seek to pull the world towards God's future!

'YOUR WILL BE DONE ON EARTH AS IT IS IN HEAVEN'

No part of the Lord's Prayer challenges modern assumptions quite so much as this one. We are obsessed with issues of human freedom and control. We will do almost anything to remain in control of our own destiny. We defend freedom of choice to the death – even unto the death of the unborn. We regard it as the highest human self-fulfilment to be a free, totally autonomous being, answerable to no one. Even the idea of self-control seems an unwarranted infringement of our liberties.

As disciples of Jesus, we may thank God both for the resilience and resistance of the human spirit in the face of oppression and for our democratic liberties while, at the same time, seeking to face the counter-cultural thrust of this prayer. The Lord's Prayer, we have said, is the *education of our desires*. Never more so than when we come to this part of the prayer. This petition is a steep learning-curve for newly forgiven sinners long nurtured in the dark arts of prideful self-sufficiency and self-promotion. Discipleship stands or falls at our willingness to pray this prayer which threatens to redefine us utterly. In Clifton Black's words, 'What we most profoundly *need* is evoked and exposed; what we most ardently *desire* is developed and disciplined.'[7] Praying this prayer draws out of us what our real needs are, not for God's sake – because He already knows what we most need before He is asked (Matt. 6:8,32) – but for our sakes so that we may distinguish real needs from felt needs, purify our desires and sanctify our ambitions. We pray this prayer not to 'get' answers in a crude sense but to achieve something much more important – *the convergence of God's will and ours.*

What we discover as we pray this prayer faithfully and sincerely is that *God's will* satisfies our deepest desires. This goes against all that a godless culture tells us is the case. Every piece of propaganda out there tries to convince us that our best interests and God's best interests are at opposite ends of the spectrum. We are sold the lie that our best interests and true happiness lie in rebelling against God's will and doing our own thing. *Jesus shows us otherwise.* To want what God wants is for Jesus the deepest satisfaction of His heart. Doing God's will is meat and drink to Him (John 4:34). The human heart was created to find its deepest desires fulfilled in doing God's will. So Jesus teaches us to pray this prayer because He knows that God's will and our best interests coincide. So it follows, as John Piper puts it, that 'God is most glorified when we are satisfied in him'.[8]

What we also discover is that faithfully praying 'your will be done' confronts us with costly choices. For Jesus praying this prayer to *Abba* led Him to Gethsemane and drew blood from Him there as well as great anguish of spirit (Matt. 26:42). Praying this prayer will lead us, at the very least, to a deeper willingness to die to self on the instalment basis; it surely commits us to a daily bearing of the cross. In this way, as C.S. Lewis characteristically reminds us, praying this prayer exposes our desires as *too weak* not as too strong.

The Christian life is not about the subjugation of desires so that we lead a dull, resigned, limp, deadened, 'feelingless' existence. Quite the reverse. Jesus comes to stir up a whirlwind of desire that inflames our desires past the point of all lesser petty satisfactions and into a passion for God and His kingdom (cf. Matt. 6:33). In Clifton Black's words, 'As we pray our Lord's Prayer, slowly, steadily, inevitably, its words form us into a people who realise that our deepest need and most basic desire is for nothing but God Himself and the grace to do God's will'.[9]

This realisation is distilled beautifully in the words of an old hymn:

I worship Thee sweet Will of God
And all Thy ways adore;
And every day I live I seem
To love Thee more and more.

I have no cares O blessed Will
For all my cares are Thine;
I live in triumph, Lord for Thou
Hast made Thy triumphs mine.

Ride on, Ride on triumphantly
Thou glorious Will, ride on;
Faith's pilgrim sons behind Thee take
The road that Thou hast gone.

He always wins who sides with God
To him chance is lost;
God's will is sweetest to him when
It triumphs at his cost.

Ill that He blesses is our good
And unblest good is ill;

And all is right that seems most wrong
If it be Thy sweet Will.

F.W. Faber (1814–1863)

So, by way of summary, when we pray this prayer we entreat the Father's will in two main senses.

Firstly, the obvious sense is seeking to lay our lives before God in such a way that He will lead us into *whatever glorifies Him*. Contrary to some 'faith teaching', it is not always wrong to insert an 'if it be your will' into some prayers. It can be sign of true humility and dependence on the Lord to lead us (cf. James 4:13–16).

In my pietistic heritage there were those teachers of 'sanctification' who encouraged the spending of inordinate time and energy – to the point, it sometimes seemed to me, of becoming neurotic – on the complex and agonising task of seeking 'guidance'. Maybe I misconstrued this advice which was given sincerely, but it felt to me, more often than not, to be like asking a blind man to stick the tail on the donkey or to tip-toe nerve-wrackingly across a minefield. It is instructive to realise that such a quest seems a fairly modern obsession. Our Puritan forefathers apparently seldom used the word, preferring instead, it seems, to rise each morning with the prayer: 'Let me glorify you today Lord in whatever I do ...' After all, God has already revealed enough about His covenant will for there to be ample scope for obedience. As I once rather abruptly advised a confused man: 'You can always start with the ten commandments!'

Secondly, we invoke the Father's will in the less obvious, but equally important sense, of wanting to align ourselves not only with what God wants but with *the way He wants to do it*. This is as much a prayer to know God's *ways* as to know His will or, indeed, His works (cf. Psa. 95:9–10). Christian history is too blood-splattered for us to be complacent about praying this prayer. It is tragically easy for zealous Christians to seek to do God's will but not in God's way. Above all, to learn to pray this prayer is to learn to trust the Holy Spirit in discerning what is the *thelema* or 'good pleasure' of God.

Therefore, I urge you, brothers, in view of God's mercy, to offer your bodies as living sacrifices, holy and pleasing to God – this is your spiritual act of worship. Do not conform any longer to the pattern of this world, but be transformed by the renewing of your mind. Then you will be able to test and approve what God's will is – his good, pleasing and perfect will.

Romans 12:1–2

God's will is not good, perfect and acceptable to …

- *the 'unsacrificed' life* – a life which is self-protective, in control of its own destiny, prizes autonomy and freedom on its own terms.
- *the unrenewed mind* – which is why the first three Godward petitions of the prayer are a priority in shaping a God-centred world-view in praying disciples.
- *the unsanctified life* – which remains wedded to the culture, follows every fashion and trend, bends to every wind and is uncritically conformist to the spirit of the age.

But to those who have, however falteringly, taken up the cross to follow Christ, who – in a sense more true than they perhaps know – have died with Christ, to those who are humbly intent on reprogramming their minds with God's truth, to those who are learning the courage to dare to be different in a radically distinctive discipleship, to them God's will seems their highest good, the complete recipe for human fulfilment, that which finds its home in God's delight. Albeit that it remains a goal; not an accomplishment.

In the end, this petition is, like the previous two, an *eschatological* prayer. In praying, 'your kingdom come, your will be done' we are praying for that day to come when heaven's will be done on earth; we are praying for that reuniting of God's will with all His creatures; we are praying for the reconciliation of all things in the harmony of love. As Ernst Lohmeyer memorably put it:

The petition presupposes that heaven and earth are still separate, or at least different, whatever the basis of this difference, whether it is divine counsel, human failure, or deliberate rebellion against God – and so it asks for this difference to be abolished at the end of time. It asks for a single will to be made powerful and effective against all divergent ones so that the world's original destiny may be fulfilled in one event.[10]

We may pray this prayer then in the words of hymnwriter Frederick Mann as a 'triumph song':

My God, my Father, make me strong;
When tasks of life seem hard and long;
To greet them with this triumph song;
Thy will be done.

Rejecting the idea that submitting to God's makes us passive, Mann goes on,

Things seemed impossible I dare;
Thine is the call and Thine the care;
Thy wisdom shall the way prepare;
Thy will be done.

And when all is said and done ...

Heaven's music chimes the glad days in;
Hope soars beyond death, pain, and sin;
Faith shouts in triumph love must win;
Thy will be done.
(Frederick Mann (1846–1928), *Baptist Hymn Book*, 480)

At this point in the prayer, the Godward aspirations for 'your' name, kingdom and will, give rise to the 'us' and 'we' petitions that reflect the basic human predicament, coloured by the special pressures of being a disciple of Jesus.

Having prioritised our praying as to the Father's royal honour and rule, Jesus now invites us to ask the Father for that which immediately concerns us – for provision, for pardon and for protection – or, if you will, for food, forgiveness and freedom.

Jesus teaches us to pray for *provision* – 'Give us today our daily bread'

Can we who live in the 'developed' world really pray this prayer for 'daily bread'? Can any of us in our consumerist Western culture pray this prayer sincerely? After all, our 'daily bread' has been in the bag or in the freezer since we last shopped or let the delivery van drop. For us, the supply chain for bread is so secure and so lengthy that praying for it on a daily basis seems odd and superfluous.

And it is, for this prayer is for 'life on the road', for disciples who have left all and followed Christ, for those who genuinely aren't sure where their next meal is going to come from.

And yet, I think, that even *we* can and must pray this prayer.

We can, I think, pray this prayer if (and only as long as) we realise that by praying it we are being *trained to trust*. This petition in other words anticipates Jesus' further teaching and is a prayerful daily step on the road to a fear-free life (Matt. 6:19–34). As Swiss pastor Walter Luthi once observed, 'When God makes the pressing needs of life the subject of a prayer, then he is transforming anxiety into trust in God.' Our Father is a rich God, Luthi goes on to say, and, 'even if all the prodigal sons the world over were to return home on the same day, that would not put the Father in an embarrassing position.'[11]

We may and must pray this prayer, I believe, if only so that by praying it we may be *trained in being 'this-worldly'*. Archbishop William Temple once provocatively but astutely called Christianity 'the most materialistic religion in the world'. He was right. Our faith is as down-to-earth as the incarnation. The ancient heresy of Gnosticism has haunted the Church from the beginning and tries to seduce us now. Gnosticism believed that salvation is a question of mind over matter, of having a special kind of knowledge that inducts you into the secrets of the spiritual realm. It downplays and downgrades our physical and bodily existence as bad and upgrades the spiritual and disembodied life as superior. But this is a blatant denial of creation and incarnation. We hold no truck with Gnostic super-spirituality or the dualistic view of reality it breeds. Jesus teaches us a 'godly materialism'. The prayer as a whole and this petition in particular train us to live a '*this*-worldly' life in an '*other*-worldly' way. If nothing else this petition saves us from the folly of trying to be more spiritual than God.

We may pray this prayer as daily training in the *detection and avoidance of idolatry.*

> Be careful that you do not ... when you eat and are satisfied, when you build fine houses and settle down ... become proud and ... forget the LORD your God, who brought you out of Egypt ... led you ... gave you manna to eat ... You may say to yourself, 'My power and the strength of my hands have produced this wealth for me.' But remember the LORD your God, for it is he who gives you the ability to produce wealth, and so confirms his covenant, which he swore to your forefathers, as it is today ...
> If you ever forget the LORD your God and follow other gods ...
>
> Deuteronomy 8:11–19

The sequence is deadly: forgetting where your bread comes from is forgetting that God is the Giver; forgetting this and becoming proud and self-sufficient, the thought takes root, 'we did this, it is our achievement ...' and before long avowedly God-fearing people lapse into idolatry. Most people in our culture are practical atheists, not positively disavowing faith in God but living as though God did not exist. But practical atheism is idolatrous by default; it honours the self and serves the creature rather than the Creator (cf. Rom. 1:21–23).

I repeat: this prayer trains us to spot and avoid idolatry.

That is, the prayer teaches us to *receive life as a gift not an entitlement and to respond to the One true Giver of life with gratitude and praise.*

'The earth is the LORD's and everything in it ...' (Psa. 24:1), the Lord owns 'the cattle on a thousand hills' (Psa. 50:10) and we are merely stewards of His good earth. To pray this petition of the prayer is to acknowledge the blessings of God and to give thanks for bread and wine and all else that is the Eucharistic gift of God.

And, we may pray this prayer sincerely – even we in our consumer comfort-zone – if we see that by praying this prayer we are *learning contentment.* Praying this prayer trains us in the good of '*the enough*'.

In his heartfelt 'thank-you' note for the financial support they have given him, Paul urges the Philippians – echoing the words of Jesus – 'Do not be anxious about anything, but in everything, by prayer and petition, with thanksgiving, present your requests to God.' He appreciates their concern for him but is glad to confess that a lifetime of prayerful dependency on the Lord's generous grace has taught him to be content in every situation. They could best 'repay' him by learning for themselves the secret of trusting a God of glorious riches to supply their every need as God has his (Phil. 4:6,10–11).

Needless to say, we may and must pray this prayer if only that by praying it we may be further *trained to embrace the needs of others*.

Hence 'our' bread – which saves the petition from being self-centred and opens us out to intercession and social action on behalf of the needy.

Lastly, and very paradoxically, praying this prayer for bread *teaches us to expect more!*

Chris Wright helpfully links the Sermon on the Mount to the book of Deuteronomy, which was much in Jesus' mind from the temptations onward where He cites the book three times. It is significant that Jesus quotes from Deuteronomy 8:3 which states that God 'fed you with manna ... to teach you that man does not live on bread alone but on every word that comes from the mouth of the LORD' (see Matt. 4:4). It is likely that this text lies behind the prayer for daily bread and influences the later teaching in the sermon on trusting God (ie Matt. 6:25–34).

Wright emphasises three things the statement in Deuteronomy is *not* doing:

- It is *not* negating bread; it acknowledges we need bread; God gives bread in the form of manna.
- It is *not* – at least in a simplistic way – contrasting human self-sufficiency with dependence on God (for God gives the manna miraculously).
- It is *not* contrasting the physical (bread) with the spiritual (word).

Rather, the sentence is not so much a contrast as a climax: '*not only bread in our mouths but the word from the Lord's mouth*'. As Chris Wright comments: 'The point was that God had given the Israelites food *in order to teach them something far more important than the mere fact that God was able to provide food for them*'.

This verse points beyond food; *it points higher*. 'Everything going forth from the mouth of God includes the declaration of God's promises, the claims of God's covenant, the guidance of God's Torah, the articulation of God's purpose for creation and humanity. Words that promised bread came from the same mouth that promised much, much more.'[12]

It is this 'much more' that Jesus is concerned to highlight. So Jesus asks a little later in the sermon 'Is not life more important than food?' (Matt. 6:25b). Praying for 'our daily bread' – paradoxically – is meant to teach us that life is indeed *more than* bread.

Praying this prayer is intended to teach us not to forget God or that life is a gift from Him; praying this prayer is meant to point us to God's larger purposes and goals; praying this prayer trains us to look beyond the basic levels of what we think are essential for living – which God is committed to providing anyway – and to give priority to 'the reign of God and God's justice – matters that undoubtedly flow from the mouth of God ...'[13]

Should we affluent Christians pray this prayer? *Yes, I think we may and I think we must pray this prayer.*

Jesus teaches us to pray for *pardon* – 'Forgive us our debts as we also have forgiven our debtors'

It is helpful in reflecting on this particular aspect of the prayer – as with all the rest of the sermon – to set it in the context of Jesus' whole ministry. Doing this enables us to see that the petition *symbolises the great new Exodus Jesus has come to achieve.*

Jesus' public proclamation of the day of salvation is a declaration that Israel's long spiritual 'exile' under God's judgment is now at an end. Forgiveness is offered, but it becomes available *not* in the appointed place, the Temple, and in defiance of the appointed agents, the priests. Jesus offers forgiveness wherever He goes and whenever He meets a repentant sinner. This petition is central to His ministry.

The petition is *a necessary confession of sin.* Praying this regularly provides us with an honest reality-check. 'Gospelised', 'Beatitude people' are being trained to pray this prayer. The mourners pray this prayer for they know only too well their own sins and the sins of the people.

The meek pray this prayer because they want the tough grace to absorb the wrong done to them without lashing back or becoming institutional victims unable to forgive others. The merciful pray this prayer for only so will they be able to be merciful in turn. The peacemakers surely pray this prayer for only forgiveness heals wounds and hopefully heals memories too. Even the persecuted find grace to pray this prayer as a way of loving their enemies by remembering the Jesus who forgave His enemies from the cross. The pure in heart are the first to pray this prayer for they want to keep short accounts with God and others and want no unconfessed sin or harboured bitterness to block their view of God.

This petition *encourages intercession; it is a prayerful cue to forgive others.*

Praying 'our sins' encourages reconciliation. Praying in this way is an incentive to repair relationships (Matt. 6:14–15; see also 5:24).

But what are we to make of 'as we also have forgiven …'? Does God's forgiveness of us depend on our forgiving others? Well, 'Yes' and 'No'. 'No' it does not, not if you mean that by forgiving others we can *earn* or *deserve* God's forgiveness for ourselves. But 'Yes' it does, in the sense that if we are forgiven by God, this forgiveness can be blocked or soured or cancelled out by our refusal to forgive others.

And why is the prayer for 'forgiveness' the only petition on which Jesus specifically elaborated (Matt. 6:14–15)? It is because, from a biblical standpoint, *forgiveness is the greatest miracle.* Which is easier to say, invites Jesus: 'Your sins are forgiven' or 'Get up, take your mat and walk'? (Mark 2:9). For us, there is no question: to say 'I forgive you' is easier than to say 'Get up and walk.'

But our response, which seems obvious to us, shows just how upside-down our world has become. For Jesus, forgiveness is by far the greater miracle, and He teaches us to pray for this miracle to be done to us and in the strength provided by being forgiven to perform the miracle of forgiving others. *For of such is the right-side up kingdom of God.*

'We have sinned in thought, word and deed', and God saves us in thought, word and deed:

- In thought – by not reckoning our sins against us.
- In word – by preaching to us the gospel of 'sins forgiven of hell subdued and peace with heaven'.
- In deed – by making peace and letting forgiveness flow from the blood of His Son's cross.

Praying this part of the prayer is a repentant, humble, abashed, yet ultimately joyful renewal of our salvation done in remembrance of Him.

Interestingly Matthew preserves the original Aramaic form of the prayer in using the word 'debts'. This leads Glen Stassen and David Gushee to point out that the 'emphasis on forgiveness has both a material and spiritual dimension'.[14] Joel Green explains that forms of enslavement and bondage were built into the Greco-Roman social system. This sustained a situation 'whereby favours done for others constituted a relationship characterised by a cycle of repayment and debt; this system condoned the widespread exercise of coercive powers by some persons over others.' Jesus' prayer, He argues, aims at 'ripping the fabric of the patronage system by treating others as (fictive) kin rather than as greater or lesser than oneself.'[15] When the need arises, forgiving others may take the form of releasing them from longstanding obligations towards us. In this kind of forgiveness we free people from what they owe us – whether it is a financial or emotional debt.

But in all this – as the apostolic teaching later shows us – *learning to be forgiven is prior to learning to forgive.* If this sequence is not followed, we may well use our willingness to forgive as a form of power to control others. This is precisely why, as Stanley Hauerwas points out, '... to be a "forgiven people" makes us lose control. To be forgiven means that I must face the fact that my life actually lies in the hands of others. I must learn to trust them as I have learned to trust God.'[16]

Thankfully, the searching 'forgive *as* ...' in the Lord's Prayer is turned by the gospel into an empowerment: '... forgiving each other, *just as* in Christ God forgave you' (Eph. 4:32, my italics).

In Gerald Sittser's words, 'Forgiveness empowers us to transcend the situation so that we can listen, learn, love and serve even when offenders show no signs of remorse or change.'

He adds,

Forgiveness is costly because it requires us to give up the right to let justice prevail, to get even. The command to forgive confronts our desire to extract payment and to punish the offender. It forces us to let God be God so that his mercy and justice, blended perfectly together, can deal with the offender in a way that both disciplines and restores.[17]

Forgiveness whether received or given is never 'cheap grace' – but it is grace. And the prayer to be a 'forgiven-forgiver' is worth praying because the answer is empowering. 'Kingdom people', say Stassen and Gushee, 'do not carry unforgiven grudges in their backpacks. They travel light in order to be of the greatest possible use to God'.[18]

Jesus teaches us to pray for *protection* – 'lead us not into temptation but deliver us from the evil one'

First, we hazard a paraphrase: 'Save is in the time of trial, let us not sin when we are tempted and deliver us from evil ...' 'Save us ...' is the first cry disciples ever utter. One thing that sharply distinguishes disciples from others is their acute sense of need, vulnerability and danger.

This is a far cry from the rose-tinted, upbeat version of Christianity which passes muster for faith even in some Evangelical and charismatic circles. In some quarters it is as passé to confess your struggles as it is to confess your sins. Coming to Christ is supposed to solve problems not give you problems; being filled with the Spirit is imagined to resolve all difficulties not plunge you into them.

Not so with Jesus, it is worth recalling. It was precisely because He was affirmed as God's Son by the voice from heaven and anointed with the Spirit that the Spirit led Him into the wilderness to be tested by the devil.

So with us, His disciples. Even the Father's adopted sons face the challenge of testing, the pressure of trials and the malevolent opposition of evil. Praying this prayer is a recognition of the difficulties we face – some of which we might never have had if we had not met Christ and been enlisted as His disciples. So this prayer emboldens us to express to the Father these elemental cries: 'help ... save us ... protect us ... deliver us ...' 'Christians are those who ask to be saved. When we pray to God to save us, we are not asking for some changed self-understanding, some new way of feeling about ourselves, something to put zest into our lives ...'.[19] This is altogether more basic, more raw-edged, more visceral, more desperate: 'Lord, save us ...'

So what are we to make of 'lead us not into temptation'? The immediate point at issue is the meaning of '*peirasmos*' – which can be translated as either 'trials' or 'testing'? Hence the attempted paraphrase above. There is, of course, clear biblical teaching on this: God does *not tempt* to sin (James 1:13); but God *does test* – as with Abraham (Gen. 22:1). So we may relate this to the 'temptation' of Jesus which Matthew has just described (Matt.

4:1–11). Jesus faced a test initiated by God, prompted – and no doubt sustained in it – by the Holy Spirit. The Satan working within these strict limits (cf. Luke 22:31) tests Jesus' 'sonship'. As Israel had been designated 'sons of God' and as the Davidic king had been titled 'son of God' so Jesus was tested as to His covenant faithfulness and messianic integrity and on both counts He succeeded where Israel and her kings failed. Jesus refused to be diverted from His God-given vocation, preferring to live by every word from God's mouth. Jesus was led by God to the trial of testing in the wilderness and in teaching His disciples to pray like this, Jesus is inviting His followers to share His own struggles and to experience for themselves that same trust in the Father and infilling of the Spirit that sustained Him.

But why not simply pray for guidance? Why this curiously negative way of putting it – 'lead us *not* …'? Because Jesus knows us too well. He knows how susceptible we are when it comes to guidance.

He knows we get the signals wrong. He knows that however sanctified we are, we can trust our own intuition once too often and end up self-deceived. He knows the devil lurks close to hand seeking to divert us from the paths of discipleship. The petition, as Dallas Willard says, is 'a vote of no confidence in our own abilities'.[20]

In similar vein, Peter Kreeft says that this is a prayer against *over-confidence*. Compare the following two prayers, he suggests, and see whether you recognise anything familiar:

(a) 'I thank thee Lord that I am not like other men. I can and will endure heroic sufferings for you. Please send them my way' – this is the prayer of a self-satisfied, over-confident Pharisee
(b) 'God be merciful to me a sinner. I am weak (like every other man). I can hardly endure even a little pain for you. Therefore, please do not send me great pain.'

Self-delusion prays, 'I am strong …' Self-knowledge prays, 'I am weak … I need deliverance … do not put me to the time of testing and save me from the evil one.'[21]

So Jesus invites us to pray a realistic and hopeful prayer; realistic because it recognises our vulnerability both internal and external; hopeful because it carries with it the promise of protection and deliverance.

In all this we can pray in the confidence – as Paul assured the Corinthians – that 'No temptation has seized you except what is common to man. And God is faithful; he will not let you be tempted beyond what you can bear. But when you are tempted, he will also provide a way out so that you can stand up under it' (1 Cor. 10:13).

Whichever nuance, then, we give to the word *peirasmos*, one thing is clear: There will never be a time when we do not need a Saviour. And Jesus assures us in teaching us this prayer that there will never be a time when we do not *have* a Saviour.

Because He was their Saviour and is our Saviour, He teaches us this prayer. Because He is our Saviour He leads us into the narrow way that leads to life and along the tough paths of righteousness. Because He was the Saviour He went bravely into the eye of the storm to fight evil to the death. Praying this prayer, then, trains us in faith. Praying this prayer leads us straight to the cross where Christ triumphed over evil and trains us to live prayerfully but fearlessly in the good of His victory.

Summary

In teaching us to pray, Jesus is making us more truthful, more faithful. Jesus is making us His disciples.

In praying, our lives are being bent away from their natural inclinations towards God. We are becoming the very holiness, obedience, forgiveness for which we ask in prayer. We find our little lives caught up in the drama of God's redemption of the world, we are swept up into an adventure more significant than our lives would have been if left to ourselves, heaven is open, the kingdom is come, and we shout, 'Amen'.[22]

SURPASSING RIGHTEOUSNESS
PRIORITIES AND NECESSITIES
(MATT. 6:19–34)

The main exhortation of Jesus in this section of the sermon is clear: *'Do not worry …'* (Matt. 6:25,27–28,31,34). But the welcome news that it is possible to be free of our perennial anxiety is prefaced by a strong *'Therefore'* (v.25a). This alerts us to the fact that the call to be free from anxiety rests firmly on what has gone before. In particular, this means that *freedom from anxiety in everyday life depends on the choices and commitments and outlook spelled out in verses 19–24.* Jesus here analyses the gravitational pull that operates deep within our personality. He exposes those habits of the heart by which we run our lives and He employs three images in doing so – each of which, significantly, has to do with economics, with money!

A. The first image is *treasure,* and where we are investing it (Matt. 6:19–21)

We are habitual investors. We value some things more than others. We entrust emotional energy in what we value most. We rightly seek security for ourselves and our family by investing for the future in ways that we hope will protect us from uncertainty and loss.

The question we face is: Where are we going to invest and in what?

Jesus poses a stark choice in this passage: Either we invest in heavenly values or in earthly ones. On the one hand we can invest everything in 'treasure on earth' and entrust our future to bank deposits, property prices, stocks and shares – that is, to money, in one form or another. Or we can store up 'treasure in heaven' by investing in the kingdom of God and its values.

Now Jesus is not for one moment encouraging irresponsibility or lack of foresight. He is, however, challenging us as to where our ultimate security lies. After all, investing everything in 'treasure on earth' is foolish, He says, because 'treasure on earth' is vulnerable and its values are limited and conditional. Moth, rust, and thieves threaten it all the time. Dale Bruner imaginatively suggests that

- *the moth* represents natural threats to our security – like floods, droughts, famines, and earthquakes
- *rust* represents the corrosion of time which causes things to lose value, to depreciate, to wear out and eventually to die
- and *the thief* represents all human threats to our security from burglars, fraudsters, and con-men through stockmarket collapses, mortgage interest rises, and inheritance tax, to the ravages of terrorism and wars.

'All three together,' he suggests, 'represent the insecurity of life lived for accumulation.'[1] But 'treasure in heaven' is not vulnerable to any of these threats (v.20b).

But just what does Jesus mean by 'treasure in heaven'? Here are four reflections:

1. Jesus is not contrasting the material over against the spiritual at this point but talking about hard cash in both cases.

2. Nor does 'in heaven' mean 'life after death'. Rather 'in heaven' means in the only realm of reality that finally exists – the kingdom of God. Not, that is, the empire of the self-styled 'eternal' Rome with its trade and taxes, which for a while seemed all encompassing, but the empire of the One Creator God, the Father of Jesus and of all who faithfully follow Him.

3. Storing up 'treasure in heaven' means investing in the value-system of the kingdom of God. And that – in particular – means *sacrificial and generous giving to others.*

Jesus makes this clear at Luke 12:33 – where laying up treasure in heaven is about selling not acquiring, about giving to the needy. 'We lay up treasures in heaven by not hoarding them here on earth, but by using our possessions sacrificially and generously.'[2]

4. Jesus is probing into the deepest movement of our hearts. His diagnosis is penetrating: 'For where your treasure is, there your heart will be also' (Matt. 6:21). Jesus' words stand in flat contradiction to the popular modern adage which urges us to do whatever our heart tells us to do, to 'follow your heart'. No, says Jesus, your heart will follow your investment. For this reason 'seek first his [God's] kingdom and his righteousness, and all these things [including the things you need, v.32] will be given to you as well' (Matt. 6:33). Where your 'treasure' is banked in the kingdom of God and in the good of others, there your heart will follow. There is no greater indicator of having invested in the kingdom God than the heartfelt joy to be found in the practice of social justice and personal giving.

B. In describing the instinctive movements of the human heart, the second image Jesus uses is that of *vision* and with what eyes we view the world (Matt. 6:22–23)

Each of us has a way of looking out at the world. We all have a particular take on reality, a habitual outlook, what – ideologically – we call a 'world-view'. We all have a world-view – whether we think we do or not – however rudimentary or sophisticated. The question is: Do we see correctly or not? Or – to use the metaphor Jesus uses – if the eye is the lamp of the body, is our eye good or bad? Is it letting in light or are we being engulfed in darkness?

This has little to do with IQ. The gospel reveals us all to be fallen in our minds as well as our wills so that we don't think straight or see clearly. Nowhere is this more obvious than with those we call intellectuals. Lesser minds are merely dimwitted, but great minds often suffer complete spiritual 'black-out' (see Eph. 4:17–24). Intellectuals think clever thoughts, say clever things, make witty remarks but their mindset, says Paul – apart from the gospel – is unenlightened, their minds are darkened, their outlook is impaired, their world-view is faulty.

Jesus made a similar observation about the scribes and Pharisees, learned men that they were, well-educated at the best rabbinic colleges no doubt, and Bible scholars too, but He calls them 'blind guides ... blind fools ... blind leaders of the blind' (Matt. 23:16–22; 15:14). So what counts is *not* how clever or well-educated you are but *how well you see.*

Our modern Western society – and, increasingly, much of the rest of the world – is ruled by one discipline: economics. The world is seen as a global market not a human family; so what counts are profit-margins, stock prices, the value of the dollar or the pound, interest rates, revenue and taxes ... the price of a barrel of oil. This perception of what matters most is what drives our world. It does so because this is how our rulers *see* the world.

This was just how the Caesars in Rome saw the world, so that a decree went out that all the world should be taxed – just as Jesus was born. And Rome's wealth was built on the backs of the poor – just as British prosperity in the eighteenth and early nineteenth century was built on the backs of the slaves – through an avaricious, exploitative and one-sided trade system that stripped the wealth of nations and sent it back to Rome. (Read Revelation 18–19 for John's take on this.)

Jesus has come announcing a change of government, preaching the gospel of another kingdom, another empire – the empire of the fatherly God in heaven whose world it is. And the 'gospelised humanity' being created by His coming is called by Jesus to exemplify an alternative way of looking at the world.

What, after all, is a 'good' or 'healthy' eye?

The parable of the Workers in the Vineyard helps us answer this (Matt. 20:1–16, NB v.15). The story Jesus tells is all about the generosity and grace of God to those workers who have arrived late in the day and don't deserve to be paid the same as the rest. Criticised for departing from accepted trade-union and accountancy procedures, Jesus has the owner of the vineyard say: 'Am I not allowed to do what I choose with what belongs to me? Or do you begrudge me my generosity?'

The footnote (in your Bible) will tell you that literally this last statement reads: 'Is your eye bad because I am good?' (Matt. 20:15, ESV). In other words a 'bad eye' represents a mean and stingy spirit; a 'good eye' means a generous attitude.

The parable opens the 'eyes of our hearts' to see that God is gracious and generous – and we catch a vivid glimpse of the divine generosity that rules the world. So kingdom disciples – 'gospelised' by this grace – look out on the world, and seeing it as it really is – awash with God's generosity – look out on it with 'generous eyes'.

You have a good or healthy eye if you look at Master-money or Master-God and see that God is more valuable.

You have a good or healthy eye if you look out on the world and see marginal people more clearly than profit margins. You have a good or healthy eye if you look out on the world and notice that someone has switched all the price-tags and that only Beatitude attitudes put the world right-side up. You have a good or healthy eye if – in other words – you view the world with a kingdom outlook.

Jesus – we recall – is describing the laws of the heart, the gravitational pull in our hearts which determines how we run our lives.

C. The third image Jesus employs is that of *service* – and asks: Can we serve two masters (Matt. 6:24)?

In memorable language, Jesus re-affirms what has already been established. Everyone instinctively gives allegiance and devotion to some person or cause or thing. A choice has to be made at this fundamental level. Jesus says: 'No-one can serve two masters.'

Of course, when faced with the challenge of 'Which master do you serve?', a smart, postmodern person would no doubt reply: 'I don't serve anyone. I am free to do what I want,' thereby disclosing that of course they *do* serve a master – it just happens to be self!

But Jesus says we cannot serve two masters at the same time. In particular we 'cannot serve God and Money' (or 'mammon'). Note the 'cannot' which states a law of the human heart; it is just not possible to divide our deepest devotion in this way.

Dale Bruner suggests that the Old Testament's 'Thou shalt have no other *gods* before me' translates into Jesus' 'Thou shalt have no other *goals* before me'.[3] As Bonhoeffer says, 'Our hearts have room only for one all-embracing devotion, and we can only cleave to one Lord.'[4]

And notice how money features again so centrally in Jesus' teaching. We serve money by worshipping money – by letting ourselves become preoccupied with money, with money lost or gained, money spent or saved, money earned or invested; we let money occupy our hearts, dominate our thinking. Or if we are rich enough not to worry about it at all then we are even more in danger of putting our ultimate trust in the stuff.

But there is an alternative way … *The 'surpassing righteousness' shown in trusting the Father of the kingdom: getting priorities right and trusting for necessities* (Matt. 6:19–34).

'… THEREFORE DO NOT WORRY …' (MATT. 6:25–34)

Freedom from anxiety, we are reminded, presupposes the choices, commitments and outlook vividly described in the images of verses 19–24. Now, having made the choices and commitments and with the outlook spelled out in verses 19–24 … 'therefore' (v.25a) … 'do not worry …' (Matt. 6:25,27–28,31,34).

With your treasure invested in the right place and your heart with it, with your vision clear so that you see the world through a generous eye, with your ultimate loyalty to God decided, it becomes possible to live free from crippling anxiety in facing the challenges of everyday living.

Anxiety is the tip of an iceberg which at its coldest depths is 'fear of death' – the root of all fears (Heb. 2:15). What we fear on whatever scale of intensity is loss of life.

The regular everyday worries of life are symptoms of a deeper existential uncertainty ('angst') that fears being cut off from all that makes life meaningful and trustworthy, and that is, at the bottom-line, a fear of being separated from the very source of our being, who is God.

Even when we have been impacted by the gospel – even when our ultimate 'fear of death' has been consoled by the hope of resurrection – we still face, in the meanwhile, the daily erosion of our confidence by domestic worries. Jesus, our Lord and Saviour and Teacher, is lovingly aware of our frailty when it comes to fretting over bread and butter issues. He wants to assure us that freedom from crippling anxiety is possible for those who have been 'gospelised' by the grace of His Father's kingdom.

Before we go any further, let's avoid misunderstanding Jesus here.

There is a big difference between not being anxious and being *idle*. Jesus is not saying that our basic needs will automatically be met regardless of whether we work or not. His words are not a recipe for being workshy.

Furthermore, there is a big difference between being anxious and being *irresponsible*. Again, to trust God does not relieve one of the responsibility to provide for one's family. Jesus is not criticising wise forethought for the future but a neurotic anxiety about it.

What Jesus is uncovering here is a deep and paralysing anxiety. The cognate noun *merimna* occurs in the Jewish tradition to mean 'sleeplessness' (1 Maccabees 6:10; Ecclesiasticus 42:9). We may joke about this ...

> I've joined the new 'don't worry' club
> In fear I hold my breath;
> I'm so afraid I'll worry,
> I'm frightened half to death ...

But Jesus is talking about a debilitating fear and worry that undermines our faith in God. Such anxiety is the result of investing our security in the wrong place, of giving our heart to the wrong objects of affection, of skewed vision, of looking in the wrong place and in the wrong way, of seeking false gods, of practising idolatry.

Two basic considerations apply here:

(a) Life is more than economics (Matt. 6:25b). But the effect of worry is to reduce life, to trivialise it, to diminish the human project, to scale down the human capacity to a tense pre-occupation with survival and basic needs. In which event, as Hans Rookmaaker once shrewdly advised a student friend, it is timely wisdom and an act of faith to buy that CD or piece of porcelain or take that holiday you can't really afford! The first economic lesson to learn is that life is more than economics.

(b) Worry gets you nowhere. Worry is futile; feeding on it won't make grow you taller or last longer (Matt. 6:27). Quite the reverse: we know now that acute and persistent tension and anxiety will shorten your life-span if not your height (though some worriers seem to fret themselves smaller).

Jesus now offers us four moves we can make to offset the encroachment of worry:

1. *Take lessons from the logic of creation* (6:26–30)
   Yes, there is a time and place to stop fretting and go out into the garden

or the countryside and spend time with nature. Because strictly speaking it is not 'Nature' in a determinist sense but creation. And it is a creation watched over by a Creator still (not Deism but Theism). The flowers can sometimes relieve our stress; the birds can teach us to trust. It may not be politically correct or ecologically cool to say so, but Jesus says it: You are 'more valuable' than the other creatures God has made. And since they don't fret to be beautiful, why should you?

2. *Take note of the lifestyle of the pagans* (6:32)

How different are we from the society around us? How counter-cultural are we when it comes to worry? How can we be salt and light if we are as neurotic as they are about daily bread?

It is striking how Jesus wants us to differentiate ourselves from the pagans all the way through the Sermon on the Mount: don't love the way the pagans love (not only close family, neighbours and friends – and, in today's world, don't sleep with your girlfriend like the pagans do, 5:47); don't pray like the pagans pray (6:7); don't seek what the pagans seek, have different ambitions (6:32) – in short, 'Do not be like them' (6:8).

3. *Take heart from the love of the Father* (6:32)

Surely this is the best medicine for anxiety: to trust the Father and to take Jesus' word for it. Jesus should know, for He knows the Father better than anyone. Jesus tells us: the Father sends sun and rain on just and unjust alike. Jesus tells us: the Father is merciful, the Father will reward you, and – when it comes to needs – '… *your Father knows what you need before you ask him*' (6:8,32, my italics).

As to the future, not even Jesus knew exactly how it will be, for 'No-one knows about that day or hour, not even … the Son, but only the Father' (Matt. 24:36). For Jesus it is enough that the Father knows, and surely that can be enough for us.

4. *Take life a day at a time* (6:34)

Take life in day-sized chunks. We find ourselves saying, 'To live in the present … if only I could … I get restless, trying to rearrange yesterday or write the script for tomorrow. This is worry.' The secret was put well by Gerald Vann who said: 'To live in the present is to live in the Presence.'[5]

Verse 33 is the key to the whole section: 'But seek first his kingdom and his righteousness, and all these things will be given to you as well.'

'Seek' is a strong word. Actively pursue the kingdom as the kingdom has actively pursued you – if we may construe Matthew 11:12 in a positive sense: '... the kingdom of heaven has been forcefully advancing, and forceful men lay hold of it.'

Seeking first God's kingdom is certainly a call to ...

- *revalue* your investment, treasure your true treasure and rekindle the passion of your heart in the fire of fresh love
- *refocus* your vision, tear out the eye that's fixated with lust and greed, or whatever blurs your single vision, fix your eyes on the generosity of God and refocus on what matters most
- *renew* your allegiance to your one Master, rededicate yourself to the God you love who loves you

In other words ...

- *re-channel* your energies into a renewed passion for the kingdom of God (6:33).

Divert some of that nervous anxiety into concern for the kingdom. Give yourselves over to 'thrusting participation in the dynamic, gracious, delivering presence of God.'[6] Participate whole-heartedly, decisively, single-mindedly in the rule and reign of God; break loose from the vicious circle of 'mammonism', consumerism and retaliation. Make a transforming initiative.

The exhortation 'do not worry' – as Glen Stassen and David Gushee point out – should be seen as *justice teaching* rather than mere psychology. In their view, this exhortation is about theology not therapy. Its intention is not that we may feel more comfortable about our money and possessions by overcoming worry. Jesus' words are a challenge to a radical way of living, summoning us to a whole new order of things.

This is a challenge to share in a new fear-free society characterised by generosity and mutual support. Here is no risk-free, 'safety-first policy' but a call to an adventurous and boundary-breaking kingdom life.

In my father's generation dedicated saints and missionaries were described as 'sold-out for God'. This isn't just for exceptional disciples but for us all. 'Seek first his kingdom ...' anticipates the punch line of the parable of Jesus in which a farmer digging his field stumbled on buried treasure and went – for sheer joy – and sold all that he had to buy the field and gain the treasure. That is precisely what seeking the kingdom means.

Sell out, then, for the kingdom; stick a 'sold-out' notice on your discipleship door! Seek to live every day under God's gracious rule and in the good of God's covenant faithfulness. Order your priorities well – God's kingdom righteousness first – then God's provision of 'all these things' that you need will flow.

And every day, keep praying the Lord's Prayer.

SURPASSING RIGHTEOUSNESS
RELATIONSHIPS (MATT. 7:1–12)

Jesus warns against 'judging' in the sense of condemning others by one who has not judged him or herself (Matt. 7:1–5). It has been said that 'human beings unhappily possess an inbred proclivity to mix ignorance of themselves with arrogance towards others'.[1] Jesus forbids His disciples the indulgence of condemning other people when they have not been willing to submit their own lives to scrutiny and judgment. If we try to do this God will judge us commensurately.

The rhetorical questions in this passage are presented in almost cartoon form (Matt. 7:3–4) and the 'Monty-Pythonish' picture continues when the positive action is urged: '… take the plank out of your own eye' (Matt. 7:5). All in all Jesus is warning *against severity* in how we assess others.

Having denounced *judgmentalism*, Jesus now goes on to advocate a right and necessary kind of 'judging' – a passing judgment which is construed as the moral and spiritual *discernment* shown by a disciple, one who is asking God for wisdom (Matt. 7:6–12). Having warned against undue severity, Jesus now seems to warn against the opposite extreme to severe condemnation of others by urging His disciples to guard against *undue laxity* (Matt. 7:6). The saying is not easy to understand but my take on it is this: Jesus is urging us not to be undiscerning in our assessments of other people; in this sense we must make judgements and perhaps particularly in offering them the gospel.

'Matthew 7:1–5 cannot be taken to mean abstinence from discernment that evaluates between good and bad. There is a legitimate judging in which Jesus' disciples are to be engaged, both in private and in public.'[2]

97

So don't be naive (cf. Phil. 1:9).

The terms used in Matthew 7:6 are undoubtedly offensive; 'dogs' is used for Gentiles and pagans (cf. Matt. 15:26; Phil. 3:2) and Jews do not keep pigs.

Two main ways of interpreting this difficult saying have been proposed:

1. It may be about *apostasy* – in which case it reflects the failure over time to value what you have in Christ, which leads to falling away and the destruction of what you once had.
2. It may be about *mission* – in which case it is saying something about not devaluing the precious gospel.

This second interpretation seems to be closer to the mark, and is favoured by many recent scholars. Don't try to force the gospel on those who have no inclination to receive it. So perhaps it anticipates, 'If the home is deserving, let your peace rest on it; if it is not, let your peace return to you. If anyone will not welcome you or listen to your words, shake the dust off your feet when you leave that home or town' (Matt. 10:13–14). Maybe there is an implied contrast with emerging revolutionary groups seeking to impose God's will by violence? Or maybe it anticipates the 'Golden Rule' (Matt. 7:12) and suggests that if we give the gospel aggressively we will be rebuffed with aggression. It may suggest also offering the gospel of the kingdom without pressing for discipleship – and thus cheapening grace. It may suggest a graphic warning against 'dumbing-down' the truth, against 'trashing' the gospel to make it fit for human consumption by those who have no intention of changing, against treating the gospel as dogmeat or pig swill!

On any reading, a point is almost certainly being made about the *infinite value* of the kingdom. The 'pearl' is elsewhere an image of the kingdom and its gospel (Matt. 13:45–46), as something especially valuable and not to be underrated. Compromise with pagans' standards will lead to you being dragged down to their level and all that you once found holy and precious will be desecrated and devalued. The priceless distinctiveness of what you have and are will be diminished by assimilation or destroyed by attack. The phrase 'trample them under their feet' echoes the fate of salt that has lost its savour (Matt. 5:13–16), and so may support this reading.

Rather we should 'seek first his kingdom and his righteousness' by esteeming it above everything else, and – to refer to a point made earlier – by being like that man who finding the buried treasure in the field, sold all he had to buy the field – in the conviction that the kingdom of God is the greatest prize of all. Don't make your holiest things and most valuable values easy meat for pagans; don't sell yourself short; don't prostitute the gospel in order to get a hearing or to make a favourable impression – they will eat you for breakfast!

There is much mileage perhaps to be explored in this text, especially when we consider the ironic state of our current society where the cardinal sin is being judgmental and where the chief virtue is being tolerant of anything and everything indiscriminately (except of course those who disagree with that stance). Jesus as the wisest teacher, strikes the perfect balance here.

The words which Jesus utters next and the stunning promise He makes (Matt. 7:7–11) are then best understood in the context of the previous verses as pointing up the need to make accurate assessments of people and situations – without on the one hand being too severe or, on the other hand, being utterly undiscerning and gullible. In which case, the invitation Jesus gives here to 'ask … seek … knock …' is not so much to engage in a prayerful life in general, but a more specific invitation to *seek from God all the wisdom we need in order to negotiate complex inter- personal relationships, especially with outsiders.* Pray to see better, pray to have logs of prejudice and self-interest removed from your eyes so as to be able to see with God's eyes. Significantly, Luke's variant of this saying is attached to the Lord's Prayer and ends, 'how much more will your Father in heaven give *the Holy Spirit* to those who ask him!' (Luke 11:13, my italics).

And so to the so-called 'Golden Rule' (Matt. 7:12). This, too, fits the context well. In the absence of any special guidance in relational matters – if all else fails – apply the Golden Rule: 'So, in everything, do to others what you would have them do to you …'.

This is not discipleship made easy: but it is discipleship made plain.

THE CALL FOR COMMITMENT
(MATT. 7:13–29)

As with the entire Sermon on the Mount, it is crucial to set these words in their first-century context. The invasion of the kingly rule of God in Jesus spells both judgment and grace for first-century Israel. The options He sets out here, therefore, are not casual lifestyle choices to be mulled over in one's leisure moments but life-or-death decisions made urgent by the national, cultural and personal crisis precipitated by the kingdom being 'at hand'. Throughout the sermon, intensifying as it draws to a close, 'the warning of catastrophe predominates'.[1]

1. Jesus says there are *two gates, two ways, two destinations* (Matt. 7:13–14)

This is serious business. The choice is sharp and proves fatal for the many, but life-giving for few – the Salt and Light Company, the marginalised disciple band of brothers and sisters. Jesus spells out how drastic the entry requirement is (narrowed down to dying to self), how tough the terrain is over which the journey is continued ('narrow and hard' and almost guaranteeing persecution!), and how crucial the destination ('destruction or life').

2. Jesus says there are *two trees* (Matt. 7:15–20)

One yields bad fruit from false prophets; the other bears good fruit from genuine prophets.

Of any teaching that professes the name of Jesus, we may legitimately ask these kingdom questions: How demanding is it to get in? To ask for anything less than total surrender and death to self is to sell the gospel short and to offer cheap grace. How tough is it to carry on? Any soft-peddling here that offers a trouble-free ride is pure fantasy which is seriously misleading and again drastically undersells the gospel. Ask too of any teaching: What does it offer to produce and what does it in fact produce? And the outcome to be looked for is not prosperity or miracles but *'fruit'* – the fruit of kingdom character and Beatitude attitudes. Anyone who offers anything less sells the gospel cheap and is likely to be, at best, misguided, at worst, a false prophet.

Above all – and this is a serious responsibility for any preacher or teacher – where will it lead? Does the teaching lead to an easy life now but destruction later, or to a disciplined life now and life for ever after?

3. Jesus says, there only *two possible foundations* (Matt. 7:21–27)

Jesus poses sharp alternatives at the end of His sermon: the alternative gates and ways which lead to opposite ends; the alternative trees which produce totally opposite fruit; and now 'The Tale of Two Builders'.

The foolish builder stupidly erects his house on sand and quickly watches it succumb to subsidence when the storm arrives. And then there is the other builder, presented as an example of sagacity and storm-proof living.

And the difference between the two builders? Not experience or expertise in Christian practice or confession; no difference there. Both call Jesus 'Lord', both do things in His name, both hear His words, but *only one of them acts on them!*

'The house that crashes,' says Dale Bruner, 'is the house of Christians who find Jesus' words important enough to hear but not realistic enough to live.'[2]

Preaching amidst the devastation of post-war Hamburg, Helmut Thielicke re-awakened his congregation's faith by declaring that 'the only Word that is rock foundation is the Word that you really stand on'.

'To dare to be obedient,' Thielicke declared, 'even when humanly speaking, it seems foolish to be obedient; to tell the truth when it is dangerous or "stupid" to tell the truth but where God really demands that it be spoken – and then with all your heart to trust that God will not let you down but will make his promises come true' – this is what it means to build on the foundation of rock.[3]

This is the way the sermon ends. But this is not the way we *want* the sermon to end.

Why did it not end where we might have preferred it to end – say at 7:12 with the Golden Rule. Then we could have gathered round Jesus and discussed it. 'Do you agree?' Jesus might have asked. 'Correct me if I'm wrong. What do you think: am I being too idealistic here?'

But Jesus does not end the sermon there; nor does He leave matters open for discussion. Jesus ends the sermon where He ends it – with our eternal destiny hanging on His every word.

This is surely absolute arrogance on the preacher's part ... unless ...

This is not the way we would encourage sermons to end!

The medium is the message but not to this degree surely.

The preacher puts Himself at the centre of the message in a unique and unprecedented and distinctly uncomfortable way.

It's all 'Me ... Me ... My words ...' – this is surely bad homiletical practice, and the height of arrogance ... unless ...

And this is not the note we usually prefer sermons to end on.

Clearly Jesus expects us when we hear His words actually to go and obey them and do them. This preacher is getting above Himself ... unless ...

And this is not the usual sanction applied by preachers when they conclude their sermons: 'I never knew you ... Away from me ...'

People often come up to me and say 'I heard you preaching and teaching ... do you remember me?' Sadly, too often, I have to confess: 'I'm sorry, I can't quite place you, I can't put a name to a face.' Apart from testifying to my poor memory, this hardly matters.

So why on earth can it matter for this preacher to say: 'I never knew you'? Why would it matter in the slightest to be banished from my presence at the end of teaching? Why does it matter to be banished from His presence?

It matters not at all ... unless ... unless ... unless ...

Unless this preacher is exactly who Matthew says He is – 'Emmanuel', God-with-us ... unless He is the One given all authority over all the nations ... unless He is the Lawgiver and Judge in person ...

In which case, not only hearing but doing His words is a matter of life and death.

Thankfully, as P.T. Forsyth mercifully reminds us: 'It is a new mercy of God (as His judgment always is) that lets the false foundation slide from us, so that we may stand in its debacle, on the Rock that nothing can shake.'[4]

None of which makes verses 21–23 less sobering.

I have spent most of my active pastoral ministry in a charismatic context. I remain totally committed to the conviction that Jesus heals today and that the charismatic gifts are the Spirit's gracious empowerment of the Church. But it clears the head rapidly to realise that Jesus did not say, 'Blessed are you if you prophesy or cast out demons in My name … or work miracles in My name.'

We may say and sing 'Lord, Lord'. Now *kurie* can mean simply, 'Mister – yes, mister' or 'Yes, Master' … right up to Caesar in Rome being addressed as *kurios*. So it is not the word that defines the Person; it is the Person that defines the word. We are listening to the One whom Thomas confessed as: 'My Lord and My God'. And only if we are committed to doing what He says are we entitled to call Him 'Lord'!

So the Sermon on the Mount *ends* but its *effects* are long-lasting and began to be felt immediately (Matt. 7:28–29).

The crowds are astonished – and what astonishes them is Jesus' *authority*. We might have known it would come down to this; this has been the underlying issue all along.

> *Jesus acts as Judge in advance of what will pertain on the last and final day (Matt. 5:3–10).*
> *Jesus claims to be the One who fulfils the God-given Law and the God-sent prophets – the lasting embodiment and final revelation of God and God's will (Matt. 5:17–20).*
> *Jesus claims to be the one true interpreter of God's Law who has the right to deepen and intensify the Torah and is qualified to bring out its truest and deepest intention with His astonishing 'I tell you the truth …' (Matt. 5:18–48).*
> *Jesus enjoys a unique relationship with God as His Father and presumes the right to invite others to share it (6:1–14).*

Finally Jesus declares that human destiny is determined by response to His words!

This is truly an astonishing authority. Unlike that of the scribes who took their stand on authorities who had written and spoken in the past, He speaks truly 'ex-*ousia*' – out of His own being – and so astonishes us with a firsthand authority that claims our lives.

HOW, THEN, DOES THE SERMON ON THE MOUNT LEAVE YOU?

I agree with the student who said at the end of Darrell Johnson's powerful lectures on the sermon: 'I can go to only one place in the Sermon – back to the beginning – and confess to being "poor in spirit".' To which Darrell Johnson replied: 'yes, and I stand there with you. I remind you only of this: that Jesus says to you "Blessings on you poor in spirit ... the kingdom is yours."'

Matthew ends his Gospel with the Great Commission, as we call it, the challenge to make disciples out of every nation. Luke ends his Gospel with the ascending Jesus lifting up His hands and blessing the gathered disciples (Luke 24:50–51). This was the last glimpse of Jesus which the upturned faces saw as the cloud enveloped Him.

Until the end of time, until He returns for us, the followers of Jesus, called to the challenging and demanding life of discipleship, live out our lives as 'Beatitude people', under the ceaseless benediction of His uplifted nail-pierced hands.

FOCAL POINT
MOUNTAIN OF TRANSFIGURATION

focal point – the place where sound and light waves converge; the centre of attention.

dictionary definition

After six days Jesus took with him Peter, James and John the brother of James, and led them up a high mountain by themselves.

Matthew 17:1

Something happened to Jesus on this mountain, something mysterious, something vivid which we call the 'transfiguration'. The face of Jesus 'shone like the sun, and his clothes became as white as the light.' 'A bright cloud enveloped' everyone there (17:2,5).

Firstly, we must consider the unique *convergence of light*. What does it signify?

The fierce sunlight and bright cloud are historic tokens of God's glorious presence experienced fleetingly before at Sinai, at the tabernacle and within the Temple (Exod. 34:5,29–35; 40:34–35; 1 Kings 8:10–13). What was being manifested in Ancient Israel and is now radiating out of Jesus is nothing less than the glory of God.

As a glowing complexion is the outer sign of inner health, so the radiance of God's glory is the outshining of God's innate holiness.

Holiness is God's essential otherness, what makes God *God* as distinct from His creation. That essential 'godness' now radiates out from Jesus to give a glimpse of what is always true about Him. The face of Jesus is not temporarily reflecting what was a borrowed light – as happened once to Moses (Exod. 34:29–35; cf. 2 Cor. 3:12–13); Jesus' face is briefly revealing what is an essential glory. Once, Moses saw and reflected God's glory so that his face shone, but even Moses in all his glory was not arrayed like this. The true God-light of God's self-disclosure, hinted at on Sinai, and in tabernacle and Temple, is here concentrated and focused on Jesus, God's Son. He shares uniquely in the glory of the One Creator God, and for an eternal moment the watching disciples see it. Here on the mountain, the spotlight of God falls on Jesus alone. It makes Him the centre of attention, as if God is directing us to 'look at him'. So even those privileged to be there finally 'saw no-one except Jesus' (Matt. 17:8).

Secondly, we note the *appearances made*. Why is Moses here? Because Moses represents the *past*. Moses was the mediator of the Law, the covenant charter of Israel's existence. Through Moses, God established the foundational revelation on which Israel's place in history is based. And Jesus has come not to abolish that Law but He has come to fulfil it. He has come to 'fulfil all righteousness' by what He is and does, and to inspire a surpassing righteousness in those who follow Him. To be sure, reading Moses throws light on Jesus. But even that God-given revelation is outshone by the sun shining in Jesus, and Jesus throws back more light on Moses than He receives from him. Jesus throws blazing light on the Law, revealing the Law's deepest intentions and long-term goals as never before as He brings them to fruition. From this moment on – as Pentecost confirms – the glory attached to the old covenant will be eclipsed by the glory of the new covenant.

Why is Elijah here? Elijah surely represents the prophets as Moses did the Law. This is no doubt true. But more specifically, Elijah represents the prophetic *future* as Moses did the historic *past*.

In the Judaism of Jesus' day, Elijah was commonly expected to return before the end as a sign of the Messiah's imminent arrival. Jesus acknowledges this common expectation but sparks a debate about the *Eschaton* (the final state of affairs) with mention of His own impending resurrection! Unable to grasp this, the disciples reflect orthodox Jewish belief by assuming He is talking about the end of history when resurrection of the dead was expected to happen. In which case, they argue, shouldn't Elijah come first (Matt. 17:9–10)? Jesus proceeds to turn the discussion on its head by identifying the future Elijah-figure with John the Baptist and He has most decidedly *already come* (Matt. 17:11–12).

The startling implication is this: if 'Elijah' has already come in the life and death of John, then in a real sense *the future is already here, and the end has already arrived in the middle of history*. And to those privileged to witness it, what this transfiguration shows in one blinding moment of the glory of that kingdom, will be decisively manifest in His own death and resurrection to those who in their turn are alive to see it (Matt. 17:12b; cf. 16:27–28)! Waves of light and sound from the past and from the future converge here on Jesus in the present. And if Moses is *eclipsed*, and Elijah is demonstrably *upstaged*, it is only so that Israel's past and Israel's future on which the world's destiny depends should converge on Jesus. Moses who never set foot in Canaan during his lifetime, now *steps out of the past* history of Israel and into the promised land for the first time, and so lives 'inside' the fulfilment of the promise because he stands within the radiance of the Messiah. Elijah who, unusually, was taken up into God's heaven without seeing death, now, *steps out of the future* of Israel, to talk of Jesus' death on which all hopes are pinned. Both Moses and Elijah are eager to discover how His suffering and death might be a new 'Exodus' and a 'new departure', the turning-point, not just for them but for the world (cf. Luke 9:30–31). All ears are now tuned to Jesus to hear the voice of authority: all eyes are turned to Jesus to see the vision of His majesty (Matt. 17:7–8).

Thirdly, we pay attention to the 'convergence of sound', to the *voices heard*. Peter – not 'untypically' – is the first voice we hear. He blurts out that he wants to stay and erect three tents – presumably to enshrine the glory and memorialise the moment. It is usual at this point to ridicule Peter for entertaining such a stupid idea, but his history and heritage had ill-prepared him to suggest otherwise. The story he knew encouraged him to respect such glimpses of glory – the kind of glory that had inspired Temples to contain them and slain to the ground the priests who ministered in them. What else was he to think?

And who would gainsay him when he says, 'it is good for us to be here.' It must have been good to breathe what the hymnwriter called that 'ampler, purer air', to see 'revealed to mortal gaze, the great old saints of other days', to soar 'on eagles' wings' with John 'whose last best word is love' – and, above all, to watch the 'human lineaments ... shine irradiant with light divine', and to 'bow before the heavenly voice which bids bewildered souls rejoice'.

However crass his response, I envy Peter his moment. I dare to say I might have felt the same, said and done what he said and did. In any event, we know from what he later tells us that it was an unforgettable and life-changing experience. Peter is an easy 'fall-guy' who makes us all feel better about ourselves and our own blundering attempts at discipleship. He usually 'boldly went' where others did not dare to go. Yes, he sank, but no other disciple ever walked on water. Some people's failures of faith take them further than other people's successes.

Decisively, *the voice from heaven* speaks as it did at Jesus' baptism (Matt. 17:5; cf. Matt. 3:17). Moses had heard that voice as a crack of thunder from a mountain wreathed in smoke. Elijah, wrapped in a self-protective cloak, had heard it not in earthquake, wind or fire but as a gentle whisper of hope. Now, the disciples hear it from a bright cloud of glory as the Father's loving commendation of His Son. The voice makes Jesus the centre of attention. The voice directs everyone with ears to hear to '*Listen to him!*'

As the terrible voice at Sinai had launched Israel on her covenant mission, as the still small voice had reawakened Elijah to his prophetic vocation, so the Father's voice commands us to hang on to Jesus' every word. Hear the call to discipleship: 'Follow me ...' Hear the Beatitudes; hear Jesus say: 'Blessed are the pure in heart for they will see God ...' Hear Him say: 'Take my yoke upon you and learn from me ...' Hear every word of Jesus spoken up to and even from the cross.

But, here, at this scene of glory on the mount of transfiguration *what does Jesus say?* Remarkably little. And even then, nothing about Himself and the huge significance of transfiguration for Him, for His identity and messiahship.

Characteristically – as with His words from the cross – He is *concerned for others*: 'Get up ... Don't be afraid' (v.7). 'Don't be afraid,' He says, which of all the things we need to hear from Jesus is the thing we need to hear most often and which unfailingly is what we most often hear Him say. And 'Get up', because face-down worship and awed adoration are the beginnings of a devotion which must be stretched into discipleship. And while it would be good to stay on mountains, there are *valleys* which need the glory and the gospel and which we must get up and go down to. The disciples learn as they descend into the vastness of human misery to say less and to let Him speak more (Matt. 17:9).

Just as Moses had come down from the glory of Sinai to confront a faithless and perverse people (Exod. 32:15ff; Deut. 32:20), so Jesus comes down from His mountain-top glory to expose the deep cultural scepticism of an 'unbelieving generation'.

Listen to Jesus, then, as He at once castigates a faith-proud people for being so faithless (Matt. 17:17), for being no less perverse than their forefathers. In a world out of control, where natural elements like fire and water sometimes appear to be allies of supernatural evil, the deliverance of one deranged boy is a foretaste of the cross where all evil and sin is met and mastered, and the world 'de-demonised'. And the raising to life of one corpse-like child heralds Jesus' resurrection and holds promise of the raising up of a whole new creation in the restoration of all things. So, *listen to Jesus*, then, as He rebukes a demon with great authority, bringing freedom and healing to a tormented boy and his distraught parents (17:18). Disciples are privileged with glimpses of glory but all too often find themselves powerless and paralysed by their own sense of helplessness, lack of faith and prayerlessness.

Listen to Jesus chiding His own 'handwringingly' impotent disciples for lacking even an ounce of dynamic faith that can – impossibly – level every mountain that obstructs God's glory (17:20–21).

And when He again speaks of His death, they listen, but find the prospect a mystery which is for the time being too painful to comprehend (Matt. 17:22–23).

All ears are now tuned to Jesus to hear the voice of authority: all eyes are turned to Jesus to see the vision of His majesty (Matt. 17:7–8).

It is Jesus who establishes the truth of the Old Testament Scriptures (hence Moses and Elijah). It is Jesus who determines the shape of the apostolic witnesses in the New Testament (hence Peter, James and John).

And John's testimony?

The Word became flesh and made his dwelling among us. We have seen his glory, the glory of the One and Only, who came from the Father, full of grace and truth …

For the law was given through Moses; grace and truth came through Jesus Christ. No-one has ever seen God, but God the One and Only, who is at the Father's side, has made him known.

John 1:14,17–18

As for Peter, he never forgot the transfiguring moment on the mount which authenticated Jesus and confirmed all that the prophets had said:

We did not follow cleverly invented stories when we told you about the power and coming of our Lord Jesus Christ, but we were eye-witnesses of his majesty. For he received honour and glory from God the Father when the voice came to him from the Majestic Glory, saying: 'This is my Son, whom I love; with him I am well pleased.' We ourselves heard this voice that came from heaven when we were with him on the sacred mountain.

And we have the word of the prophets made more certain, and you will do well to pay attention to it, as to a light shining in a dark place, until the day dawns and the morning star rises in your hearts.

2 Peter 1:16–19

The light of God's glory is focused here; the sound of God's truth is concentrated here – in the transfigured Jesus.

With one voice – lawgivers, prophets and apostles – they point to Jesus and say: 'Look at him!': they all say what the Father says of His beloved Son, 'Listen to him!' *Look only to Jesus: Listen only to Jesus.* He is the focal point of God's grace and glory. The bright shining of God's revelation – flickeringly heralded by Moses and Elijah – and the unveiling of the future glory of God's kingdom converge here in this luminous present moment.

As we descend from the mountain, P.T. Forsyth says,

… let us go down to know that there is nothing in all the raging valley – neither the devilry of the world nor the impotence of the Church

– that can destroy our confidence, quench our power, or derange our peace. Let us go down to know that the meanest or the most terrible things of life now move beneath the eternal mastery and triumphant composure of an almighty Saviour and a final salvation which is assured in heavenly places in Jesus Christ our Lord.[1]

Until that final day, we can say – like Paul, who later had his own 'transfiguration moment' – we have seen enough of the glory of God in the face of Jesus Christ to have a gospel to proclaim in the dark, yet-to-be redeemed valleys of our world (2 Cor. 4:4–7). Until then we have this treasure in the clay pots of our current frailty through which, from time to time, the unquenchable light shines through as we pray and work for the kingdom fully to come.

PART TWO

CRUCIAL WORDS
FROM SKULL HILL

INTRODUCTION
AND OUTLINE

Carrying his cross, Jesus went out to the place called Skull Hill (the name in Hebrew is Golgotha), where they crucified him …

John 19:17, *The Message*

Any road that leads us to the heart of our faith is surely worth pursuing. And the *seven words of Jesus from the cross* surely do just that, for the saving death of Jesus on the cross is the beating heart of the Christian faith and gospel.

Classic voices in the Church confirm this. As the great Scottish theologian, James Denney, put it in his seminal work on the death of Christ, the cross 'shifts the centre of gravity in the New Testament … It is not in his being here but in his being here as a propitiation for the sins of the world, that the love of God is revealed. Not Bethlehem but Calvary is the focus of revelation, and any construction of Christianity which ignores or denies this, distorts Christianity by putting it out of focus.'[1]

As the celebrated Princeton theologian, B.B. Warfield, once said: 'not only is the doctrine of the sacrificial death of Christ embodied in Christianity as an essential element of the system, but in a very real sense it constitutes Christianity. It is this which differentiates Christianity from other religions.'[2]

As the greatest British theologian of the cross, P.T. Forsyth said, summing up his many profound reflections on the subject, 'it is the cross, then, that is the key to Christ.'[3]

And as the leading German theologian of our day, Jurgen Moltmann, asserts on the opening page of his most famous book *The Crucified God*, echoing Luther, 'the cross is the test of everything which deserves to be called Christian.'[4]

But in celebrating the cross, we do not overlook its grim actuality. Calvary was a banal and wretched spot, a squalid scenario where sordid and pitiless things were done. Crucifixion conjures up gruesome and often gratuitous violence and images from more recent history are parasitic on it like flies to decomposing meat. Laughing SS troops taunting an elderly Jewish man on the streets of Munich as they hack off his long-flowing beard, while he pitifully tries to cover his shame. Conscripted riflemen in a firing squad taking aim at a baby-faced, shell-shocked 'Tommy' being executed for cowardice amid the mud of Flanders by his fellow British 'pals'. Naked Iraqi detainees piled humiliatingly on top of one another at the command and to the amusement of their derisive US guards. And much, much more, both before and since.

It's all here at Calvary: the concentrated hatred, the cruel mockery, the crude injustice, the callous violence, the accumulated sin and evil – all being drawn down onto the head of God's own innocent, pure, dear and beloved Son. And, atop the hill called Golgotha, silhouetted against the skyline, three roughly manufactured cross-pieces, which capped the whole ugly process.

Crucifixion was designed as a vicious torture to maximise and prolong the excruciating pain – some of which, perhaps, Mel Gibson's film *The Passion of the Christ* managed to portray.

Crucifixion was a savage punishment reserved for especially violent criminals, runaway slaves or political rebels against Rome. The German New Testament scholar, Martin Hengel, in his definitive study of crucifixion in the ancient world, concluded that '... crucifixion satisfied the primitive lust for revenge and sadistic cruelty of individual rulers and the masses ... a form of execution which manifests the demonic character of human cruelty and bestiality.'[5] Hengel shows how the cross represented extreme humiliation, the victim being exposed naked to public gaze.

Not surprisingly, throughout the ancient world where it was practised, crucifixion was regarded with horror as the most barbaric and contemptible way in which anyone could conceivably die. No wonder the apostle Paul spoke of the folly and the scandal of the cross (see 1 Cor. 1:18–25; Gal. 5:11).

In a world drenched in blood, much of it captured on newsreels or lately by round-the-clock media watch, we moderns have perhaps become inured to the grim reality that was the cross. ,

Well, what's new?

'It is curious,' novelist Dorothy L. Sayers once noted, 'that people who are filled with horrified indignation whenever a cat kills a sparrow can hear the story of the killing of God ... and not experience any shock at all.'[6]

The fashion for bloodless forms of spirituality is gaining a resurgence in our day. The unhistorical, fallacious but intriguing blend of ancient Gnosticism and natural-born paganism, which explains so much of the attraction of such widely-read nonsense as Dan Brown's *The da Vinci Code*, is a case in point. As Luke Johnson points out:

> Even more strikingly, the Gnostic gospels lack passion accounts. The death of Jesus is either omitted or touched on only lightly. Their emphasis is on the revelation of the divine ... The emphasis of the canonical Gospels is on the suffering of the Messiah ... In Gnostic Christianity, the enlightenment of the mind enables the avoidance of suffering.
>
> ... the canonical gospels view Jesus from the perspective of the resurrection ... but in sharp contrast to the Gnostic gospels, which have only that perspective, the canonical gospels hold that vision of power in tension with the reality of Jesus' suffering and death ...
>
> In none of the canonical gospels is the scandal of the cross removed in favour of the divine glory[7]

So we approach this well-worn story willing once again to be shocked into paying attention to it. And the emphasis is on *paying attention*. The passion narratives do have shock value – as perhaps we moderns needed reminding by Mel Gibson's film. But they are written not merely in order to arouse deep emotions in us; still less that we might feel sorry for Jesus, a pity which He specifically disdained and discouraged in one of His last pronouncements before the cross (cf. Luke 23:28). Rather, the Passion narratives are written to engage our minds, hearts and wills and to move us to faith, as John reminds us right in the thick of the action he is describing (cf. John 19:35).

My point, and it is an important one, is this. Without minimising the gruesome realities of crucifixion, the evangelists and apostles proclaim the drama of Good Friday *not as a bare fact but as a meaningful event.* They are not reporters only. But, as is evident time and again, they are interpreters of the Passion. In fact, they are sparing in their descriptions of the gruesome details, not because they are squeamish but because they are convinced that there were reasons behind the madness of Calvary; and that those reasons might well be God-given, biblical, and saving reasons. In speaking of the cross, the apostles are therefore more concerned to convey a message than to make an impression.

Mystery, metaphor, meaning

The Church's subsequent attempts to build on this apostolic conviction by developing doctrines of the atonement are easily parodied. For liberal Christian critics, concerned to accommodate the faith to the prevailing cultural mores and supposed sensitivities, the classic doctrine of penal substitution, in particular, has been a regular target. They have recently been joined not only by feminist theologians but by avowed Evangelicals of a revisionist inclination, who range from the scholarly Joel Green to the populist Steve Chalke.

Apart from specific criticisms, what these critics share is a common suspicion of what they consider to be over-intellectualised, rigid 'theories' of atonement. They downplay atonement doctrines in favour of metaphor and mystery. They stress the variety of *metaphors* used in the New Testament – metaphors taken not only from the lawcourts (penal substitution and satisfaction, which are deemed especially unsuitable for today's postmodern audience) but from the marketplace (redemption), the realm of personal relationships (reconciliation) and warfare (the *Christus Victor* view which heralds the triumph of the cross and resurrection). They are as one in emphasising the sheer *mystery* of what went on at the cross which, they assert, no metaphor can unravel.

Many of the points raised are uncontentious and they are not decisive for the argument being made. All our language about God and His activity is metaphorical. But metaphors are metaphors of *something* not nothing. The cross being a divine, even an intra-Trinitarian action – is of necessity an unfathomable mystery. But it is a revealed mystery, a stateable mystery, that enables us to say that through the cross God was in Christ – a Christ without sin who was made sin for us – and that in *this* Christ, God was reconciling the world unto Himself (cf. 2 Cor. 5:17–21).

To think otherwise by polarising 'theory' and 'mystery', is once again to fall into the logical fallacy of assuming that because we cannot know everything it follows that we cannot know *anything*.

To think otherwise, is to fail to confront the numerous New Testament texts which proclaim the significance of Christ's death as a central feature of the gospel of salvation.

1 Corinthians 15:3–5 sets the pattern here. 'For what I received I passed on to you as of first importance: that Christ died for our sins according to the Scriptures, that he was buried, that he was raised on the third day according to the Scriptures, and that he appeared to Peter and then to the Twelve.'

Each of these terms is loaded with theological significance.

'Christ died' – He really died and was buried; and what was raised was a dead and buried body of Christ.

And He died as *the Christ* – highlighting the significance of the crucified victim – among the many nailed up that year – as the representative messianic king of Israel and the last Adam of us all.

He died *'for our sins …'* implying that this death was no ordinary death but crucial to atone for human sin, a substitutionary death – 'in my place condemned he stood … sealed my pardon through his blood … Hallelujah! What a Saviour' (Philip Bliss).

And all of this was *'according to the Scriptures …'* not simply to tick off the proof texts which anticipated His dying in this way but to show that His story from birth to Passion makes sense only if seen as the crucial chapter in God's larger covenantal and redemptive story told throughout the Old Testament Scriptures.

James Denney said it well:

The death of Christ was never presented to the world as a spectacle. It was never presented by any apostle or evangelist apart from an interpretation. It was the death of Christ so interpreted as to appeal irresistibly to the heart, the conscience, the imagination, perhaps we should include even the very senses … which exercised the emancipatory power.[8]

We may speak, I suggest, of a Christian *apprehension* of the cross of Christ, using several meanings of the complex word 'apprehension'.

We come in apprehension, with 'anxiety and trepidation' which, in this instance, perhaps suggests a properly humble and reverential approach.

We come to 'apprehend', intent on 'arrest or seizure' – in this case, not so much in grasping the cross as in being captured *by* the cross.

We come wanting to 'apprehend', seeking 'knowledge and understanding' – in this case not by attempting to dissolve the mystery of the cross but by coming to its foot and 'standing under' the lordly revelation and power of the crucified One so that we intelligibly receive what it says and does to us.

So it is appropriate to listen to the cries from the cross, which rent the humid air and stifling darkness, for the light they shed on the mystery and miracle of Jesus' dying for us.

'Seven times He spoke, seven words of love ...' is Frederick Faber's view ('O come and mourn with me awhile', *Baptist Hymn Book*, 144). These seven words from the cross are like seven pillars of wisdom upon which a theology of the cross can be supported.[9] The seven words are spread over all four Gospels. One, the cry of dereliction occurs, in two Gospels, Matthew and Mark. Three are in Luke: 'Father forgive them ... Today you will be with me in paradise ... Into your hands I commit my spirit.' Three are in John: 'Dear woman , here is your son ... son, behold your mother ... I thirst ... It is finished.'

Each evangelist offers us as a slightly different angle of vision on the cross. The evangelists themselves were not, of course, among the spectators at the crucifixion. They draw on reliable but second-hand eyewitness testimony (eg John 19:35) and choose to highlight certain features rather than others. In this sense, Derek Tidball likens the evangelists to four witnesses looking down from four sides of a public square at what is going on there:

They witness the identical event. But from high above, four people throw open the windows, one on each side of the square, and describe what they see. The reports have plenty in common, but each records what he sees as he views it from his own angle.

One Gospel writer allows his eye to linger over a detail his fellow-evangelists miss, and another strains his ear to pick up a saying to which the others are deaf. No doubt each is alert to those aspects of the scene that fit his own interests and strike him as particularly relevant to the audience for whom he writes.[10]

The variety and slight differences between the reports, therefore, serve only to endorse their authenticity. As Tidball adds, '… the differing perspectives on the cross which each Gospel writer provides gives us a complete and multifaceted view of what happened on that first Good Friday.'[11]

In these seven words, as if echoing the seven days of creation, we hear the overture to a new creation. We hear our Saviour as He …

- petitions His Father for the pardon of His enemies
- redeems a wasted life and ushers a man of extreme violence into the kingdom of peace
- provides for His mother's wellbeing and oversees the creation of a new family
- cries out like a curse-bearing scapegoat driven into the hellish far country of our God-forsaken exile
- shares our physical distress and utters His soul's craving that the Father's saving will be fully done
- sees of the travail of his soul, is satisfied and casts His defiant victory cry to the four winds
- surrenders to the Father's safe-keeping in a final tribute of trust to the Father's good future

'Seven words of love' that contribute to the one 'word' of the cross, the saving message of Easter.

Faber ends his hymn,

O love of God! O sin of man!
In this dread act your strength is tried,
And victory remains with love,
For He, our Lord, is crucified.

And one last note.

All the way through this second part we shall need to remind ourselves that this is the action of the Trinitarian God. All this is from God and involves all of God (2 Cor. 5:18; Acts 2:23ff). As P.T. Forsyth said: 'No half God could redeem a world it took a whole God to create.'

Listen to Forsyth again:

> No heart but that of a holy God is equal to inviting into it all that labour and are heavy laden, to pitying on an adequate scale the awful tragedy of man or measuring man's suffering with that informed sympathy which is the condition of healing it.
>
> None can pity our human case to saving purpose but a God who treats it with more holy grace even than heart pity, and who is stronger to save our conscience than He is quick to feel our wounds. Our suffering can only be finally dealt with by Him who is more concerned about our sin; who is strong enough to resist pity till grief has done its gracious work even in His own Son; and who can endure not only to see the world's suffering go on for its moral ends, but to take its agony upon His own heart and feel it even as the victims do not, for the holy purpose, final blessing, and the far victory of His love. And this is what we have in the atoning cross of Christ.[12]

Kathleen Norris bemoans the bland, insipid, cross-less religiosity that has drained the colour and vitality from much mainline Protestantism and is such a poor imitation of the real thing. She notes how heartened she was to read the American-Mexican writer Ruben Martinez describe himself as 'not just a cultural Catholic ... but a flesh-eating, blood-drinking practitioner of the faith'.[13]

And if that's too Catholic for you, let's reflect on the words themselves.

Outline of the Crucial Words

Word of Atonement

'Father, forgive them, for they do not know what they are doing.'

Luke 23:34

Word of Acceptance

Then he said, 'Jesus, remember me when you come into your kingdom.' Jesus answered him, 'I tell you the truth, today you will be with me in paradise.'

Luke 23:42–43

Word of Affection

When Jesus saw his mother and the disciple whom he loved standing nearby, he said to his mother, 'Woman, behold your son!' Then he said to the disciple, 'Behold, your mother!'

John 19:26–27, ESV

Word of Abandonment

From the sixth hour until the ninth hour darkness came over all the land. About the ninth hour, Jesus cried out in a loud voice, 'Eloi, Eloi, lama sabachthani?' – which means, 'My God, my God, why have you forsaken me?'

Matthew 27:45–46

Word of Affliction

Later, knowing that all was now completed, and so that the Scripture would be fulfilled, Jesus said: 'I am thirsty.'

John 19:28

Word of Achievement

When he had received the drink, Jesus said, 'It is finished.'

John 19:30

Word of Assurance

Jesus called out with a loud voice, 'Father, into your hands I commit my spirit.' When he had said this, he breathed his last.

Luke 23:46

MORAL MIRACLE
WORD OF ATONEMENT

'Father, forgive them, for they do not know what they are doing.'
Luke 23:34

Our first reaction to these words of Jesus is, surely, astonishment that in His own extreme agony He is still able to think of others and their needs. He does not unleash a stream of invective, angrily denouncing His enemies but, instead, prays for them to be forgiven. He neither rages against fate nor hurls abuse back at those mocking and torturing Him. He calls down no curses from heaven but pleads the blessing of God on them.

The hate-filled taunts hurled at the cross rebound from His heart as whispers of grace. Like stones thrown down a bottomless well, the malicious insults lose their echo, swallowed up in an unfathomable love. The vicious cycle of violence is finally broken in the crucified Jesus; the toxic-hate is absorbed and not passed on, the vicious poison neutralised.

The apostle Peter who was near enough to know, later recalled – with the wonder still fresh – that 'When they hurled their insults at him, he did not retaliate; when he suffered, he made no threats' (1 Pet. 2:23). What amazing grace!

That's the first thing that strikes us; but there is more, much more.

Forgiveness is what Jesus seeks for His enemies. When Gordon Wilson gravely and soberly said that by God's grace he was able to forgive the IRA bombers who killed his daughter at a Remembrance Day parade in Inniskillen ... when Anthony Walker's mother, Gee, forgave in the name of Jesus the race-hate-fuelled thugs who had murdered her son in

127

Merseyside ... we are moved – and doubt whether we could possibly have done the same. When Gee Walker was asked, after her son's killers were sentenced, to explain why she chose to forgive, she quoted these very words of Jesus from the cross. From afar, we stand amazed that anyone can learn to forgive as these wounded people have.

At the same time we understand only too well the Reverend Julie Nicolson, who stepped down as an Anglican vicar because she felt she could not officiate at the Eucharist while being unable to forgive the suicide bombers who had murdered her daughter in the London bombings of July 2005.

The reason we are baffled and astonished when some people find it in their hearts to forgive those who have grievously wronged them, and the reason why we sympathise with even good and godly people when they cannot find it in the hearts to forgive – is precisely because forgiving one's enemies seems difficult, even impossible to contemplate. And that's because it is.

Forgiveness is a *moral miracle.*

Above all, forgiveness is a divine act. The Reverend Nicolson, in her integrity, got that right: 'Forgiving another human being for violating your child is almost beyond human capabilities ... I will leave potential forgiveness in God's hands ...'[1] Only God can ultimately forgive sin, for the simple reason that all sin is ultimately sin against God. It is both harder and easier for God to forgive. It is harder because God is infinitely holy and feels the wound more uniquely. It is easier because only He can express the holy love and exert the moral power to forgive such dire affront.

This is why it is important to note that we are not told that Jesus forgave His tormentors directly – though who could doubt that He did – but that He asked the Father to do so. Note the words carefully: *'Father ... forgive ...'* They tell us all we need to know about what the theologians call the Person and work of Christ.

'Father ...' says it all about His unique personal relationship with God, His own intimate faith, if you will, that was given exceptional expression in the *'abba'* that rose up from His heart in times of crisis and which orientated His long obedience in the Father's direction. Now He places that unique sonship on the line for the sake of sinners.

'Forgive them ...' sums up His life's work to make His soul an offering for sin, a ransom for many; it forms His final appeal to His Father to

make good His own Last Supper pledge that His body be broken and His blood be poured out for the forgiveness of sins as the foundation of a new covenant.

So, the first words of Jesus from the cross are a *prayer*. As Isaiah had anticipated and His own baptism sealed, God's Suffering Servant, Jesus, was being numbered with transgressors and was making intercession for them. Prayer, as P.T. Forsyth argued, is the heart of the atonement. In Miroslav Volf's words, 'the passion of Christ is the agony of a tortured soul and wrecked body offered as *a prayer for the forgiveness of the torturers*.'[2] Here is further vital truth. For Jesus, the first effect of His death was not intended for us, or else He might have said more about it. *The first effect of the cross was on God the Father.* The death of Jesus was a prayer, a dealing with God. On the cross, Jesus offered Himself to God as a perfect sacrifice for sin. He paid homage to the moral order of the universe. He hallowed the Father's holy name. His sacrificial death constituted an appeal to the holy heart of His holy Father that would serve as the ground on which a holy God might forgive sin. His death is first directed Godward, and that is where the greatest work of atonement was done. The greatest thing that happened on Good Friday was done out of sight and sound, as the Father's answer to the Son's prayer.

Here is a Trinitarian wonder; and it is all God's doing. Jesus did not die to make God into our Father but in His death Father and Son worked together to enable God, without compromising His justice, to *treat us sinners as sons*. Or, as Paul later probed the mystery: 'God presented him [Jesus] as a sacrifice of atonement, through faith in his blood. He did this … so as to be just and the one who justifies those who have faith in Jesus' (Rom. 3:25–26). This is a truly divine answer to prayer achieved by Father and Son in the Holy Spirit. Samuel Davies' (1723–1761) great hymn says it well:

> *Great God of wonders, all Thy ways*
> *Are matchless, godlike, and divine;*
> *But the fair glories of Thy grace*
> *More godlike and unrivalled shine:*
>
> Who is a pardoning God like Thee?
> Or who has grace so rich and free?

Such dire offences to forgive,
Such guilty daring souls to save
This is Thy grand prerogative,
And none shall in the honour share

    Who is a pardoning God like Thee?
    Or who has grace so rich and free?

In wonder lost, with trembling joy,
We take the pardon of our God.
Pardon for sins of deepest dye;
A pardon sealed with Jesus' blood;

    Who is a pardoning God like Thee?
    Or who has grace so rich and free?

And as if to raise the stakes even higher, we must note Jesus' disclaimer: '*... they do not know what they are doing.*' This too is astonishing, isn't it? What an audacious statement! What mercy! Surely they knew? Didn't the soldiers know what they were doing? Surely the chief priests and rulers did, they who had plotted for this moment? Yet the gracious prayer of Jesus from the cross implies that no one really knew what was going on.

Even the *weeping women* – semi-official mourners attending the condemned Man – had not known what was going on. They meant well, pitying Him as they did, but they were misjudging the situation. It was not Jesus who was being judged but His judges. 'For if men do these things when the tree is green, what will happen when it is dry?' (Luke 23:31), which translates: 'Save your pity for yourselves and your generation, for the shadow of a terrible fate looms over you which I would spare you from if only you knew.'

Could the *soldiers* really have known? After all, they were merely doing a job of work, subsuming any niggling self-doubts under the honour of serving imperial power. Theirs was just one example of countless routine crimes committed – as Adolf Eichmann excused his murder of Jews – by people simply obeying orders.

And what of the *religious leaders* who engineered this event – they surely knew what was happening? But could even they have known what an outrage they were perpetrating that Good Friday against their own Creator God, so thoroughly had power-politics and vested self-interest clouded their judgment. Assuming God and the Bible are on your side can only increase the blindness if malevolence holds the heart hostage. Like modern suicide bombers, they could even claim religious endorsement for their extremism. A line runs straight from them through Christian crusaders to Islamic terrorists. As Pascal once chillingly observed, 'Men and women never delight in doing evil as much as if they can do it for religious reasons.'

None of us can ever be sure we really know what we are doing! God's secret wisdom was being stunningly unveiled at the cross but, as Paul put it, 'None of the rulers of this age understood it, for if they had, they would not have crucified the Lord of glory' (1 Cor. 2:8). Sin is irrational, the moth beating itself to death against the lamp, the ultimate absurdity. So in being saved we must be saved out of our ignorance. The Law recognised that even sins committed unwittingly or unknowingly nevertheless still need to be atoned for (Num. 15:22–29). In the Bible, ignorance is no excuse. As Hitler's close aide Albert Speer admitted after the war, when asked about the death-camps: 'I didn't know but I could have found out.' Ignorance in biblical terms is not an intellectual failure but a moral one born of a hardened or unenlightened conscience.

So none of us know what we are doing: all have sinned; all of us need saving. H.R. Macintosh once said wisely that we fail to understand the cross not because we are not clever enough but because we are *not good enough*.[3] We are nowhere near good enough to appreciate the enormity of sin. If only we knew how terrible sin is then no one would have connived at nailing Jesus to the cross. It is inconceivable that those who hounded Jesus to His death with due process, legal or otherwise, should not have known they were doing wrong. They surely did. But they did not know what they were doing in the sense that they failed to realise the *enormity* of what they were doing. They minimised sin – as we all do: 'We never thought it would come to this.' Does this not help to explain Judas' drastic reaction to what he had done? We didn't realise that our sins amounted to this, that we were implicated on this scale, that our sins counted enough to have Jesus crucified! We never realised that our accumulated and – to us – minor acts of selfishness could mount up to this monstrous end. But then, as Robert Murray M'Cheyne said: 'Call no sin trivial; it has eternal consequences.'

It is then to be regretted that *the doctrine of sin* is too often toned down, muted or shunted to the sidelines altogether in our user-friendly, contemporary Evangelicalism. It is an unspoken assumption that dare not speak its name, deemed too morbid and introspective, too negative and offensive in a therapeutic culture bent on feeling good about itself. Don't beat yourself up; beat up Christ instead.

The turning-point in Jesus' most famous parable comes when the rebellious prodigal comes to his senses, appalled not only at the mess his sin has got him into but also at the offence and insult to the father of squandering his God-given life in such tawdry ways: 'I have sinned against heaven and against you …'

To forgive is costly, and God in Christ bore the cost so that we might be forgiven no less than through His blood. *But being forgiven too comes at a price, that of knowing the reality of what we have done.* He makes light of the cost but we should not.

We tried to kill God our Maker. We nailed up the only perfect Man who has ever lived. We loved darkness rather than light, and sought to snuff out the Light of Life.

But Jesus prays for His enemies to be forgiven and dies to make it possible. And if Jesus dies for the forgiveness of the Gentile Romans, ignorant pagans that they were, who mocked and tortured and executed Him, then surely He died for God's own people who did not know they were complicit in the murder of their own Messiah? 'Now, brothers,' concedes Peter after Pentecost, 'I know that you acted in *ignorance*, as did your leaders …' but, since this was in God's saving plan, 'Repent … and turn to God, so that your sins may be wiped out …' (Acts 3:17,19, my italics).

The fierce mercy of the cross which exposes our culpable ignorance lavishes grace on us. So Paul never forget: 'Even though I was once a blasphemer and a persecutor and a violent man, I was shown mercy because I acted in ignorance and unbelief. The grace of our Lord was poured out on me abundantly, along with the faith and love that are in Christ Jesus' (1 Tim. 1:13–14).

'O happy fault' for: *if, when we sinned we did not know what we were doing, we now know what God was doing to save us.* We know now that there is forgiveness through His blood.

- Forgiveness is God's gracious release from guilt and debt, liberating us from the eternal moral consequences of sin, freeing us to enter God's future with joyful hope.
- Freed by forgiveness from the bondage of the past, we are empowered to restore broken relationship and to be reconciled, even to former enemies.
- Freed from condemnation, we are called to live by grace and by grace to become, in our turn, forgiven-forgivers of others.

Forgiven much, we love much. We cheerfully join Philip Bliss (1838–1876) in singing:

In my place condemned he stood,
sealed my pardon with his blood …
Hallelujah! What a Saviour.

So we eagerly celebrate with Isaac Watts (1674–1748)

the joyful news of sins forgiven,
of hell subdued, and peace with heaven …

The cross is both the Son's prayer and the Father's answer. What was done there was done by an eternal God in an eternal Christ with eternal consequences. And the forgiveness that was won then in the historic, dying Jesus is immortalised and perpetuated in His ascended high-priestly ministry. As our great High Priest He ever lives to make intercession for us, guaranteeing and applying the atonement secured at the cross.

Five bleeding wounds he bears,
Received on Calvary;
They pour effectual prayers
They strongly plead for me;
'Forgive him, O Forgive! They cry
Nor let the ransomed sinner die'

Charles Wesley (1707–1788)

Coda

Forgive us our sins as we forgive those who sin against us; blessed are the merciful, for they will be shown mercy.

FIRST ONE HOME
WORD OF ACCEPTANCE

Then he said, 'Jesus, remember me when you come into your kingdom.'
Jesus answered him, 'I tell you the truth, today you will be with me in paradise.'

Luke 23:42–43

Sound familiar? A fanatical political terrorist facing death with the final wish of going to paradise. But this is no Islamist suicide-bomber dreaming of the virginal pleasures awaiting him on the other side. To be sure, what we have here is a revolutionary, a man of violent extremes, being executed for crimes against the state. However, here what is being offered is not wishful thinking but something 'far better' – immediate entry to paradise with Jesus Christ.

On Good Friday 1957, Karl Barth, then the most famous Protestant theologian in the world, made one of his regular visits to Basel Prison to preach to the inmates. What he had come to tell the prisoners, he said, was that Jesus had been crucified with criminals, one on either side of him. Then he asked, 'Which is more amazing, to find Jesus in such bad company, or to find the criminals in such good company?'[1]

Of course, as Barth adds, both are true. Jesus and the two wrongdoers share a solidarity of suffering which Barth suggests should never be undone, so that there will for ever be three crosses on that hill. Yet, looking back at the road Jesus has travelled, we should perhaps not be so surprised that He ended up in such company. After all, at His baptism, Jesus, the righteous One, had shown Himself willing – as Isaiah had prophesied – to be 'numbered with the transgressors'. Thereafter He became known, to the scandal of the respectable, as the 'friend of sinners'. Now, at the last, He is counted among their number again. Jesus dies, the just for the unjust, by sharing their fate and dying alongside them.

And so, as Richard John Neuhaus has it, 'the first one home was a thief'.[2] Some thief! Luke calls the two men crucified beside Jesus 'wrongdoers', but the other evangelists describe them as robbers or bandits (*lêstai* cf. also Barrabas, John 18:40, NRSV). In all likelihood they were political revolutionaries whose armed robberies had funded insurrection against Rome. They were just the sort of criminals for whom crucifixion was fiendishly intended. The first one home was – in today's parlance – a terrorist.

There is nothing original about the way one of the criminals taunts Jesus. He merely echoes what he has heard shouted by the religious leaders mocking Jesus' messiahship and the Roman soldiers cynically urging Jesus to save Himself. The derision serves to compound the isolation of Jesus, cut off from friends and now surrounded by His enemies, like baying dogs cornering a stag (cf. Psa 22:7,12–13; 69:10; 89:50–51). But suddenly and surprisingly – in Luke's taut narrative – one of the two thieves rebukes his comrade and calls out to Jesus '... remember me ...' Isn't that the cry that rises up from the depths of each unique soul, not least in the face of imminent death – a cry not to be forgotten, not to be cast into oblivion? 'Remember me for what I might have been, and if you can, for what I was; remember me kindly if you can, not cruelly', and here – in its ultimate need – 'Remember me eternally and save me'.

What on earth suddenly changed this man's attitude and caused him to call on Jesus in this way? Was it blind panic or a residue of faith? At what point did mockery give way to hope? Had he heard Jesus pray for His enemies to be forgiven? Was it, in James Nelson's words, the 'sight of embodied love' that moved his heart? Could he see the cynical logo above the head of Jesus – 'King of the Jews' – and did that title, for a fleeting moment, lose its irony and seem luminously true?

'Jesus ...' – the thief calls out – 'Jesus ...' a direct use of Jesus' personal name, which is unique in Luke's Gospel, and in R.E. Brown's view, is 'stunning in its intimacy'. As Brown notes, 'The first person with the confidence to be so familiar is a convicted criminal who is also the last person to speak to Jesus before he dies.'[3]

'Jesus, remember me when you come into your kingdom.' The scholars discuss whether the text should read 'into' or 'in'. 'Into' implies that Jesus is going somewhere, that He is on His way to the kingdom; 'in' might imply that He is coming, bringing His kingly rule as in the *parousia* or perhaps in the resurrection. It is not possible to be conclusive about this, not least because of the mysterious 'today' which Jesus immediately utters. In the layers of meaning favoured by the evangelist, perhaps several options can be included. The evangelist often foreshortens events for theological reasons. Even if we opt for the future coming of God's kingdom in Christ, the prior truth is foundational to it; namely that in one profound sense Jesus ascends to the throne of His glory on and through the cross itself. Indeed, Luke records Jesus saying before the ascension that He had suffered and 'entered his glory' (Luke 24:26). Note, too, that this is an especially paradoxical feature of John's Gospel.

'I tell you the truth, today you will be with me in paradise.'

What a wonderful response? What amazing grace. What are we to make of the term 'paradise'? It appears to be a Persian loan word for a walled garden, and is used in the Old Testament of the Garden of Eden (Isa. 51:3, LXX). It likely symbolises heaven or God's presence (2 Cor. 12:4), and points forward to God's ultimate 'Eden' of the 'new heavens and new earth' (cf. Rev. 2:7). What an extraordinary conjunction of images: the bliss of Eden and the agony of Golgotha! For those who die with trust in Jesus the door is open 'today'. This is great consolation but we need to see that paradisal blessedness is an interim state in a transformation that goes beyond 'today'. As Tom Wright explains, '"Paradise" is the blissful garden where God's people rest before the resurrection.'[4] When believers die, their immediate destination is to be 'with the Lord' or 'with Christ' (which Paul says is far better [Phil. 1:21–23]) but their ultimate destiny is the resurrection of the body, the 'putting' on of immortality to match the putting off of mortality, both of which are physical, though only the former is 'spiritual'. In other words, whereas 'paradise' is life after death, resurrection is life *after* life after death. The classic hymn 'For all the saints who from their labours rest' by William Walsham How (1823–1897) gets it about right. The hymnwriter relishes the immediate entry into Lord's presence at death:

Soon, soon to faithful warriors comes their rest.
Sweet is the calm of paradise the blest.

But he does not confuse this with the final state, as the next stanza correctly points beyond the blissful rest:

But lo! There breaks a yet more glorious day:
the saints triumphant rise in bright array ...

It is this 'rising' in a new creation at the glorious last day that is the Christian prospect and that constitutes 'the sure and certain hope of the resurrection of the dead' – of which the 'Today ... with me in paradise' is the token and foretaste.

As Bonhoeffer reflects:

A strange paradise, this hill of Golgotha, this cross, this blood, this broken body; a strange tree of life on which God himself had to suffer and die – and yet here is bequeathed anew by God in grace: the kingdom of life, of resurrection, an open door of imperishable hope, of waiting, of patience. Tree of life, cross of Christ, the center of God's fallen and preserved world, that is the end of the story of paradise for us.[5]

It was Jacob, the founder of the nation, who, as a fugitive from justice, dreamed a dream and found the very stairway to heaven in the most unlikely place (Gen. 28:10–19). Given the cross, it is surely possible, even in the most nightmarish surroundings, to awake to a true dream and say 'Surely the LORD is in this place, and I was not aware of it ... How awesome is this place! This is none other than the house of God; this is the gate of heaven' (cf. Gen. 28:16). As that gifted preacher of an earlier generation, Ian Macpherson said: 'long before the nails held the carpenter, the carpenter held the nails'. It led him to ponder what the carpenter made of His cross, and he concluded that He made a 'ladder by which a sinful soul could scale the skies'.[6]

As to the holy patriarch that wondrous dream was given,
So seems my Saviour's Cross to me, a ladder up to heaven.[7]

Having said all this, we might detect an even deeper note – if not in the thief's mind, perhaps in John the evangelist's many-layered presentation. Andrew Perriman notes that the word 'paradise' can indicate what lies beyond death, but suggests that it may be signifying something even more striking. He points out that the word 'paradise' occurs in Isaiah 51:3, (LXX) in a context which has to do not with the fate of individuals but with the destiny of the nation of Israel. He suggests that in what would be a highly concentrated reference, the word evokes the restoration of Israel as God's people from a wilderness to a transformed garden, a restoration to be achieved not – as in the thief's case – through revolutionary violence but through the sacrificial actions of God's Suffering Servant Jesus.[8] Such an idea would once again remind us of the larger dimension of what is happening at the cross – though whether one word can carry so much theological weight is uncertain.

Be that as it may, we may well linger long over the '… with me …' From here onwards, being 'with Jesus' will be the key signature of salvation throughout the New Testament, a vibrant expectation in the hearts of the early Christians (see 1 Thess. 4:17; Phil. 1:23; 2 Cor. 4:17; 2 Cor. 5:8). He wants this dying man to be with Him. Acceptance is surely the breathtaking heart of love when someone loves you enough to want you to be with them for ever. Postmodern people are losing the sweet taste of it because they are increasingly reluctant to commit themselves to one another for the long-term. But if love has accepted you just as you are, pledged to be with you for better or for worse, for richer for poorer, in sickness and in health, has kept and is keeping its vows, then you have truly fallen into a covenant-love which is faithful and true and made of 'God-stuff'. Even more so in the case of our Lord Jesus Christ, the one who comes 'among us' where we are, who stands 'alongside us' in our suffering and who dies 'instead of us' in His dying. He dies as an insurrectionist though He was not one. He repudiated the way of the sword, declined even to call down twelve legions of angelic warriors to assist Him and scorned the armed mob coming to arrest Him as if He were leading a rebellion (Matt. 26:52–55). In the end, He takes the place of a known revolutionary, Barabbas, as one of three killed that day.

As Tom Wright graphically describes it:

Jesus, the innocent one, the one person who has done nothing wrong, the one innocent of the crimes of which Israel as a whole is guilty, has become identified with rebel Israel who represents God's whole rebel world; with us who are rebels, unclean, unfaithful, unloving, unholy

– so that he might take that sin as it were into himself and deal with it … He is numbered with transgressors, so that we might be with him in paradise.[9]

In Miroslav Volf's words: '… the arms of the crucified are open – a sign of a space in God's self and an invitation for the enemy to come in.'[10] Outstretched arms are the sure sign of welcome and acceptance, as were the father's for the returning prodigal. So with Jesus on the cross. Fixed where He is, with opened arms of welcome and embrace, He says, in effect, 'Come with me and I will take you home.' And the first one home was a terrorist.

And there is no delay but a clear, if mysterious, 'Today'. This is a favourite Lucan note. 'Today, salvation has come to this house …' Jesus tells Zacchaeus (Luke 19:9). The day of salvation has truly dawned in Jesus, as is clear from the manifesto of ministry Jesus gave to the astonished and then outraged members of His hometown synagogue in Nazareth:

'The Spirit of the Lord is on me, because he has anointed me to preach good news to the poor. He has sent me to proclaim freedom for the prisoners and recovery of sight for the blind, to release the oppressed, to proclaim the year of the Lord's favour … Today, this Scripture is fulfilled in your hearing.'

Luke 4:18–21

Salvation's year is here: today is the day of grace – even for desperate last-minute claimants seeking release from captivity and oppression!

So 'today' means what it says; no purgatory to undergo, no limbo in the land of *sheol* in which to languish, but today you will be with Me. Typically, and in line with His original grace-filled manifesto, Jesus chooses as His first companion a convicted felon! The question is often asked as to whether or to what degree this one dying criminal repented. Scraps of repentance are perhaps to be found. Is there a faint pulse to this man's conscience? He does recognise the justice of his conviction and sentence; he acknowledges that unlike him and his companion Jesus is innocent; he rebukes his fellow-robber for not 'fearing God'. Reality is now staring him in the face as he painfully realises where his misplaced zeal and passion have brought him. Revolutionaries pose as defenders of the poor and spokesmen for the oppressed and powerless. And they often are. They rightly rant against the blatant sins of the wicked, the rich and the powerful, who are expropriating the land of the peasant farmers and exacting harsh and unbearable taxes. But they can be blind to the sins of the poor. The powerless victims, says Miroslav Volf, are prey to two main sins: envy and enmity.[11] This was what fuelled the passion of the two men crucified alongside Jesus. For the sake of the poor they would rob and steal to fund a hate-filled revolution which would restore power to the people. But then and since – as the bloody history of the twentieth century testifies – the resentment which feeds violence spawns revolutions which inflict as much, if not more, suffering and establish as much, if not more, tyranny and injustice than the systems they were naively intended to replace.

The turning of the one terrorist to Jesus as King was a slender repentance, but it was enough. Jesus calls all sinners to repentance, whether those who repress the poor or those who represent the poor. In each and every case, to repent is to renounce worldly values and methods and to embrace God's kingly rule in Jesus Christ.[12] This surely is what the dying thief did. 'I surrender my vision of the kingdom: let your kingdom come … let your cross-shaped will, not my violence-fuelled zeal, be done … may your God-given kingdom come, not my man-made Utopia, wrought by inflicting pain on others.'

Jesus ushered this man of violence into the kingdom of peace. Jesus' first words in Luke promised deliverance to the captives (Luke 4:16ff); it is only fitting that His last words addressed to another human being were to a captive criminal, offering him the freedom of paradise. There were three crosses on that hill. Jesus was the 'man in the middle'. God was in Christ, the Man in the middle, reconciling the world unto Himself. God was in Christ, the Middleman, not imputing violent sin to a hardened criminal. God was in Christ – for there is one mediator between God and men, the Man Christ Jesus – the tortured, crucified Man in the middle, who gave Himself as a ransom for all men (1 Tim. 2:5–6). 'Today' if you hear His voice … do not harden your hearts. There were two thieves said Augustine: one was saved so that we might not despair, the other was not so that we might not presume.

We are promised by the gospel that 'if we die with Christ we shall also surely live with him'. Barth ended his sermon to the prisoners in Basel

Gaol with these words: 'Those receive the promise who regard themselves as neither so exalted nor so debased that they cannot "get in line behind" the two criminals who were first on Golgotha'.[13]

Coda

Blessed are those who are persecuted because of righteousness, who endure suffering rather than inflicting it, for theirs is the kingdom of heaven and when all men disapprove heaven applauds. Blessed are you when others revile and persecute you ... rejoice and be glad for your reward is great in heaven. Blessed is He who, for the joy set before Him, endured the cross, despising the shame, and is now seated at the right hand of the throne of God.

FAMILY TREE
WORD OF AFFECTION

When Jesus saw his mother and the disciple whom he loved standing nearby, he said to his mother, 'Woman, behold your son!' Then he said to the disciple, 'Behold, your mother!'

John 19:26–27, ESV

In times of crisis we are consoled by having our family and friends around us. Often they can *do* very little, but they are *there*. They would best say little but they are with us; that's what counts. Jesus, too, must surely have been comforted in His agony on the cross to see His mother and closest associate standing there. Turning the spotlight on them serves to highlight two contrasting groups of people caught up in the drama of the day.

Four soldiers (vv.23–24)	Four women (v.25)
His enemies, the outsiders	His friends, the insiders
Standing against Him	Standing with Him
Stripping His humanity	Supporting His humanity
Their ruthless disposal of few possessions left	His tender concern for those He is leaving behind

There is moving intimacy and tenderness being shown here in the most cruel circumstances.

The spotlight falls on two characters in the crowd who have drawn 'near' to the cross (25a,26b). Jesus notices them and speaks to them –

- *Mary, His mother* had come to see her Son. Seeing Him reduced to this mangled wreck of a man must have been heartbreaking for her. When she had presented Him as a seven-day-old child for dedication at the Temple, the devout old priest Simeon had warned her prophetically that her child would cause national upheaval and be 'misunderstood and contradicted' (Luke 2:34, *The Message*). During the last three years her faith in Him had often been baffled and strained by His actions and words. Simeon had also prophesied that a sword would pierce her own soul, too. If that had ever been true it was true now! How she must have hurt to see her own flesh-and-blood Son torn and bleeding before her very eyes in a humiliating and scandalous execution. No intimacy or privacy is possible with such an indecently public exposure but she drew as 'near' as she could to her beleaguered Son.

- As for the *beloved disciple*, he had always been closest to Jesus (cf. John 13:23–25). Now he too moves as near as he can to the appalling scene. With the courage of a true friend, he stands his ground faithfully to the bitter end, sensing perhaps, that the least he can do for his beloved Master is to wait and watch and tell the world the saving truth of this story (John 19:35).

But, typically, Jesus is thinking more of them than Himself, and comforts them with amazing and creative words. Speaking to His mother, He says: 'Woman, behold, your son!' and to the disciple, 'Behold, your mother!' (John 19:26–27, ESV). 'Behold' (*ide*) is a key indicator in John's Gospel: 'Behold, the Lamb of God … (1:29); 'Behold, the man!' (19:5); 'Behold your King!' (19:14).

'Behold' highlights the significance of the word spoken. Here, it highlights first the *intimacy and tenderness* of filial piety and brotherly love. Jesus' mother as a widow would be especially vulnerable in society when her eldest Son died. Jesus movingly shows concern for her needs and provides for her care. The beloved disciple is given a great responsibility but one which honours him immensely, being entrusted with the mother of his Lord. In the words of Richard Bauckham and Trevor Hart, 'Jesus in his dying did not put human affection to death. He brought it to new life, set it free to run in new channels, at once deepened and extended.'[1]

Yet, at the same time as emphasising the intimacy and tenderness that bridges the gap between the tortured man on the cross and His mother and disciple, John seems also to be presenting us with a picture of Jesus as isolated and uniquely lonely.

Jesus' 'behold', secondly, highlights that there is a necessary but painful distancing going on here. For this reason, some scholars emphasise the *Christological significance* of Jesus' words. Beverly Roberts Gaventa views the scene as completing the 'crucifixion separation of Jesus from all that belongs to his earthly life. Just as he is stripped of his clothing, he divests himself of his mother and his beloved disciple … at the "hour" of his return to the Father'.[2] As he had done when he was twelve years old in the Temple, Jesus strangely distances Himself from His earthly family. It is as if Jesus says all over again – as when He was twelve years old – 'What has this to do with you? I must be about my Father's business.' He did this at the wedding feast in Cana, when, as here, He called his mother 'woman' – not rude or disrespectful but rather formal. More severely still, He once rebuffed His mother and sharply distinguished His natural family from whoever does the will of God and is, therefore, truly His mother and brothers and sister (Mark 3:31–35).

Even more shocking to modern ears are those harsh-sounding words about 'hating' one's family with which He exposed the potential idolatry of family allegiance that deterred potential recruits from paying the price of discipleship by foregoing home comforts to follow the call of God in Him (Luke 14:25–26). In which case, this word is not about being nice to Mum (although that wouldn't come amiss in some quarters). For sure, as Fleming Rutledge says, Good Friday is not Mothering Sunday! Perhaps, then, as Gaventa suggests, these words from the cross constitute the completion of that process of *distancing* necessary to the carrying out of His messianic mission, a distancing born, therefore, not of unfeeling and unkindness but of a sense of destiny.

Which leads us to think that the 'behold' points out to us that *there is a strange sovereignty being exercised here by Jesus.* R.E. Brown notes that 'the atmosphere is testamentary as the dying Jesus makes disposition of the two unnamed figures who are known only through their relationship with Him (*His* mother, the disciple *He* loves).'[3] Paul Wells writes: 'Quite apart from the human drama of these words, they convey that from the cross Jesus acts as Lord over his people. He heals and reorders their lives. As the mediator … Jesus acts as their Lord, even during moments of intense suffering. He holds the future history of humanity in his hands; he has the power to save; his church will be a community organised under his Lordship in a way different from worldly standards.'[4]

There is a uniquely cross-shaped community being created here. Mary is given to the beloved disciple and he is given to her. Mother and disciple are entrusted to each other. Just here on the level ground at the foot of the cross, the Church was born. Consider the words of Richard Bauckham and Trevor Hart:

> Just as Jesus' mother and the Beloved Disciple would not otherwise have been related, had not Jesus at his death brought them together, and charged them with being mother and son to each other, so the church is the community of people who would not otherwise be related but whom the crucified Jesus brings together, forging new relationships through his death for us.[5]

We are His gifts to one another! In relating to Him we are called as Christ's followers to treat one another as if they were His mother and best friend. Decades later, the young pastor, Timothy, was being exhorted to 'Treat younger men as brothers, older women as mothers, and younger women as sisters …' (1 Tim. 5:1–2). Indeed, so closely are Christ's people associated with Him that to hurt them is to hurt Him as Saul of Tarsus found out (Acts 9). So close is the union of Christ and His own that to minister to them is – even unknowingly – to minister to Him. If we ask, 'Lord, when did we see you hungry … or thirsty … a stranger … or needing clothes … sick or in prison …?' He replies that whatever we did it to the least member of His new extended family of faith, we did it to Him (Matt. 25:31–46).

So for us there is both joy and obligation. As Ronald Wallace says, '… if Mary turned away from the cross that day with some of her burden lifted, John turned away from it with a new and heavy responsibility thrust into his personal home life.'[6] So for us the Church is no abstraction but flesh and blood relations, characterised by family affection, brotherly love and bonds of trusting friendship. The new covenant community created here by the cross is where those starving of deep human affection can find it; where the loveless can find genuine love; where the homeless are taken in; where those without friends find friends, where widows and orphans particularly are welcomed and cared for.

God is a relational God, in essence a social God – Father, Son and Holy Spirit – a holy Trinity of love where in the unfathomable mystery of God's dealings with history, the 'once bereaved' Father (if we may put it like that) and the once 'orphaned' Son (as it were) feel the pain of a broken creation and store up as in a bottle the tears shed by wounded hearts of love. What other incentive do we need than the cross to seek the unity of all Christians? Our fellowship is formed by the one broken body which does not need to be torn apart again by our fractiousness and divisions. Let's return to the level ground beneath the cross, so to drink of the one fountain of love, that the world may know we are His disciples by our love for one another. In Father Neuhaus's words, 'It is the cross that binds John to Mary, and binds all disciples to one another in a mutual gift of self. Christ is the gift and Christ enables us to give the gift, which is finally the gift of Christ.'[7] The Holy Spirit, who is the Spirit of unity and fellowship, will see to that, if we let Him. As John Taylor put it in his classic study of the work of the Holy Spirit: 'Not in our greater goodness, then, but in our openness to one another in Christ's name, the Spirit possesses us. But,' he went on, 'the Spirit does not give himself where our encounters are glib, masked exchanges of second-hand thoughts. Our defences must be down, broken entirely by intense joy or by despair. One way or the other we must come to the end of ourselves.'[8]

The cross does bring us to a dead end before it offers us a new beginning. Drawn into Christ's death, we find our defences are broken down and our lives opened out to one another in the loving space made for us by Father and Son. So John took Mary home with him that Good Friday night. Together they faced an uncertain future. But, as Christopher Seitz says, 'Whatever tears they shed that night, they shed under the shadow of a new day, a new hope, and a complete reconstituting of what family means in Jesus Christ'.[9]

So, barely six weeks later, with the other women, *Mary* was to be found in the Upper Room on the day of Pentecost (Acts 1:14). Once more she makes herself open and receptive to be overshadowed by the Holy Spirit as she had been thirty years earlier. This time, when the ascended Lord pours out the power from on high upon her, she is made part of His body as He had once been made part of hers. Losing her one, special Son, she regains Him in the countless sons and daughters in whom His strange glory shines.[10]

As for the *beloved disciple*, he watches appalled as the soldiers thrust a spear into Jesus' side. He witnesses the blood and water flowing from the lanced side of Jesus. As if standing in for all in Israel who have failed to recognise their Messiah,[11] he forces himself to 'look on the one they have pierced' (John 19:37; Zech. 12:10) and, in looking, he believes and gives his testimony to the truth of the matter so that others too might believe (v.35).

The flow of 'blood and water' undoubtedly carry symbolic significance. John has already indicated that 'streams of living water will flow from within him' (John 7:37–39) by which was meant the Spirit, not yet given because Jesus had not yet been glorified. Now in that paradoxical conflation of crucifixion and glory for which John's Gospel is noted (cf. John 3:14), the beloved disciple sees the water and blood flow from the side of Jesus lifted up in strange glory on the cross. Atonement at the cross opens the cleansing fountain (Zech. 13:1). Out of Him – crucified and bleeding to death for us – flows the water of the life-giving Spirit to empower sinners washed and cleansed by His blood with His new life.

Having seen this – and Scripture's fulfilment in Jesus – the beloved disciple lives to bear witness to the truth of this saving story and to bring others to saving faith in His Saviour and Lord. So much hangs on the original witnesses, and so much depends on the Church's ongoing faith and testimony. Plunged beneath baptismal waters, infused with the life-giving Spirit of God and regularly renewed in faith by the bread and wine of the Eucharist, we are sealed as witnesses to this truth. Christ died; He shed His blood for the sins of the world – do you believe it? Is this true truth for you? Jesus does not, at this point, vindicate Himself. He lets the Father do that in resurrection. The only hermeneutic of the gospel – that which proved this to be true – is the existence of a witnessing Church that stands under the cross and shows by its cruciform life and faithful testimony the authentic glory of the crucified and risen One.

As Bonhoeffer characteristically said: 'We are the Church beneath the Cross.'[12] At the very least, as Bonhoeffer did, we can stand by God in His hour of grieving over a wounded world.

Coda

Blessed are those who mourn, who feel they've lost what's most dear to them, for they shall be comforted and embraced by the One most dear to them. Blessed are those who 'show people how to cooperate instead of compete or fight' for that's when they discover their 'place in God's family' (see Matt. 5:1–9, *The Message*).

ECLIPSE OF THE SON
WORD OF ABANDONMENT

From the sixth hour until the ninth hour darkness came over all the land. About the ninth hour Jesus cried out in a loud voice, 'Eloi, Eloi, lama sabachthani?' – which means, 'My God, my God, why have you forsaken me?'

Matthew 27:45–46

This is a Job-like cry wrenched from the heart of a righteous Man on whom the sky has fallen in. It expresses an unfathomable mystery. It conceals as much as it reveals, and we scarcely know how to approach it. The least we can do out of respect for it is not put any kind of 'gloss' on it. The cry was evoked by something which was real and deeply felt. So whatever else we cannot say, we can, I think, say this right at the outset: Jesus shares to the full our human experiences of God-forsakenness. That in itself is a bold claim. Can it really be true? We have evidence enough of hellish experiences that we suffer from emotional overload and compassion fatigue. The bleak horror that was Auschwitz, the carnage of Iwa Jima or Omaha Beach on D-Day, the towering infernos of 9/11, the weeping child cringing from more abuse, the rape victim crazed with fear and shame, the blindfolded hostage blank with desperation ... and on and pitilessly on ... the inventory is unending and unmitigated.

Without doubt we sense we are living in a God-forsaken world. God seems absent or non-existent or, at best, distant, uncaring and unwilling to be involved. We stare nihilism in the face and find no loving eyes return our gaze in a world without God. The irrationality of evil and the randomness of suffering make pain so much harder to bear. Why now? Why me? Why my child? Why no answers to prayer? Why do the innocent suffer? Why do the wicked prosper? 'How long?' – is the martyr's cry; why the delay? And the final default position: What's the point of it all? Yet we still complain as if responding to an instinctive need to know and an inbuilt demand for explanation. So stung by blatant injustice, seared by perplexity, we clamour with raw emotions for real reasons, we claw for a scrap of meaning in the madness. Our only hope is to be found in the fact that Jesus, our Saviour also asked 'Why?'

As Frederick Dale Bruner points out: '… when Jesus died asking questions, we learn that Jesus not only took on our flesh and blood but also our nervous systems. He came not only giving us answers; he came also asking our questions and questions seem weaker than exclamations.' But then, as Bruner adds, 'Jesus has been redefining strength his whole life.'[1]

From deep within His consciousness rise unbidden the stored away memories of Scripture – in this case, Psalm 22. Psalm 22 is the song of a righteous sufferer which finds an echo in many hearts. The victim's pain is acute; no one is answering prayer, no one is offering help (Psa. 22:2,11). The mere fact of His quoting a psalm which expresses common if unusually severe pain, encourages us to believe that Jesus shares fully in all our own God-forsaken experiences. Every aspect of the psalm resonates with crucifixion details. Scorn, mockery, ravaging thirst, raging enemies besieging Him. The cry of forsakenness in the psalm uttered again on the cross represents 'limit experiences', where we are taken to the very edge of sanity and humanity. The psalmist feels himself to be on the brink of losing the last vestige of his self-esteem: '… I am a worm, not a man …' (Psa. 22:6). The psalmist scarcely feels human anymore. With the cry of forsakenness on the cross, the incarnation reaches its extreme limit; incarnation can go no further than this. This is the very limit of where becoming human can take you – to the point of losing it again.

In His forsakenness, the Lord Jesus goes to the very furthest reaches of our broken and fallen humanness. His cry, as Spurgeon has it, distils 'the concentrated anguish of the world'.[2] In Peter Bolt's words, here 'on the cross God entered into solidarity with us human beings in our suffering. In the person of his Son, God took on flesh and blood, and gathered up all our cries of Godforsakenness.'[3] In her classic account, *The Hiding Place*, Corrie ten Boom tells the story of her family's trauma in being arrested for assisting Jews in Nazi-ruled Holland and their incarceration in Ravensbruck Concentration Camp. She describes the horrors of such a place and the remarkable resilience of faith. She recalls bending down to her sister Betsie lying emaciated and dying on a stretcher and hearing Betsie whisper: '... we must tell people what we have learned here. We must tell them that *there is no pit so deep that He is not deeper still ... They will listen to us, Corrie, for we have been here ...*'.[4]

Perhaps our reflection on the cry of dereliction can now be taken to an even deeper level. We have acknowledged that Jesus' God-forsakenness is – to use Peter Bolt's expression – *a concrete event in human history*; it really happened and represents a common human experience.[5] Now, tentatively, we need to make the more difficult step and see in this cry not only an external event in the history of humanity but – as it were – *an internal event in the history of the Trinity.*

If, on the one hand, Jesus, in dying, shares to the full our human experiences of God-forsakenness, then the cross is an *inclusive* event – embracing our common suffering. On the other hand, since the cry from the cross expresses a unique wrath-bearing then the cross is an *exclusive* event and Jesus a unique sufferer. In the one case, He is alongside us and acts in solidarity *with* us; in the other He acts uniquely and alone *instead* of us. Bruce Milne acknowledges how terrible our extreme experiences can be, but goes on to suggest that, 'Only once in all history has there truly been "hell on earth" – when Jesus Christ took our place on the Cross and bore the wrath due to our sins.'[6]

So though He shares to the full our human experience of forsakenness, we must go on to say this: *Jesus uniquely bears the full weight of God's wrath and curse on sin and the God-forsakenness which results. This 'exclusive place-taking' matches the 'inclusive place-taking' that we have looked at.*[7] Jesus bears the wrath of God on our behalf.

Biblical images support this understanding.

The Cup that Jesus pledged to drink and prayed to be spared in the Garden of Gethsemane, but which He accepted from the Father's hand is, according to the prophets, the cup of God's wrath against sin (Isa. 51:17,22; Jer. 25:18; Zech. 12:2).

Tom Wright speaks of Jesus being overwhelmed by '... a horror of drinking the cup of God's wrath, of sharing the depths of suffering, mental and emotional, as well as physical, that characterised the world in general and Israel in particular.' 'Evil itself', he goes on, 'greater than the sum of its parts, cut him off from the one he called "abba" in a way he had never known before. And welling up from his lifetime of biblically based prayer there came … a cry not of rebellion but of despair and sorrow, yet still a despair that, having lost contact with God, still asks God why this should be.'[8] The cup our sins had mingled Jesus now drinks to the dregs on the cross, with all its bitter aftertaste of God-forsakenness.

Baptism as a metaphor tells the same story. The baptism which Jesus pledges to undergo (Mark 10:38) and for which His own baptism was – as it were prophetically – a trial run, is also an image of judgment and wrath in Psalm 69 where it is linked to the hiding of God's face (Psa. 69:1–2,14–17).

Exile as curse is a significant resonance here too. The cry of forsakenness may be approached as the bearing of the judgmental curse of exile upon a rebellious Israel. The Torah warned that persistent breaking of the covenant would bring curses not blessings, and would lead eventually to the final curse of exile from the promised land (Deut. 28:63–64; 29:27–28). Strikingly, the text warns that there the Lord will give 'an anxious mind, eyes weary with longing, and a despairing heart' (Deut. 28:65). As the psalmist concludes, 'Therefore the LORD was angry with his people and abhorred his inheritance. He handed them over to the nations, and their foes ruled over them' (Psa. 106:40–41). There is an intriguing document from the Dead Sea Scrolls collection at Qumran, which has the Old Testament character, Joseph, after his brothers have placed him into the hands of strangers, lamenting: 'My Father and my God, do not abandon me to the hands of the nations.'[9]

The evangelists present Jesus as the embodiment of Israel's destiny who suffers Israel's exile under the curse.[10] It is in line with this that the passion predictions anticipate the Son of Man being handed over to the Gentiles (Mark 10:33). 'Just as Israel was once delivered over into the hands of the nations, under the wrath of God, so the Son of Man, the suffering servant, the Christ, will be handed over into the hands of the nations by Israel's leaders'.[11] Significantly, Deuteronomy also legislates that anyone convicted of a crime who is hung on a tree is under God's curse (Deut. 21:23). This covenantal curse of exile from God's presence and land is borne by Jesus and reversed (as Paul expounds it in Galatians 3:13).

The *darkness* that descends over Judah for three hours is also very evocative. It contrasts with the Bethlehem glory thirty-three years earlier as Douglas Webster notes: 'At the birth of the Son of God there was brightness at midnight; at the death of the Son of God there was darkness at noon.'[12] Darkness spoke of God's judgment on Israel. The long-hoped-for day of the Lord, warned Amos, will in fact turn out to be darkness rather than light so that it will be night time at noon (Amos 5:18; 8:9; cf. Jer. 15:9). One feature of the judgmental curses incurred by covenantal disobedience is that 'At midday you will grope about like a blind man in the dark' (Deut. 28:29). Other commentators detect an even older resonance which echoes God's judgment on Egypt at the Exodus. Gordon Royce Gruenler writes: 'The plague of darkness that fell upon Egypt before the Passover (Exod. 10:21–23) falls on the land of Judah when Jesus becomes the final Passover and substitutionary curse. Nature participates in the prelude to Jesus' cry of dereliction as He suffers divine wrath on behalf of sinners.'[13] The darkness here can be contrasted also with the bright cloud overshadowing Jesus at the transfiguration, which betokened His glory and made Him the focal point of God's self-revelation. So here the darkness that falls over the land is clearly symbolic of the darkness that envelops the consciousness of Jesus, shutting out the light and hiding the Father's face. The hiding of God's face is one of the Old Testament's metaphors of relational separation which portray God's disfavour and which baffled Job and the psalmist alike (Job 13:24; Psa. 13:1).

Now as the Father gives Jesus up to bear the full weight of the God-forsakenness due to sin, the 'darkness' is the sign. He is 'stricken by God … pierced for our transgressions … crushed for our iniquities', 'the punishment that brought us peace was upon him, and by his wounds we are healed' (Isa. 53:4–5). The cry of abandonment from the cross, says Thomas Weinandy, was 'no mere charade, but the authentic lamentation of one who was suffering the wages of humankind's sin'.[14]

We refuse to see any conflict in God here. Still less can we detect any form of 'cosmic child abuse' as some superficially now allege. There is nothing in the classic orthodox Christian understanding of this mystery that even remotely summons up the image of an emotionally volatile, trigger-happy God, who arbitrarily punishes a random victim who happens to be Jesus. No, if this is anything, it is *an internal event within the history and mystery of the Holy Trinity.*[15] It is the union of Father and Son that makes the cry so terrible.[16] The hints we receive here of a differentiation in the sin-bearers within the one Godhead becomes for the sin-bearing Son an unbearable dislocation. What is a Trinitarian distinction for us is existential pain for Him. But concealed within this mystery is the mediatorial victory. 'The mediation through Christ and his cross is central and represents the continuing trinitarian construal of the atonement'.[17] It is precisely the failure to appreciate the Trinitarian – indeed inter-trinitarian – dynamics of the atonement which lead to some of the crass and simplistic objections to its substitutionary force. As Moltmann states it, 'The mystery of God's atoning intervention for the world is unfolded once we grasp that the event on the cross is an event in God, and interpret it in trinitarian terms.'[18] Even to emphasise the suffering of God in the cross or to speak of the Father's grief is not the whole picture. Since the Son was not merely a passive victim but an enduring victor, the Father in the apostolic witness is not so much pained as pleased with the Son's sacrificial achievement.

Holding fast to the Trinity is crucial then. Even more so if we consider *the role of the Holy Spirit* at just such a moment when the cry of dereliction was being offered. The Spirit is usually the missing link in our understanding as in our experience, and it may well be the case here. The writer to the Hebrews offers us a clue which is worth following up. In explicating the superior atonement offered for sins by the blood of Jesus shed in sacrifice, he speaks of Christ who *'through the eternal Spirit* offered himself unblemished to God ...' (Heb. 9:14, my italics). In a moving passage, John Taylor ventures to ask, 'What was the Holy Spirit doing at Calvary?' Taylor suggests tentatively that 'in a mystery that we cannot plumb, he must have been about his eternal employ between the Father and the Son, holding each in awareness of the other, in an agony of bliss and love that must for ever lie infinitely beyond our understanding. For Jesus this included both the forsakenness and the ultimate trust.'[19] The Holy Spirit then was *not* the missing link at the cross. Whatever else was missing at that moment in the Father–Son relationship, whether immediacy or intimacy, the Trinitarian communion was never broken because the Holy Spirit maintained it even in the excruciating estrangement of exile and atonement: 'Where can I go from your Spirit? ... if I make my bed in the depths, you are there' (Psa. 139:7). In Moltmann's words, 'The Holy Spirit is therefore the link in the separation. He is the link joining the bond between the Father and the Son, with their separation.'[20] He adds, 'The Father is crucifying love, the Son is crucified love, and the Holy Spirit is the unvanquishable power of the cross.' So, Moltmann concludes, 'The common sacrifice of the Father and the Son comes about through the Holy Spirit, who joins and unites the Son in his forsakenness with the Father.'[21]

Do the reactions of the bystanders add anything to our understanding of what is going on? Intriguingly, the cry of forsakenness lies at the centre of the third of three apocalyptic events – all significant unveilings of ultimate reality which structure the Gospel account especially Mark.[22] The following chart seeks to show this:

(cf. Matt. 3:13–17; 17:1–13; 27:45–54; Mark 1:9–11; 9:2–13; 15:33–39.) In each context Elijah features significantly.

Baptism	Transfiguration	Cross
Heavens rent, dove descends	Clothes white, cloud descends	Rent veil in Temple, darkness descends
Voice from heaven	Voice from heaven	Voice from the cross (Jesus)
'You are my Son whom I love' (divine voice)	'This is my Son ... Listen to him!' (divine voice)	'Surely this man was the Son of God! (human voice)
Father's favour	Father's focus	Forsaken by God
John the Baptist as Elijah (John as Elijah who has come – Matt. 17:12)	Elijah there	'Is he calling on Elijah?'

These are three great apocalyptic events – moments of divine disclosure when we see what God is really like and what determines the final outcome and the ultimate state of affairs.

A clue to such significance – often overlooked – may be found in the detail of how the bystanders misunderstand the cry and think Jesus is calling for Elijah. This may well be – at least as the evangelist sees it – not merely a linguistic mistake but a theological mistake as well.

Tom Wright points out that Elijah was the figure expected as the end-time prophet who would herald God's kingdom. When this expectation is raised with Jesus at His transfiguration, as we discovered earlier, where Elijah appears with Him, Jesus tells His disciples that the expected Elijah ministry has already happened in the person of John the Baptist – whom, He adds, was summarily dealt with. Wright also points out that each Passover the hoped-for arrival of Elijah to usher in the kingdom is evoked in the liturgy and symbolised by the open door left for his entry and the final hopeful toast: 'next year in Jerusalem!' Now listen to Jesus before the transfiguration: *'I tell you the truth, some who are standing here will not taste death before they see the Son of Man coming in his kingdom'* (Matt. 16:28; Mark 9:1). Was the apocalyptic unveiling on the Mount of Transfiguration at least a partial fulfilment of that pledge? Now listen to Jesus again at the Last Supper: *'I tell you, I will not drink of this fruit of this vine from now on until that day when I drink it anew with you in my Father's kingdom'* (Matt. 26:29). The final and ultimate Passover will not be *next year* in Jerusalem but *next day* when the true Passover Lamb is offered up. To misinterpret His cry of forsakenness as a cry for Elijah is misguided but understandable. All the more so if we recall that Elijah routed God's enemies by calling down the fire of judgment on their heads. By contrast to Elijah, however, Jesus does not call down the fire of divine judgment on His enemies; rather He pleads their forgiveness and lets that fierce and fiery final judgment fall on His own head. The kingdom that comes, therefore, is not one that is brought about by savagery and sword, nor even a massive and overt demonstration of overwhelmingly superior angelic forces – not even by God's fiery presence.

In Tom Wright's words:

> Just as Elijah challenged the powers of darkness to that great contest, in which the god who answered by fire was to be God, so now Jesus takes on the rulers of the world: the might of Rome, the law of Israel, and behind both the usurping and destroying power of Satan. And this time the rules of the contest are: *the god who answers by love, let him be God.*[23]

The kingdom comes, then, paradoxically in the foolishness of the cross, where God's own weakness and absence achieve more than man's brutal attempts to do His work for Him. Here at the cross, God's own wisdom made flesh in a despairing question proves to be the practical solution to the mystery of iniquity. Our anguished 'Whys?' would fade on the air were they not gathered in by His heartfelt cry into God's holy heart. Uninvolved? Uncaring? Distant? How more involved could God be than in His own Son to venture deep into the frightening wasteland of His absence and to bear the full horror of His own God-forsaking wrath and judgment? 'And,' in Peter Bolt's words, 'Jesus goes where the many will not go, so that the many might never have to go there at all.'[24]

This is truly an intra-trinitarian wonder that we cannot fathom but it saves us – however much out-of-our-depth we are. *'No pit so deep that he is not deeper still …'*

I will never forget hearing Jurgen Moltmann, great theologian of our time, give his testimony to this when he recalled his first visit to Britain as a seventeen-year-old youth. Drafted into Hitler's armies in the last frantic days of the Reich, the teenage Moltmann was captured by the allies in Belgium and ended up in a prisoner-of-war camp in Scotland. Desperate, lonely and afraid, his state of mind was hardly improved by the guards who showed him newly-taken photographs of the recently discovered extermination camps at Auschwitz and Belsen. Moltmann recalled feeling terrifyingly alone, ashamed to be German, repulsed by the thought of going home and wanting only to die. The padre caused only added disappointment by offering not cigarettes but copies of the New Testament. But Moltmann took one and began to read. Coming, he said, from a non-church-going family, he read for the first time the story of Jesus, suffering and dying on the cross. Moltmann was gripped especially by Jesus' words of abandonment 'My God, my God why have you forsaken me?' There, at that point, Moltmann confessed, 'I found that Jesus was my friend.' Amazingly, at the very place and under the very conditions which threaten to make atheists of us all, God makes believers of us all.

Meanwhile, how does all this work – savingly – for us? In a word, because *Jesus, the Son never forsook the Father so that we are saved by faith – His faith.* This is vital element in His mediatoral achievement.

Paul Wells offers further helpful insight into the cry of dereliction along these lines from a staunchly Reformed perspective by utilising as symbolism the placing of this cry – the fourth – at the centre of the seven last words. On this basis, Wells suggests that the first three words of Jesus (to the Father forgiving His enemies, to the thief promising paradise, and to His mother and disciple giving them to each other) – these first three words sum up what He has been doing *up to the cross*. 'In the first three utterances of the Messiah from the cross we behold the astonishing spectacle of Jesus acting to close down His earthly ministry.'[25] But the final three words, suggests Wells, 'express a different orientation': they are essentially Godward and forward-looking in direction. They 'concern the way Jesus looks forward to the end of his ministry'. That is, the last three cries concern what Jesus is doing on the cross and might further be thought to be the inception of what Jesus will be doing afterwards in virtue of His cross in his heavenly ministry. The point of this analysis is that it highlights the 'central utterance as *the expression of the trials of the Mediator*'.[26] 'As go-between,' Wells says, 'Christ finds himself in his personal experience in a "no-man's land" with a view to doing a work that, by necessity, only he can do.'[27] Jesus is a mediator who can be trusted absolutely because He Himself trusted absolutely even when He felt forsaken. The non-intervention of the Father at this point, the silence of heaven, the seeming absence of God – all call forth a remarkable act of faith on the Son's part who, despite everything, still wants to say 'My God, my God'. 'Jesus does not waver in faith. He feels the opposite of what he knows yet he continues to trust.'[28] Even in the darkest depths of forsakenness, Jesus never abandons faith in His Father. Frederick Dale Bruner comments well, 'The God whose presence Jesus does not feel, Jesus addresses. The God whom Jesus does not experience, Jesus invokes'. Jesus teaches us, Bruner adds, 'exactly what faith at its deepest level is: it is believing in God even when we do not feel him'.[29]

In the teeth of climactic unbelief and divine abandonment, Jesus hangs on to a narrow ledge of biblically inspired faith and trust. It is as if the Father says to the Son: 'You are on Your own from here on in ... You are going to this for Me but without Me.' It is as if the Father can trust the Son to go ahead into the dread darkness alone and to complete the work unaided. Jesus can be trusted to do His Father's will and to love to the uttermost. God forsaken by God and, says Paul Wells, only Jesus 'could have stood up to this soul-destroying paradox without losing confidence in the Father'.[30] *One would have to be extraordinarily pastorally insensitive not to value the theology of the atonement at this point.* Listen to Dale Bruner again, 'Jesus' last words before death teach us the gospel within the Gospel. They tell us that Jesus took on *our* abandonment, *our* questions, *our* feelings of God's betrayal, *our* most agonising experiences, and still believed in the God he could not feel and was surely tempted to disbelieve.'[31]

Renowned Christian novelist Frederick Beuchner tells of the sense of anguish and helplessness as he and his wife paced up and down a hospital corridor outside the room where their daughter lay gravely ill. But when the worst happens or is about to happen, he says, 'a kind of peace comes. I had,' he confesses,

> passed beyond grief, beyond terror, all but beyond hope, and it was there, in that wilderness, that for the first time in my life I caught sight of something of what it must be like to love God truly ... I loved him because there was nothing else left. I loved him because he seemed to have made himself as helpless in his might as I was in my helplessness. I loved him not so much in spite of there being nothing in it for me, but almost because there was nothing in it for me. For the first time in my life, there in that wilderness, I caught a glimpse of what it must be like to love God truly, for his own sake, to love him no matter what.[32]

'My God, my God ...', because Jesus believed, we are saved. The cross is the only theodicy we are going to get short of the second coming. The cross offers us no neat intellectual answers to the theoretical problem of evil but a practical solution that works and saves. God's will is inscrutable and His ways past finding out, but His work in Jesus Christ finds us and evokes our desperate heartfelt trust. By Christ's faithfulness in the outer darkness we have been given – as P.T. Forsyth put it – *a cross we can cling to even when we cannot feel – or indeed – think anymore.* And, blessed be His name, that is enough for our salvation, come what may. 'My God, my God, why have you forsaken me?' are, says Beuchner, the words of 'a love song, the greatest love song of them all. In a way they are the words we must all speak before we know what it means to love God as we are commanded to love him'.[33]

Coda
Blessed are the pure in heart for they shall see God, and blessed is the Purest in heart for He surely shows us God. Blessed is the Peacemaker for He is truly called the Son of God.

STRICKEN DEER
WORD OF AFFLICTION

Later, knowing that all was now completed, and so that the Scripture would be fulfilled, Jesus said, 'I am thirsty'.

John 19:28

Eighteen hours without food or water, beaten, battered, enervated, exhausted, in excruciating pain, desperately weak, He finally gasps 'I am thirsty.' This is the only time during His ordeal that Jesus refers to His physical sufferings. The evangelists, too, are reticent about them, though some Christian traditions practise what seems a rather morbid devotion to the wounds of Jesus and construct elaborate rituals around them.

'I am thirsty' at an elemental level is *a sign of Jesus' real humanity.*

Our bodies are seventy-five per cent water, and we need water to live; to regulate our body temperature and to transport oxygen and nutrients that safeguard vital organs. When Olympic oarsman James Cracknell and TV vet Ben Fogle pulled off the amazing feat of rowing across the Atlantic, they faced extreme danger and fearsome challenges. One of their most difficult moments came when their de-salinator broke down, depriving them of their usual supply of drinking water. On Christmas Day, they began to feel the first effects of real thirst; the best Christmas present they said they could have dreamed of would have been fresh water!

In 1906, W.J. McGee, Director of the St Louis Public Museum, published one of the most detailed and graphic descriptions of the ravages of extreme dehydration ever recorded. McGee's account was based on the experiences of Pablo Valencia, a forty-year-old sailor-turned-prospector, who survived almost seven days in the Arizona desert without water ...

Saliva becomes thick and foul-tasting; the tongue clings irritatingly to the teeth and the roof of the mouth ... A lump seems to form in the throat ... severe pain is felt in the head and neck. The face feels full due to the shrinking of the skin. Hearing is affected, and many people begin to hallucinate ... [then come] the agonies of a mouth that has ceased to generate saliva. The tongue hardens into what McGee describes as 'a senseless weight, swinging on the still-soft root and striking foreignly against the teeth.' Speech becomes impossible, although sufferers have been known to moan and bellow.

Crucifixion was a long drawn out agony. Preceded by hours of torture and sleep deprivation, it came to a hideous climax as the condemned man was forced to drag his own cross to the place of execution, where he was laid and bound onto the crosspieces. Eight-inch nails were driven into his wrists, stretching the median nerve agonisingly over the nail heads. The victim was then hoisted up, and his feet nailed to the upright pole. Left hanging from three tearing wounds, the pain would become unbearable. The ribs are drawn upwards so that the chest is fixed in the position of having taken a long breath. The victim soon begins to choke. The body lacks oxygen, severe cramp sets in, and the victim – to get air – pushes up on his nailed feet until the excruciating pain forces him to drop. This sequence goes on so that the victim slowly dies of suffocation. Body temperature rises, sweat and blood run down the body, blood pressure falls, the heart pounds faster, the lungs begin to fill with fluid, the death rattle starts. Finally, in Jesus' case, He gasps 'I am thirsty', is offered a sponge soaked in wine vinegar, bows His head and before long dies.[1] 'Since the children have flesh and blood, he too *shared [our] humanity* so that by his death he might destroy him who holds the power of death – that is, the devil – and free those who all their lives were held in slavery by their fear of death' (Heb. 2:14, my italics). Jesus shared our flesh and blood humanity to the full, and that is why He is qualified to be our Saviour and High Priest.

But why do we need to emphasise that He 'shared our humanity'? Because, remarkably enough, the first battles the apostles had to fight in the Early Church were not with those who denied the divinity of Jesus but with those who doubted His humanity. They were called 'docetists' – from the Greek verb *dokeo* which means 'to appear to be' or ' to seem to be'. Docetic thinkers held that Jesus was only a phantom Man, and that His sufferings were not real. At best, this inadequate view arose because believers so overstressed Jesus' divine nature that they played down His real and true humanness. As Evangelicals, always keen to stress Jesus' unique Godness, this is always our biggest danger too: so to elevate His divine status that we distance Him from the real flesh-and-blood humanity He took to Himself at incarnation and glorified in His resurrection. John would have had none of this (cf. 1 John 4:1–4).

Gnosticism – a later development, ruled as heresy by the Great Councils of the Early Church, but much favoured in our day as the seedbed of New Age spirituality – downplayed the physical in favour of the spiritual, and so badly misconstrued the apostolic testimony to the incarnation of Jesus. Luke Johnson's point, cited earlier, bears repetition:

> Even more strikingly, the Gnostic gospels lack passion accounts. The death of Jesus is either omitted or touched on only lightly. Their emphasis is on the revelation of the divine ... The emphasis of the canonical Gospels is on the suffering of the Messiah ... In Gnostic Christianity, the enlightenment of the mind enables the avoidance of suffering.
>
> ... the canonical gospels view Jesus from the perspective of the resurrection ... but in sharp contrast to the Gnostic gospels, which have only that perspective, the canonical gospels hold that vision of power in tension with the reality of Jesus' suffering and death ...
>
> In none of the canonical gospels is the scandal of the cross removed in favour of the divine glory.[2]

As Douglas John Hall sharply reminds us, 'One glimpses the God whom Jesus represents as one follows the (genuinely) human life he leads, the relationships he forms, the responses he makes to power, to weakness, to illness and death, to sin, to the demonic ... So, if I am asked,' Hall adds, '"Do you believe in the divinity of Christ?" I answer: "yes, otherwise, how could he have been so wonderfully human?"'[3] We might want to say more than that: but we would not want to say less.

'I am thirsty' is clearly a *symptom of Jesus' utter self-giving for us*.

Hans Urs von Balthasar, the great Catholic theologian, suggests that this word from the cross matches the cry of dereliction: 'The source of living water, springing up to eternal life, of which all are invited to drink (John 4:10–13; 7:37–39) has audibly drained away and become parched ground.[4] Jesus tasted death for every man. What is the taste of death if not its dried up desolation, its desert of scorched dreams, its bitter cup, its foulness, its countless humiliations, its sordid, God-forsaken horror. And He tastes that for us and for our salvation.

In a true sense, Jesus has always been giving His life away, always been laying down His life for others. Now, at the last, He summons His innermost being to His final sacrifice. The effort not only drained His physical strength, it taxed His central energies, drew on the deepest reservoirs of spiritual vitality in Him, so that He exhausted Himself in lavish self-expenditure. Isaiah's Suffering Servant is graphically described as having 'poured out His soul unto death …' In Forsyth's words, it is 'as if the limpid water that transfigured every pebble ran off and left but the muddy bed and debris of death'.[5]

His thirst and the self-giving it represents is our salvation. Von Balthasar notes the 'water and blood' flowing from Christ's wounded side, which shows us, he adds, how 'it is at the moment when he suffers the most absolute thirst that Jesus pours himself forth as the everlasting spring'.[6]

I want to suggest, too, that 'thirst' is *a symbol of Jesus' unquenchable desire for God and desire to do His will.*

The psalms have made us familiar with the image of thirst as metaphor for desire and longing for God. For example: 'As the deer pants for streams of water, so my soul pants for you, O God. My soul thirsts for God, for the living God' (Psa. 42:1–2). And again, 'O God, you are my God, earnestly I seek you; my soul thirsts for you, my body longs for you, in a dry and weary land where there is no water' (Psa. 63:1).

Almost certainly John is suggesting that we apply this deeper level of meaning to the cry of Jesus. He indicates this by setting what sounds like a simple matter-of-fact statement 'I am thirsty' in the context of Jesus' awareness that His work was now being completed and that the Scriptures were therefore being fulfilled. In other words, we can say of Jesus that it was His thirst for God that put Him on the cross. What brought Him to this point of agony was precisely His unquenchable desire to do His Father's will, His passion for the kingdom.

Even Psalm 69, which is traditionally associated with this word from the cross tells the same story. It describes the physical thirst of a righteous sufferer: 'I am worn out calling for help; my throat is parched' – a thirst made worst by his enemies, who he says 'put gall in my food and gave me vinegar for my thirst' (Psa. 69:3,21). But His suffering is suffering in God's cause: '... I endure scorn for your sake ... for zeal for your house consumes me, and the insults of those who insult you fall on me' (Psa. 69:7,9 – a statement already applied to Jesus by John, John 2:17).

Jesus' ministry had begun in sustained hunger; it ends in intense thirst. The self-chosen fast of forty days showed His determination to be the Living Word of God which He embodied and to live by every written word of God which enabled Him to withstand the demonic temptation to choose an easier route. His ministry is sealed three years later in Gethsemane by His costly refusal to embrace an alternative to the cup the Father hands Him. Now He refuses the drugged wine that might have mitigated the pain and distorted His self-offering. His physical thirst, then, is emblematic of His spiritual thirst – a thirst He refuses to slake at any other source whatever it costs Him.

Lesslie Newbigin comments: 'The physical thirst of a man hanging on the cross in the fierce heat of the afternoon disappears in the thirst of the Son to complete the work for which he came.'[7] Donald Senior: 'The cry of thirst that echoes over Golgotha is no longer a cry of torment – as the onlookers wrongly suppose – but a final cry of commitment. Jesus thirsts for God, and he thirsts out of love for "his own in this world".'[8] Stephen Cottrell says of Jesus, 'He thirsts to do the will of God ... He had to thirst for the salvation of the world with the self-same longing of God.'[9]

Paul Wells looks a little further, 'Everything was accomplished and he thirsted for communion with the Father and his own in the kingdom.'[10]

As I pondered further this cry and looked for more about 'thirst' and its significance, I came across a remarkable book by James Nelson, a Presbyterian minister and recovering alcoholic, called *Thirst: God and the Alcoholic Experience*.

Addiction covers a wide range of human trauma, from substance addictions (alcohol, food, tobacco, drugs) to addictive behaviour (sex, gambling, work – as in 'workaholism' – shopping, and even religion). But, says Nelson, what they all have in common, at root, is a 'haunting sense of incompleteness, a yearning for completion, for certainty, a brokenness hungering for wholeness ...'.[11] Addictions are false alternative ways of quenching the deep thirst in our hearts.

Cracknell and Fogle adrift in the Atlantic had – as the old line goes – 'water, water everywhere and not a drop to drink'! Their de-salinator used to convert sea water to drinking water had failed. This seems to me to be a parable of life; all around is an ocean of seemingly satisfying experiences, relationships, possessions, and we desperately try to 'de-salinate' such things. By 'de-salinating' them we hope to convert them from the brackish, unpalatable things they are into what will quench our inner thirst and satisfy the soul. For some people it is sex or money or drugs or alcohol. Take the encounter of Jesus with the Samaritan woman as an example (John 4). In this extraordinary narrative, thirst is explored at three levels: the purely physical, the emotional and sexual, and the spiritual! The woman comes to the well to ask Jesus for a drink. But what is her thirst and how is it to be quenched. Beyond physical water there is living water, and the satisfaction she has sought through sex with five men has not quenched her inner thirst! Only the water Jesus gives can satisfy her soul, and before we know where we are, the encounter takes a startling turn and Jesus is telling her that she can not only receive this deeply satisfying water but can cease being a taker and consumer, can cease being addictively dependent on any sensation or person. Instead, by drinking of the water He offers, she can in fact become a source and giver of life to others – even to God in worship! Three levels of thirst have been uncovered: physical, emotional and sexual, and spiritual! The woman's thirst may thus be 'part of the thirst Jesus felt on the cross'.[12] Even more provocatively, Jesus interrupts the high feast day of Tabernacles where the souls of the devout were being replenished by the Torah and its water-symbolism. In the middle of the proceedings, He shouts a better offer: 'Whoever believes in me ... streams of living water will flow from within him' (John 7:37).

Addictions are at root a substitute for the real thing. They represent – in Jeremiah's powerful imagery – a forsaking of the fountain of living waters and an attempt to dig our own cisterns which all too often turn out to be broken cisterns that hold no water (Jer. 2:13). It is often only when our 'de-salinator' breaks down that we start longing for the real thing. Then we may come to recognise, as James Nelson finally did through attending AA, that 'desire, is at the core of our spirituality, a burning desire for that which promises to bring us closer to completion and certainty and wholeness, a desire for what feels most life-giving'.[13] Then, if we choose aright, we may find the courage and receive the grace to discover that all along our hearts were longing for God Himself who alone can satisfy our deepest needs.

The gospel depends – our salvation depends – on the fact that Jesus accepted no substitutes, embraced no alternatives, but remained 'addicted' – if we may put it that way – only to love and the broken creation God Himself still loves. Listen to Donald Senior again: 'Jesus' cry of thirst is a deliberate act, reaffirming in the face of death his complete freedom and unswerving commitment to the mission God had entrusted to him. He thirsts because he desires to "drink" the cup given him – the cup that will complete the work he has been given to do ...'.[14]

SO HOW MAY WE RESPOND?

Let us ... *reaffirm our faith in this God and this Saviour.* John Stott, in an oft-quoted statement, sums up how all this affects us:

I could never myself believe in God, if it were not for the cross. The only God I believe in is the one Nietzsche ridiculed as 'God on the cross'. In the real world of pain, how could one worship a God who was immune to it?

I have entered many Buddhist temples ... and stood respectfully before the statue of the Buddha, his legs crossed, arms folded, eyes closed, the ghost of a smile playing around his mouth, a remote look on his face, detached from the agonies of the world.

But each time, after a while, I have had to turn away.

And in imagination I have turned instead to that lonely, twisted, tortured figure on the cross, nails through hands and feet, back lacerated, limbs wrenched, brow bleeding from thorn-pricks, mouth dry and intolerably thirsty, plunged in God-forsaken darkness.

That is the God for me!

He laid aside his immunity to pain. He entered our world of flesh and blood, tears and death. He suffered for us. Our sufferings become more manageable in the light of his. There is still a question mark against human suffering, but over it we boldly stamp another mark, the cross, which symbolises divine suffering.

Stott concludes by quoting P.T. Forsyth who said, 'The cross of Christ
... is God's only self-justification in such a world as ours.'[15]

Let us ... *rekindle our longing after God and thirst for Him.* 'If anyone
is thirsty, let him come to me and drink. Whoever believes in me, as the
Scripture has said, streams of living water will flow from within him'
(John 7:37f). But the satisfaction may well turn out to be commensurate
with the dissatisfaction. In which case, more often than not – and if we
are tolerably willing – He will lead us to the place – usually some desert
of sorts – where He can purge our cravings and boil all our idolatrous
desires dry into a searing, intolerable, thirst for God alone.

And the reason for this is our need to ... *recognise that we may well have
to live with a sense of discontent until the final kingdom comes.*

James Nelson concludes,

So we live with imperfection, and our thirst continues. But that too
is a strange gift. With perfection we would have no spiritual life, for
our spirituality is grounded in our thirst for completion. When such a
thirst is not present, there is no spirituality. So precisely in and through
our imperfection, God gives us a continuing spiritual life. The healing
waters ... soothe parched throats but they do not remove our thirst
completely.[16]

That dear and saintly, but melancholy Evangelical poet, William
Cowper described himself thus:

I was a stricken deer that left the herd
long since; with many an arrow deep infixt
my panting side was charged; when I withdrew
to seek a tranquil death in distant shades.
William Cowper (1731–1800), The Task Book 3

But elsewhere he was able to write:

I thirst, but not as once I did,
The vain delights of earth to share;
Thy wounds, Emmanuel, all forbid
That I should seek my pleasure there.

It was the sight of Thy dear Cross
First weaned my soul from earthly things
And taught me to esteem as dross
The mirth of fools, and pomp of kings.

I want that grace that springs from Thee,
That quickens all things where it flows,
And makes a wretched thorn like me
Bloom as myrtle or the rose.

Dear fountain of delights unknown!
No longer sink below the brim,
But overflow and pour me down
A living and life-giving stream.

For sure, of all the plants that share
The notice of Thy Father's eye,
None proves less grateful to His care
Or yields him meaner fruit than I.

Here is the grace of the cross. We can so rest in Christ's completeness that we can live with our own sense of incompleteness, with unsatisfied longings which need not destroy us, but which can even be redemptive if we let them drive us closer to Him to die with Him.

Let us ... *reach out to the suffering Church around us.* For, if we were to ask of Jesus now: 'When did we see You thirsty?' He would answer: 'Not only when you saw Me thirsty on the cross ... but when you gave even a cup of cold water to any one of these little ones because he was My disciple ... you truly did it unto Me' (see Matt. 10:42; 25:37–40). At the entrance to the chapel of Mother Teresa's Missionaries of Charity in the Bronx – and of all her chapels throughout the world – are the words: 'I thirst, I quench.' 'In this way,' said Mother Teresa, 'we want to salute the thirst of Jesus on the cross for the souls of others. In offering drink to others, our thirst is quenched.'[17]

Coda

Blessed are those who hunger and thirst for righteousness for they shall be filled. Blessed is He who thirsted after God even unto death, for He will see of the travail of His soul and be satisfied.

MISSION ACCOMPLISHED
WORD OF ACHIEVEMENT

When he had received the drink, Jesus said, 'It is finished [tetelestai].'

John 19:30

This is truly the end; *tetelestai* – one word in the Greek text of John's Gospel.

What does it mean?

Is it a cry of relief? Is Jesus saying that His ordeal is over? Well, partly, perhaps.

It has been a terrible last eighteen hours. The long night in Gethsemane with its agonised wrestling in prayer; torches flashing in the darkened garden; a glint of steel; a rattle of armour; a traitor's kiss; an arrest as if He were a bandit. Interrogation in the middle of a sleep-deprived night; trumped-up charges; false witnesses; a nightmare of injustice unfolding; a beating by the mocking guards, relieving their pent-up boredom and frustration; a tense waiting for daybreak. Early morning questioning, shuttled roughly here and there between a dramatic encounter with Pilate and a tense confrontation with Herod; mockery, torture, Pilate's verdict; a hostile mob baying for blood; the public humiliation intensifies. Then the exhausting, mind-numbing climb to Calvary; the unspeakable pain of the nails; the withering agony of hanging under a scorching sun; the fever and finality of death squeezes from Him His cry of thirst. Small wonder that it is said that Jesus 'endured the cross', for there was so much to endure; or that He 'despised the shame' – there was so much shame to despise! Now, it's coming to an end. Who isn't glad that His ordeal is almost over, that His sufferings will not go on for ever. So the cry might well have captured the echo of a sigh of relief. And yet, I doubt that the evangelist John sees it that way at all.

Is this a cry of despair, a final admission that He is 'done for', that this is the end of everything and He can be written off? No. I am confident that Jesus is not voicing any failure or disillusionment here. Not least this is because elsewhere in John's Gospel – as we shall see – the word John uses here is used of the completion of a task. So this must be read not as concession of failure but as a cry of victory: 'It is accomplished, it is achieved.' In a word, as in the Greek text, 'done' – not 'done-for' but 'done'.

Perhaps after all, there was in Jesus' consciousness more than merely the first line of Psalm 22. Perhaps He did have the rest of the psalm swirling through His pain-distracted mind? Perhaps the bystanders heard Him croak through swollen lips not only the psalm's opening lament, 'My God, my God, why have you forsaken me?' but also the triumphant conclusion of the psalm: '... for he has done it' (Psa. 22:31).

If so, they were the first of millions since who hang their helpless souls on Him, trust in His finished work on the cross and for ever remain confident that what He passively endured masked a stupendous achievement. In the end His Passion was His most crucial action!

John intends us, I have no doubt, to construe this cry as a cry of victory; Jesus' messianic task is truly 'mission accomplished'.

From the start He has had one goal in mind; it has been His meat and drink to do the Father's will and, as He puts it Himself, 'to finish his work' (John 4:34). Or again: 'The very work that the Father has given me to finish, and which I am doing, testifies that the Father has sent me' (John 5:36). All the way through his narrative John insists that we view Jesus not as a helpless victim of fate but as the chief actor in the drama that is unfolding. So the Passion predictions in the Synoptic Gospels have their counterpart in John's record of Jesus saying: 'The reason my Father loves me is that I lay down my life – only to take it up again. No-one takes it from me, but I lay it down of my own accord' (John 10:17).

How had Jesus viewed His messianic mission? He viewed it as *a price to be paid*: 'For even the Son of Man did not come to be served, but to serve, and to give his life as a ransom for many' (Mark 10:45). There was a redemption price to be paid to set free all held hostage by sin; on the cross that saving service is rendered, that redemptive work is completed, 'it is finished', *the price is paid!*

He spoke of His mission as *a baptism He had to undergo*: 'I have a baptism to undergo, and how distressed I am until it is completed!' (Luke 12:50). Now from the cross, He heralds the completion of that task. The cup our sins had mingled He has drunk to the last drop; the baptism of overwhelming suffering has engulfed Him; 'it is finished'!

Jesus regarded His mission as *a road He had to travel.* In Luke especially we trace *the journey* Jesus embarks on virtually from the start of His ministry which will lead Him to a prophet's death in Jerusalem. Luke sees Him as always 'on the way'. This, Jesus, tells us, is the God-given path mapped out in Scripture that He has to take. At one point the disciples noticed how resolutely Jesus set out for Jerusalem, as if, W.E. Sangster said, 'his destination was in his face' (cf. Luke 9:51). And no one could deter Him. 'Go tell that fox' – He says dismissively of Herod who had sought to block His path – 'Go tell that fox, "I will drive out demons and heal people today and tomorrow, and on the third day I will reach my goal." In any case, I must keep going today and tomorrow and the next day – for surely no prophet can die outside Jerusalem!' (Luke 13:32–33). When the paths diverged, Jesus took 'the road less travelled' which was the redemptive road that led Him to Calvary. Now He has faithfully walked the road to its bitter but saving end: 'It is finished.'

With His special attention to detail, John picks up how often Jesus spoke of His hour (ESV). Along the way, because His 'hour' had not yet come,

- He rebuffs His mother's impatience (John 2:4)
- He avoids open attendance at the feast (John 7:6,8)
- He remains seemingly immune from arrest (John 8:20)

But one day His 'hour' does come. At last, in the Upper Room, He is able to pray for the sacrifice to be made complete: 'Father, the hour has come; glorify your Son that the Son may glorify you … I have glorified you on earth, having accomplished the work that you gave me to do' (John 17:1,4, ESV). Now from the cross, knowing that all was now completed, Jesus said, 'It is finished'!

We can see Christ's achievement as *the securing of a great objective.* In this connection it is important to note an intriguing piece of John's text which acts as preface to our word of Jesus from the cross: '... knowing that all was now completed, and so that Scripture would be fulfilled ... Jesus said "It is finished."' That telltale phrase, 'that Scripture would be fulfilled' sets the achievement of Jesus in the largest possible context of the age-old, redemptive plan of God. The messianic mission that Jesus was successfully accomplishing on the cross was the crucial key chapter in the larger story told in the Scriptures of Israel of what the One Creator God has been doing and planning to do to restore Israel and to redeem His creation. The scope of scriptural fulfilment, as John and the other evangelists see it, goes well beyond mere proof-texting; it encompasses God's purposes from creation, His saving strategy since Abraham, His decisive covenantal commitments made to Israel and her kings, and the hope of salvation and renewal made through the prophets. This is the large-scale, long-term, far-reaching plan of God, which is reaching its climactic fulfilment on the cross![1]

John weaves his whole Gospel out of such rich cloth. From the overture which signals a transition from the first creation to new creation (1:1–18), Jesus is seen as the One who is bringing all God's promises and prophetic patterns to fruition through His Israel-specific ministry and world-impacting Easter triumph. The Lamb of God is offered, the final Passover is here. The age of the Spirit has arrived and is on Him in fullest measure enabling Him to dispense the Spirit in turn. Jesus is the true and faithful Israel encapsulated in Him, the long-awaited Messiah, God's royal Son. The long-promised new covenant is inaugurated (1:16–51) which is new wine for a new age (2:1–11). The old Temple must give way to the promised new Temple (2:12ff). In a stunning way, Jesus personifies all the holy seasons and holy sites of Judaism. In this new day even devout and biblical people need a new birth (3:1ff); even ostracised Samaritans can receive living water and be part of a new kind of worship (chapter 4). Sabbath is a new Sabbath, not so much a day of rest as of restoration (chapter 5).

Jesus fulfils and replaces the significance and purpose of all of Israel's feasts and institutions and so brings the whole Scriptural narrative of the Old Testament to its intended goal and climax. It is in this comprehensive and conclusive way that the Scriptures 'testify' to Jesus (5:39). John never lets up and leaves us in no doubt about this as his Gospel moves to its climax. Jesus leads a new exodus, offering fresh manna (6:1ff), new light and living water to sustain the pilgrimage of God's people (chapters 7–8). Jesus, Israel's new Shepherd representing God, displaces the false shepherds, and saves the sheep at the cost of His life (chapters 9–10). To cap it all, Jesus is the resurrection and the life, ushering in the new creation (11:1ff).

From hereon in, we half expect what John shows us: a new commandment for a new covenant community, a new High Priest praying, a new King enthroned in paradoxical glory on the cross, and in His sacrificial death and resurrection bringing the old Temple worship to its fulfilment, achieving what was always intended for it to achieve – ultimate atonement for sins and the spiritual worship that would flow from it.

All this and more John intends us to assume by this 'knowing that all was now completed, and so that the Scripture would be fulfilled'. No wonder Jesus cries: 'It is finished.' Even as tiny and seemingly as insignificant a detail as the soaked sponge offered to Jesus echoes with these same scriptural resonances. In R.E. Brown's words, 'When Jesus drinks from the sponge put on a hyssop, he is symbolically playing the scriptural role of the paschal lamb predicted at the beginning of his career, and so has finished the commitment made when the word became flesh'.[2] John's skill in showing us all this serves to reinforce what we noted earlier: the portrayal of Jesus as not so much passively submitting to events which are beyond His control as sovereignly in command. Everything moves under the ruling aegis of scriptural mandate and fulfilment. Everything says: This is God's work, and in the suffering dying Jesus, seemingly a mere pawn in the hands of His enemies, God is doing it.

And if we can speak of mission accomplished and objective secured, then we call also speak of *battle won*.

About this Jesus had earlier spoken prophetically: 'Now is the time for judgment on this world; now the prince of this world will be driven out' (John 12:31).

The word *krisis*, usually translated 'judgment', denotes crisis, and decision. It is used in conjunction with the word *krino*, 'to judge' (cf. 3:17–21; 5:22–30; 7:24; 8:16). Now from the cross Jesus can profess to have made good His prophetic pledge. Now in the cross the hour of final resolution has come. The final judgment has already happened in the cross. But it is a saving judgement, as P.T. Forsyth observed: 'In him the world passed its judgement on God, and Christ took it. But still more in Him, God passed his judgement on the world and Christ took that also.'[3]

We see the cross as the saving judgment of God even more when we realise that in the cross the power of evil has been defeated. Evil did its worst and lost. Freedom dawns for sin's captives. The ruler of this world who holds all in his grip is routed and His rule based on falsehood and deception is broken by the truth. It is in this confidence Jesus comes to the cross (14:30). His final words to them as a group are: 'I have told you these things, so that in me you may have peace. In this world you will have trouble. But take heart! I have overcome the world' (16:33).

The cross is the victory. 'The evil world will not win at last, because it failed to win at the only time it ever could. It is a vanquished world where men play their devilries. Christ has overcome it. It can make tribulation, but desolation it can never make.'[4] It really is 'finished'!

And if what we have said is true then *the picture is complete.*

In other words, since Jesus came to show us the Father, we get our best view of God when Jesus is on the cross! Now, do we really believe *that*! In Jesus we read the story of God. If, as Don Carson says, 'Jesus is the narration of God'[5] then it must be true that His finished work is God's finest hour. If we read God's story perfectly in the human story of Jesus because Jesus obediently walks in a unique relationship of intimacy and love (5:19–20) … if Jesus does only what He sees the Father doing and says only what He hears the Father say … if when we see Jesus, we see God for 'Anyone who has seen me has seen the Father' (14:7–9) – then the sight and sounds of Jesus on the cross are the consummate revelation of God.

If we can look at Jesus, the Word-made-flesh, and say: 'This is your God' then we know that there is in God no 'un-Christlikeness' at all. Jesus did not publish a new idea about God, He embodied God as His Son and exhibited His glory (John 1:14; 2:11).

As is well known, John loves to conflate the cross and glory (John 3:14; 8:28; 12:27,32; 13:31; 17:1). The implications are revealing. If the hour of Jesus' death is in fact the hour of the mutual glorification of Father and Son for which Jesus prayed, a startling new light falls on God. We can look at Jesus on the cross and see that the biblical picture of God is complete. The portrait is a finished portrait; it shows us once and for all what kind of god God really is. God the Father in His Son is willing to pay the price to redeem the world He made. God is not first and foremost a God who demands sacrifice but a God who makes sacrifice! As Forsyth put it of

Jesus in His death: '… he colours with the crimson of sacrifice the pale centres of deity.'[6]

In a very real sense Good Friday and Easter Sunday do mark the *end of the world*. At least the end of the world 'as we know it'. The God who had the first word on creation will have the last word. For as Chesterton said, 'The world had died in the night …' and a new world was being made at Easter. Prophetically and in advance Jesus pronounces over it His triumphant 'It is finished.' No wonder our forefathers in the faith spoke so wonderingly of the 'finished work of Christ'.

HOW MIGHT WE RESPOND?

Firstly, let us not forget for one moment that we are saved not by our works whether meritorious or not but by His work alone. 'For it is by grace you have been saved, through faith – and this not from yourselves, it is the gift of God – not by works, so that no-one can boast' (Eph. 2:8). 'The Gospel began its career as a finished work.'[7]

Furthermore, *let us not imagine for one moment that God has no hands but our hands to do His work.* That is 'greetings-card' Christianity. If God did His greatest work out of our sight and out of mind then surely we may suspect that there is a lot more going on than we may deduce from surveying the desultory results of the Church's evangelism. And yet it goes without saying that there is still much to be accomplished. As Father Tim, the lead character in Jan Karon's much-loved Mitford stories, typically responds, 'consider it done'. And so may we when it comes to salvation, 'consider it done'. But this – as with the catchphrase in everyday life – is itself a commitment to further action – both on God's part by working in all things until He can unveil the new heavens and new earth, and on our part as we work with Him and with His energies within us on those small-scale enactments and prayers which say: 'Your kingdom come, O Lord.'

Further encouragement may be derived from a possible reading of what appears next in John's text at this point: 'With that, he bowed his head and gave up his spirit' (John 19:30b). Unlike Luke, John does not mention the recipient of Jesus' gift (in Luke it is the Father). Now John, like Luke, may simply be saying that Jesus 'gave up' His life in death. But, intriguingly, the word John uses for 'gave up' is not normally used in reference to death.

The verb usually means (as elsewhere in the New Testament) to 'hand something on to a successor' and is used, for example, of the handing on of a tradition. Gary Burge suggests, therefore, that John's symbolic eye and characteristic double-meaning are in play here. In which case, John is wanting us to know that as Jesus bows His head in the direction of those disciples still standing beneath the cross (John and Jesus' mother) He is, in effect, handing on to them His Spirit to carry on His mission. John elsewhere connects the giving of the Holy Spirit with the giving of Jesus on the cross (John 7:37–39; and perhaps also John 19:34; cf. 1 John 5:8). From John's perspective, then, the finished work on the cross is not the end but the start of the Holy Spirit's ministry to glorify Jesus before a watching world. The Spirit is the fruit of the cross.[8]

In addition, *let us not imagine for one moment that God's future is in jeopardy or that He is defeated by the way the world looks now.* Because Jesus said 'It is finished', I can do no better than commend to you the confidence of Peter Taylor Forsyth when he said in words I have kept close to my heart for over forty years:

> I sink under what has to be done for the world, 'til I realise it is all less than what has been done and put into the charge of our faith and word. The world's awful need is less than Christ's awful victory. And the devils we meet were all foredamned in the Satan he ruined.[9]

Believers do not go from battle to victory; we go from the victory to the battle!

Finally, *let us not grow weary in well-doing ourselves.* Endurance is called for and given to us to press on, knowing that even with us God has no 'unfinished business' and that He who began a good work in us will bring it to completion at the day of Christ.

Thirty-five years ago nearly to the day, in ending a sermon on this word from the cross, I left with my first small congregation this encouraging word from the famous British New Testament scholar, T.W. Manson; I leave the same words with you: 'To follow Christ is not to go in search of an ideal but to share in the results of an achievement.'

Coda

Blessed are the meek, for they shall inherit the earth, blessed are those who are brave enough to forego their own plans for God's plans, who embark on the risky adventure of accomplishing all that God gives them to do. Blessed be the great Musicmaker who has no unfinished symphonies for those who stay in tune with Him.

SUCCESSFUL HANDOVER
WORD OF ASSURANCE

Jesus called out with a loud voice, 'Father, into your hands I commit my spirit.' When he had said this, he breathed his last.

Luke 23:46

The prospect of death prompts varying emotions. In the poet Dylan Thomas it evoked anger as he urged his dying father: 'Do not go gentle into that good night/Rage, rage against the dying of the light.' Comedians try to be flip about it. Spike Milligan's self-chosen epitaph was 'I told you I was ill'! Woody Allen confesses not to be afraid of dying, he just doesn't want to be there when it happens! So, with fear or disdain or anger we seek to come to terms with what confronts us.

Jesus undoubtedly showed great courage in dying. But bravery in the face of painful death is not uncommon. That is not what makes this death special. We do not have to embroider His death by making Jesus into some kind of macho superhero in order to make His death special. His cross was a rugged cross not a gilt-edged one.

Facing imminent death, it is said, concentrates the mind like nothing else does and tells so much about ourselves. Especially, it reveals what kind of person we have been all along. History teaches this simple principle and clinical research confirms it, that whatever you are in life is liable to be how you are in dying. What you are *every* day is likely to determine how you are on the *final* day. Bertrand Russell once memorably outlined his defining conviction: 'No fire of heroism, no intensity of thought or feeling can preserve an individual life beyond the grave … all the labours of the age, all the devotion, all the inspiration, all the noonday brightness of human genius, are destined to extinction in the vast death of the solar

183

system …' Well, if you live by that bleak creed, it's hardly surprising that Russell's funeral was a largely silent affair. In complete contrast was the death of my friend and colleague Selwyn Hughes, much-loved founder of CWR. Among his many achievements in Christian ministry, the one which was most dear to his heart was his writing for over forty years of the bestselling daily devotional booklet *Every Day with Jesus*. When I had the privilege of talking and laughing and praying with him a day or two before he died, I tentatively asked him how he was facing death. His reply was immediate and characteristic: 'Well, I've written about Jesus long enough: I can't wait to meet Him.'

No wonder Karl Barth famously said that the chief purpose of Christian ministry was to major on ultimate not penultimate issues; in short to prepare people for death: 'It is evident that they do not need us to help them live, but seem rather to need us to help them die; for their whole life is lived in the shadow of death.'[1]

Clearly, in doing the one thing – preparing for death – we are engaged in life-long discipleship. How we face death is shaped by how we have approached life. Never was this principle more true than with Jesus. What makes the way He faced death special is what it reveals about the one dying there. 'His death is shown to be utterly consistent with his life.'[2] His death was all of a piece with His life like the seamless garment He had worn.

His first and last words from the cross were addressed to His *'Father'*. This was altogether characteristic of His life. 'His Father's business' was how He had began to articulate who He was and why He had come, even at the age of twelve confounding – and no doubt irritating – His parents – by insisting 'I had to be in my Father's house' (Luke 2:49).

'He had always thought of himself in this way; not in the hands of men, nor in the hands of chance, but in the hands of the loving and Almighty Father.'[3] Now, as He had anticipated, He has been 'betrayed into the hands of men' (Luke 9:44), 'handed over' to Gentiles for rough treatment and summary justice. But even here, at the last, while pinned to a cross, He evades their clutches and consciously places Himself in His Fathers hands! As He has lived so He dies.

Jesus' first and last words from the cross are quoted from the Psalms. Nor should this surprise us. He met and mastered demonic evil in the Judean wilderness by wielding only one sword, that of the Spirit which is the written, inscripturated Word of God. Three temptations countered by three citations from the book of Deuteronomy. Moving at once to His hometown synagogue in Nazareth, Luke shows Jesus setting out His messianic manifesto in the scriptural hopes and dreams of the biblical prophets so that He could say 'Today this scripture is fulfilled in your hearing' (Luke 4:18–21).

As Spurgeon noted, what was once said of John Bunyan could certainly have been said of Jesus, that 'his blood was Bibline, the very essence of the Bible flows through him'.[4] Now on the cross the psalms which had been woven deep into the texture of His mind come to the surface to fortify and express His faith in the Father in the words of Psalm 31:5. Again the habits of a lifetime shape the frame of mind in which He dies.

Furthermore Jesus had had a keen sense of His impending death from early in His ministry. He had read His prophetic history and knew from early opposition that He might have to walk the way of the persecuted prophets before Him. 'Go tell that fox' – he says of Herod – 'I will drive out demons and heal people today and tomorrow, and on the third day I will reach my goal. In any case, I must keep going today and tomorrow and the next day – for surely no prophet can die outside Jerusalem!' (Luke 13:32–33). His passion predictions spelt this out to disbelieving and baffled disciples (Mark 8:31f; 9:31f; 10:33f). Jerusalem – He is aware – has a reputation for killing prophets, and He soon senses that He is to be no exception.

This lifetime of intimacy with the Father and biblically nourished confidence is gathered up in this one last prayer as He summons His final reserves of spirit and places Himself in the Father's hands.

Psalm 31 was all the rock He needed to withstand the storm: '… into your hands I commit my spirit … I trust in the LORD.' Every line of the psalm resonates with significance for Jesus. The psalmist is ravaged by bodily weakness (vv.9–10); He is trapped (v.4), bedevilled by lying intrigue and conspiracy (vv.13,18,20); He is scorned by friend and enemy alike (v.11). But the Lord provides safety and security: 'In you O LORD, I have taken refuge …' (v.1). The Lord gives space to breathe: 'You … have set my feet in a spacious place' (v.8b). And the Lord provides a strange, secret sanctuary which shields from harm: 'In the shelter of your presence you hide them …' (v.20). So the psalmist takes heart. Despite everything, '… I trust in you, LORD … My times are in your hands … You have not handed me over to the enemy ...' (vv.14–15,8). Drawing on this psalm from somewhere deep within Himself, Jesus finds His trust strengthened and expressed.

Right to the bitter end, Jesus had alternatives put to Him. Matthew's narrative tells this best (Matt. 27:40–43). Taunting words are relentlessly flung at Him on the cross: 'Come down from the cross, if you are the Son of God!' (v.40). On what terms will we believe in You: on the basis of a sonship which evades the cross.

'He saved others ... he can't save himself!' (v.42). What are our terms for trusting You? That You save Yourself. How ironic this is: it was, in fact, the precise opposite of the truth; Jesus saved others only because He refused to save Himself.

'He's the King of Israel! Let him come down now from the cross, and we will believe in him' (v.42b). The basis for our believing is that You conform to our predetermined ideas about how messiahs are supposed to behave. And the final taunt ... 'He trusts in God. Let God rescue him now if we wants him, for he said, "I am the Son of God"' (v.43). If God wants Him? No one, surely, wants and loves Him more than the Father? Will He save Himself? No, He will not save Himself. And because He refuses to save Himself, He will save others. Would we believe Him if He came down? No. It is precisely because He stayed up that we believe in Him.

And so Jesus prayed this prayer of humble trust and confident assurance as if He were about to go to sleep! 'Father, into your hands I commit my spirit.' And so in the last analysis, we believe in Jesus as our Saviour because He believed in God His Father.

He trusted Himself entirely to the Father's hand. *We trust in His trust.* Our salvation depends on this total and complete act of trust by Jesus. And so does the future of the world.

Paul Wells intriguingly links the seven words of Jesus from the cross to the seven days of creation. Like the Sabbath, this seventh cry brings finality to the others. Six days of creation were followed by a rest day. So, Wells suggests, by giving up His spirit to the Father, Jesus entered into divine rest after His labour. Of course redemption goes far beyond the original creation in fulfilling its promise and potential. Wells has it, 'Jesus' seventh word is the beginning of a new creation, and Jesus is the first to enter it.'[5] This seventh word brings Jesus to His place of rest after His redemptive achievement. As Wells wonderfully concludes: 'Christ rests his case, a perfect humanity, in the hands of God.' He died as He had lived, and His trust is the turning point of the world.

Poet and churchman, John Donne wrestled long with God over his protracted illness, asking all the troubled and convoluted questions of 'Why?' and 'Who?' in relation to trial. Commenting on Donne's story, Philip Yancey says that Donne moved eventually towards the question of response, 'the defining issue which confronts every person who suffers.' In Yancey's words, '… will I trust God with my crisis, and the fear it provokes? Or will I turn away from God in bitterness and anger?' 'Donne decided,' Yancey observes, 'that it did not matter whether his sickness was a chastening or merely a natural occurrence. In either case he would trust God, for in the end trust represents the proper fear of the Lord.'[6]

Donne says it well in his own poem.

Death be not proud, though some have called thee
Mighty and dreadful, for, thou are not so …
One short sleep past, we wake eternally,
And death shall be no more, Death thou shalt die.

During a televised masterclass, Pablo Casals told a young cellist – who to many watchers seemed to have played superbly – 'You are playing the notes but not the music.'

So trust is better than explanation. But it is – we know – not always easy to trust. We find trust difficult because it means we have to give up control. However, just as mistrust was the original sin, so trust is the final challenge. In all of the awesome words from the cross – not least this one – 'deep calls to deep'. What is deep and unfathomable and often inarticulate in us finds its true voice in the cries of Jesus from the cross and finds its lasting echo in the depths of God's heart.

To trust God even when our questions go unanswered – as Jesus did – is the ultimate way to glorify the Father. But then our assurance, as H.R. Macintosh once said, is that 'God is a Father worthy of the perfect trust of Jesus.' And because He is, we can do likewise and commit our whole selves into the safe and eternal keeping of *this* Father and *this* Son. You can hear the 'voice from the hills' in the valley of the shadow of death – any 'death'.

I was once mired in a deep valley of sin but I heard the voice from the hills say 'If you judge yourself you will not come under judgment' and 'Father, forgive him for he does not what he is doing' and 'Go and sin no more'. I trudged for a long time through a deep valley of suicidal depression, unable to pray or read my Bible, and I heard the 'voice from the hills' say, 'Just speak My name', and I did – 'Jesus, Jesus, Jesus …' over and over again … and I began to stutter the 'Jesus Prayer' as my breathing became more regular, and time and again the name saved me, saved me *from* myself and saved me *for* myself.

I was, I recall, a somewhat timid child, not cut out for over-heroic action. I identify with Stanley Hauerwas, certainly no shrinking violet, when he confesses that the only reason he would not have been among the mob baying for Jesus' blood is that he doesn't like crowds! Looking back, I very much doubt whether I would ever have had the nerve to go through with being a political rebel, but as I approach the end of my life not entirely free of my fears, I take my stand with the dying thief – which, by the way, sounds much less grandiose, far more banal and, come the last analysis, humiliatingly more realistic than revolutionary or terrorist. With the dying thief – ruined of big ideas and grand schemes and reduced at the last to being the penitent which we all are – I am listening in the shadowed valley for the voice from the hills to assure me: 'Today you will be with Me in paradise.'

The apostle Paul, facing death as he faced life, was able boldly to claim: 'For to me, to live is Christ and to die is gain … I desire to depart and be with Christ, which is better by far …' (Phil. 1:21,23). The gospel had made him confident that death has no dominion because death had no mastery over Jesus (Rom. 6:9). Bonhoeffer's last recorded words are justly famous, spoken as he was about to be taken out to be cynically and brutally murdered by the Nazis within earshot of the artillery fire of the advancing Allied armies: 'This is the end; for me the beginning of life.'

Knowing this may even give you 'life *before* death'. The high cliffs at Beachy Head on the south coast of England are famous for the views they offer of the English Channel. But these same cliffs are also notorious as the place where up to twenty desperate people a year choose to take their own lives. After Brian Lane's wife committed suicide off the cliffs, he set up patrols to seek to discourage others from taking the terminal jump. As a sign which he hoped might make someone stop and reconsider, he planted a cross with his wife Maggie's name on it. One day, he returned to the clifftop to find the cross had gone. Under a pile of stones where it had stood he found a note which read: 'I came to kill myself. I saw the cross. It gave me hope. I want to live. Sorry, but I took the cross home with me.'

That is just what the voice from the hills says to each of us: 'Take the cross home with you. Your name is on it too. Never let go of it. I died that you might live.' So don't count the notes: listen to the music: *Father, into your hands I commit my spirit …'*

Coda
Blessed are the poor in spirit, for theirs is the kingdom of heaven; blessed are those who leave life as they arrived, in the care of another; blessed are they who, having begun life involuntarily entrusted to an earthly mother's arms, end it with willing commitment in their heavenly Father's hands.

VANTAGE POINT
MOUNTAIN OF TRIUMPH

vantage point – a position of superiority that offers an overall view of a scene or situation.

dictionary definition

Then the eleven disciples went to Galilee, to the mountain where Jesus had told them to go.

Matthew 28:16

Is the mountain to which Jesus directs His disciples post-Easter the same mountain from which He gave the Sermon on the Mount? We cannot be sure but it is an appealing idea. Since the 'Great Commission' – as it is known – gives a central place to the commands and teaching of Jesus, locating the Commission on the same mountain where Jesus gave that teaching in the Sermon is an attractive thought and makes sense. Of course, as before, this is not merely a matter of geography. Matthew consistently uses 'mountain settings' to provide typological and theological colour to his narrative. This makes it likely that with this final reference to a 'mountain' scene, Matthew intends us to hear once again echoes of Sinai and Zion – Mount Sinai with reference to commandments and teaching and Mount Zion with its resonances of authority, kingship and worship.

Let's start with worship and the remarkable devotion shown to a man who only three years previously had been an unknown jobbing builder from up-country Galilee. Matthew's word for 'worship' implies more than saying flattering things about someone or voicing adulation to their face, this could be no more than fawning. Nor is this simply the knee-jerk reaction to a 'resurrected wonder-kid' who has jumped out of the blue like a man from Mars. Jesus is Someone they have known and loved, with whom they have walked and eaten meals, with whom they have argued and who they have observed at close quarters with amazement and incredulity. This is Someone whose messianic claims and outrageous Passion predictions have been vindicated. As Michael Polanyi showed us, all objects of study deserve the relational response appropriate to them if we are to gain knowledge of them. Most objects we observe, whether animate or inanimate are 'known' by a scientific approach that analyses and studies them. But God is not an 'object' we can observe in this way, and in His infinite mystery and transcendence calls forth a different stance, a different way of knowing – one that involves respect, even faith, even love, even worship. So Matthew's word for 'worship' rightly involves the same kind of response from all the disciples that the special three disciples had made to the vision of God's glory and the voice of God from the bright cloud – they fell on their faces, bowing to the ground in adoration. It is *'godness'* not mere strangeness they are reacting to. 'But some doubted' (v.11) – what are we to make of that?

My first reflection is this: *doubt keeps worship honest.*

All the disciples are involved here – 'some' is not in the original text. But what does 'doubted' tell us of their state of mind. It is unlikely that we should connect their attitude with modern, post-Enlightenment atheism or even agnosticism. There *were* those in Jesus' day among the Greek-trained philosophers and among the Jewish religious leaders – the Sadducees spring to mind – who had rational and ideological objections to the notion of resurrection in the same way as moderns do. First-century thinkers were not naturally more gullible because they lived in a pre-scientific era.

Rather, what Matthew records is evidence of open-mouthed incredulity not close-mindedness on the part of the disciples. Theirs is a humble recognition of mystery rather than an imposition of scepticism. This is disbelieving joy not unbelieving prejudice (Luke 24:41). It is a vital aspect of a healthy faith. I am convinced of the ongoing need to heed the advice of the poet W.H. Auden when he said, '… unless you can say "there must be some mistake", then you are mistaken!' Only those who react to the event of Easter by feeling 'this is too good to be true' come to realise that it is 'too good *not* to be true'.

So the resurrection vantage-point encourages Christians to leave room for mystery and uncertainty. As Mark Allan Powell expresses it, this 'mystery is what allows … worshippers who know that they do not know everything and who do not need to know everything to recognise that they are in the presence of God'.[1] In this way, Powell suggests, worship is kept free of self-satisfaction and superficiality and disciples of Jesus are kept grounded in reality. Faith is not promised absolute certainty. Overly-dogmatic believers go wrong at this point, too eager to have every question answered and every loose end nailed down with fundamentalist inerrancy. They fall into the same trap as their atheistic opponents. But because we are not sure of *everything* does not mean we are not sure of *something*. Absolute certainty is not ours to possess; only God has that. What we can have is absolute confidence in *His absolute certainty*. We trust in His trust.

Doubt is not merely inevitable as if it were a faultline in the Christian mind; doubt is essential to maintaining a healthy Christian mind. Christian doubt helps us within the circle of the Church in the ongoing task of 'discerning the spirits' and being preserved from sharks and imposters who claim Christ's name and cause in the publicity handouts. In this way, Christian doubt serves as a quality control on our own faith, saving us from being gullible. Furthermore, doubt helps us to 'think Christianly' when it comes to evaluating the ideas and propaganda which bombard our minds from outside the Church. Acclaimed Christian novelist, Flannery O'Connor once remarked that it was doubt that preserved her Christian faith when she first went away to university by making her question the flagrant secularism thrown at it. So in resurrection-mode of thinking we can afford to sit light to over-dogmatism and at the same time to 'doubt our doubts'. Thinking like this will make us relentlessly suspicious of spin and 'hype', even when – particularly when – it comes with a Christian label. At the same time, we can be genuinely open to the 'newness' generated by resurrection and can expect to be joyfully surprised at every turn of the road. The miracle of resurrection, then, is not calling Christians *not to think*. Quite the reverse. It is calling us to think more deeply, more Christianly, more rigorously, more self-critically, more counter-culturally, more wonderingly, more worshipfully about everything. We should never lose the wonder of discovery, that fear of the Lord that is the end of arrogant intellectualism and the beginning of wisdom and a life-long curiosity about the mysteries of grace.

My second reflection is this: *discipleship keeps authority Christlike*. 'All authority ... has been given to me ... Therefore go and make disciples ...' Jesus' commands, spoken on a mountain, recall Moses on the verge of the promised land reiterating the Law to the Israelites poised to enter and take possession of it. His words also strongly echo the royal tradition of the king ruling from Mount Zion and Daniel 7:13–14 where the Son of Man is vindicated after suffering by being given dominion, glory and a kingdom, and promised the allegiance of the nations. The scope of this authority – all nations – also consciously connects with the foundational promise made to Abraham that through him all the families of the earth will be blessed (Gen. 12:1–3; cf. Matt. 1:1; 8:11; Rev. 7:9). And, as Chris Wright says, 'The Great Commission ... could even be regarded as the promulgation of the new covenant by the *risen* Jesus, just as his words at the Last Supper were the institution of the new covenant in relation to his *death*'. Greg Beale speaks of the disciples being 'commissioned as a representative bridgehead of the new humanity, the New Israel' and of the Great Commission being a renewal of the creation mandate given to Adam.[2] New Moses, new covenant, new David, new Adam, new creation – a profusion of rich biblical images come together as Jesus makes known His authority to His disciples.

Discipleship is a necessary outcome of authority. Jesus makes the astonishing claim that He has been entrusted with full and final authority in all the realms over which God is Creator. This in itself often seems 'too good to be true', so much is the evidence in our world against it. But our puzzlement over how to match the undisputed lordship of Jesus that we confess to the unsubjugated world we live in is already a clue as to how that authority operates. That is, slowly, incrementally, non-violently, non-coercively: with the infinite patience of the cross that subverts received wisdom and with the ingenuity of the resurrection that – like grass springing up through cracks in concrete – finds ways to initiate life through the deadest of hardened-over disappointment. Everywhere, in every age, the lordly rule of Jesus confounds the principalities and powers-that-be, undermines their assumed claims to control, and raises up faithful dissidents and holy fools, saints 'in ordinary' and martyrs 'in extraordinary' who defy the odds and sign the kingdom in. Discipleship is the necessary corollary to how the authority of Jesus works. It involves practising all that Jesus commanded us to be and do – not least in the Sermon on the Mount (Matt. 25:20).

A firmer commitment to 'making disciples' might have saved the Church both ancient and modern from major errors. For example, *prioritising discipleship might have saved the Church from the error of confusing Christ's authority with its own.* That Jesus is Lord does not mean that Christians can control history or make it turn out the way they see fit. Discipleship is not about wielding power but about acknowledging the authority of the Servant King. Not about following a programme but following a Person. Not about maintaining the status quo but about fomenting a silent but steady revolution.

Sadly, too soon after the centuries of initial growth in the post-apostolic era, the Church relaxed the need for thoroughgoing discipleship. And when 'making disciples' the 'Jesus way' slips down the Church's agenda, the temptation grows for Christians to seize power, to promote state religion, to be satisfied with being chaplain to the culture and to relish the chance to make the rules. A real willingness to embrace discipleship and a refusal to relegate the plain commands and teaching of Jesus to an idealistic 'otherplace', might have spared the world Constantinianism, the Crusades and Inquisitions – whether Catholic or otherwise – which have tried to impose morality by legislation or to enforce conversion at the point of a sword. This is not how the authority of the Lamb on the throne is meant to work. It is a far cry from the Sermon on the Mount or the words from the cross.

Another error which discipleship might have avoided is a more modern and more evangelical one. *A firmer commitment to 'making disciples' might have saved the Church from superficial evangelism.* In its heartfelt, God-given, cross-generated passion for the lost, Evangelicalism has led the quest for personal conversions. Millions have just cause to be thankful for this and for contemporary initiatives, such as Alpha, that are inspiring a new zeal for evangelism. But too much evidence exists that the 'back door' of the Church is as wide, if not wider, than the 'front door', for questions not to be raised about how deep the 'conversions' go. The drop-out rate is alarming even where, perhaps especially where, the intake is notable. Might not one reason be the demise of discipleship?

A recurrent debate – renewed a few years back – concerns what cliché lovers term 'lordship theology'. One wonders how the debate ever got started but it involved the unapostolic idea that you can know Jesus as Saviour without submitting to Him as Lord – a theological perversion which is often foisted onto the dying thief for support! A more unsustainable or alien notion never crept over the borders of orthodoxy than this one. This is an extreme example but it highlights a perennial danger within Evangelical Christianity. Under pressure for church growth, it is difficult to resist the temptation to go for quick-fix evangelism and to fast-track conversions. As the old adage went: to opt for decisions rather than disciples. Failure here results in the current scandal of supposedly 'born-again' people – whether in the United States or elsewhere – who continue to live lives which in all significant respects are virtually indistinguishable from their pagan neighbours, except they 'do' church at weekends. Nor will the promotion of celebrity Christians fill the gap or make us any more convincing. Discipleship is *slow*-business not 'show-business'. The pragmatic rush for results has a predictable outcome: superficiality. To repeat: the way the authority of Christ works in the world is slow and incremental. Discipleship is intended to demonstrate how that lordship works. Discipleship will necessarily be time-consuming and labour-intensive, involving the gradual business of getting to know people and mentoring them over time into the words and ways of Jesus. It will involve teaching a new language – not the 'language of Zion' which is easy to parody – but the counter-cultural *lingua franca* of the kingdom of God with its strange terminology of servanthood, humility, endurance, truth-telling, forgiveness and so on. On this account, evangelism is more of an educational process than an evangelistic crisis. If there is a critical point, then it is arrived at in *baptism*, construed as death to an old self-determined way of living and the beginning of a discipled life. Baptism is both the long-term goal of evangelism and a drastic initiation into the life-long learning adventure of becoming truly human again; of taking on the shape of the gospel and the likeness of Christ.

Having the resurrection vantage-point gives us a superior vantage-point but does not make *us superior* to other people. To be a disciple means to take orders from Jesus. And Christians never stop being disciples, never stop being learners, never stop being students, never stop being trainees, never graduate to disdainful heights of advanced knowledge. Maturity is called for in discipleship but it means to see Christ more clearly, to love Him more dearly and to follow Him more nearly. Discipleship is not about showing how right Christians are about ethics or morality – nor for that matter how *right-wing* they are about politics and social issues! Discipleship is 'the Jesus way' to demonstrate how the triumph of the Crucified truly works in a world that as yet does not acknowledge His lordship (hence Phil. 2:1–4 arises out of 2:5–11). It works when the Sermon on the Mount is implemented in those who have died with Christ and come alive to His risen authority as Lord. Only discipleship keeps authority Christlike.

My third reflection: *Christ's authority extends to all nations for all time.* As has been rightly said: Christians do not go to make Jesus Lord, they go because He already is Lord. They go to make disciples of 'all nations' until the 'end' of time not because – as is often alleged – they presume the right to tell other people how to believe, but because they dare not deny the world the truth or deprive it of such good news. But the Great Commission is far more than a 'get up and go' rallying call. It sows the seeds of what – for want of a better term – we may call *an entire Christian world-view*.

Disciples are those who are privileged to see things from a new vantage-point and know that the world is under new management; no longer is Caesar lord but 'Jesus is Lord' and He is alive and well and reigning. A Christian world-view starts with the fact and reality of *the resurrection of Jesus Christ from the dead*. Critics – ancient and modern – sneeringly say that the resurrection of Jesus cannot be fitted into their understanding of how the world works. Christians can only agree! The resurrection of Jesus is outside everyone's frame of reference. The resurrection never did and never will fit into a rationalistic or closed-system view of the world. That is because *the resurrection of Jesus is the starting-point of an entirely new way of looking at the world.*

And *from this vantage point even the cross looks different.* What seemed a failure was in fact an achievement. No one needs to realise this more than Christians, for we often go wrong at this point. The resurrection did not turn an apparent defeat into a victory, as if it were the happy ending to a tragic but thankfully brief episode. No: the resurrection reveals that the cross *was* the victory. It was there at the cross – in the apparent defeat – that sin was atoned for, the devil discredited, the powers dethroned and death overcome.

Furthermore, the resurrection did not cancel out the cross for Christians – as if Jesus did all the dying and now we do all the living on the resurrection side of things. On the contrary, the resurrection endorsed the cross-bearing way, as *the* way to live life to the full, the way Jesus did. Paul understood the order of things better than anyone when he prayed: '… that I may know him and the power of his resurrection, and may share his sufferings, becoming like him in his death, that by any means possible I may attain the resurrection from the dead' (Phil. 3:10–11, ESV). The spiritual logic clear. The resurrection of Jesus illuminates the cross as the Christlike and cruciform way of living, and empowers one to enter more fully into it.

The vantage point of resurrection, then, enables disciples to see the cross differently and in so doing to see the world, and their place in it, in a wholly new light. *The cross is a whole new way of looking at God and at ourselves, at our world and what makes this world work.*

Since the cross in every way *cuts across* accepted norms, it cannot fail to be counter-cultural. 'Jews demand miraculous signs and Greeks look for wisdom, but we preach Christ crucified: a stumbling-block to Jews and foolishness to the Gentiles, but to those whom God has called, both Jews and Greeks, Christ the power of God and the wisdom of God' (1 Cor. 1:22–24). Richard Hays comments:

> 'Christian apologetics, if it is to be done at all, cannot proceed in such a way that we identify the culture's questions and then provide satisfying 'answers'… In fact, according to Paul, neither Jews nor Greeks will get the answers they seek. What we have to offer, instead, is the story of Jesus. To believe that story is to find one's whole life reframed, one's questions radically reformulated. Therefore, much of the work of Christian apologetics will be to say to people: 'No, you are asking the wrong questions, looking for the wrong thing.'[3]

What the world means by power and wisdom is radically redefined by the cross of Jesus. Sin is exposed for what it is – a self-protective or self-promoting preference for darkness over light; evil is exposed as the futile attempt to kill God; the powers are exposed for their ruinous determination to run the world without Him; death's all-oppressive grip is broken and the ghosts of fear that stalk our death-haunted world are exorcised and robbed of victims.

From this vantage-point, on the mountain of resurrection victory, the *teaching of Jesus* no longer looks an impossible ideal but the only way to life a truly human life like Jesus. Jesus wants to remake repentant sinners into disciples who will do 'everything [he has] commanded' (Matt. 28:20). The Sermon on the Mount is a kingdom manifesto that can now be put into effect in 'disciples of all nations' (v.19).

In this regard it is worth pointing out that while Christian mission seeks to respect national differences, it nevertheless, humbly but defiantly, acknowledges a supra-national authority. Christians will seek to incarnate themselves (as their Lord did) in actual human conditions and be sensitive to local culture (as Paul did cf. 1 Cor. 9:19–24) but will refuse to assimilate to any cultural norms or conform to any particular context. The gospel does transcribe into a variety of settings but Christians serve a transnational Lord of all space. The world has a new 'Time Lord' proclaimed in a cross-generational gospel. A plethora of voices now tell us that the world has altered so unrecognisably in a postmodern, post-Christendom, post-everything era that all bets are off as to the likelihood of their being one story for one world. But as Stanley Hauerwas said in reply to those who said that 9/11 had changed the world: 'Christians do not believe that September 11th 2001 changed the world because the world was changed in 33 A.D.' Furthermore, Hauerwas maintained, 'We ... Christians believe we can only know what happened on September 11th 2001 because God acted decisively on behalf of the world in 33 A.D.'[4] And 'we can only know what happened' in our modern world, because we are looking at that world from the vantage-point of the Easter Jesus. And only by looking to Him and listening to Him can we hope to find a better way of 'loving' our enemies than by bombing them into oblivion.

All authority belongs to Jesus ... all nations must yield up disciples ... all that Jesus has commanded is the standard of truth ... and all this in every age and intellectual climate until the world's end! There is something deeply radical here – in the true sense of deeply-rooted – that survives the frosts of cultural mood swings, that resists niche-marketing and fashionable re-branding. Here is something comprehensive, universal, exclusive, authoritative, trans-cultural and cross-generational – enough here to affront virtually all postmodern sensitivities! And yet, at the same time, this world-view and the gospel from which it derives is rooted firmly in what postmodernity demands – a very particularised and localised narrative about one special Person. Following Him whenever and wherever He calls you is what discipleship will always be about.

And the 'always' prompts my final reflection: *presence makes delay bearable, mission possible and discipleship enjoyable.*

'And surely I am with you always ...' (Matt. 28:20). I admit to being haunted as much as consoled by that 'always'. It betokens a long stretch ... a horizonless landscape ... no quick return ... the 'long march' of faith ... a discipleship that demands a 'long obedience in the same direction'.

Vantage point, it may be, that we have, but after 2,000 years the world seems smaller and the waiting gets longer. And the making and the going and the teaching and the baptising and the observing – or otherwise – of Jesus' commands goes on. And what is our consolation? His promise to be *'with us'. The presence* – or the snatches of His presence that our inattention allows us to know – the presence is what sustains us. It is a 'presence that disturbs' no doubt. It is a presence – which, as they say – disturbs the comfortable and comforts the disturbed and, more often than we realise, does this simultaneously to each individual who is saved as a result and enlisted as a disciple. Here and there, day after day, among every nation and tribe, ethnic unit or language group on the face of the planet, someone settled in their work and domestic routine hears a rumour of good news, is ruffled by the disturbing presence, feels a fresh breeze blowing and finally hears Him name their name and say, 'Follow Me' – and they do.

And the 'presence' means that His is not just a truthful way of *looking at* the world but a true way of *living in* the world. It is worth noticing that these supra-rational experiences of the transcendent, of the risenness of Jesus, do not initiate an undogmatic, contentless Christian mysticism. Quite the contrary. It is the Risen Jesus – almost ethereal in His otherness – who yet climbs mountains, eats breakfast and calls for adherence to His specific teaching and commands. For all the explosion of new creation life they sparked off, neither Easter nor Pentecost launched the Church on a non-didactic, non-conceptual or otherwise head-in-the-clouds kind of discipleship. The Risen Jesus did not initiate a spirituality that was undifferentiated or unmediated. He planned embodied rites of passage (baptism) and mind-renewing, behaviour-shaping practices (teaching and discipling) for the post-Easter, post-Pentecost adventure He instigates. Can you be any more postmodern than post-Easter?

And who can finally *know where his 'being with us' will take us?* Into all nations? Into uncharted territory beyond our comfort-zones? Charles Talbert helpfully suggests that the Great Commission actually amounts to a *Great Empowerment*. What we have here is an indicative not just an imperative. Talbert cites previous scholarship to show that the expressions 'with us', or 'with you' or 'in your midst' are synonymous and that the over one hundred occurrences of the phrases – mainly in the historical books of the Old Testament – signify the 'empowerment of God's people, individual or corporate'.[5] Furthermore, earlier research made the connection between these formulae and *the presence and power of God's Spirit*. This connection, Talbert argues, is too frequent to be accidental. He concludes that '... the expression "with you" or "in your midst" refers to the dynamic activity of God's Spirit enabling people to do God's work by protecting, assisting, and blessing them'.[6] This is consistent with how Jesus Himself was empowered for His messianic ministry (cf. Acts 1:1). Peter makes the same connections when he declares of Jesus that 'God anointed Jesus of Nazareth with *the Holy Spirit* and power ... he went around doing good and healing all who were under the power of the devil, because God was *with him*' (Acts 10:38, my italics). Additional support for these connections comes from recalling that 'in the name of' – applied here to baptism – signifies not only 'ownership', so that we belong to God, but 'presence and authorisation', so that our baptismal immersion is into the all-embracing life, love and power of the Trinity!

Discipleship from the start was a call to personal relationship and friendship with Jesus. To enjoy the risen presence of Jesus is to feel the Presence, and that Presence not only disturbs and comforts but energises and empowers. And, paradoxically, it is His seeming absence – an absence which often weighs so heavily on us – that makes the Church's mission possible. From His exalted status through the Spirit, the Lord of glory, unconstrained by geographical limitation, continues in the Church what He 'began to do and to teach' (Acts 1:1; cf. 2:33). 'The Acts of the Apostles' is something of a misnomer; it might better be called 'The Acts of the Ascended Christ' in, through, and with His appointed apostles and

Church. He will be 'with us', enabling us both to be disciples and in turn to make disciples, and He will never leave us nor forsake us as we fulfil our mission till the end of time.

So how does Matthew end? Matthew ends his Jesus story where he began, with 'Emmanuel' – *'God with us'*. Through word and deed, transfigured and crucified, *Jesus is shown to be with us as God is with us*. So Matthew ends his account as if he were comparing Jesus to Moses standing on Mount Nebo looking wistfully over into Canaan. But where Moses had said, in effect, 'Go into the promised land and teach everything God has commanded and God be with you', Jesus makes an astonishing Christological claim and says: 'All authority has been given to me … Go into the *promised world* and make disciples of all nations teaching them to observe all that *I* have commanded you and *I* will be with you always.'

'Nostalgia' was a term first coined by Johannes Hofer in Switzerland in 1678. He employed it to describe the depressed mental state of Swiss mountaineers forced to live in the lowlands. Disciples are those who are learning to defy 'spiritual gravity' by living in the lowlands and valleys of our world without succumbing to nostalgia for mountain-peak experiences and without failing to hear the 'voice from the hills'.

Coda
From a hillside behind the village of Missouri in Northern India, early one morning, I once saw the Himalayas mountain range, some 90 to 100 miles away. I watched as the rising sun glinted on the snow-capped peaks in the distance, and knew that the full light of dawn was at hand. I recalled an old hymn by H. Burton which I had not sung since childhood and which I mentally edited even as I remembered it, though most of it stands up well to scrutiny.

> *There's a light upon the mountains*
> *and the day is at the spring,*
> *When our eyes shall see the beauty*
> *and the glory of the King;*
> *Weary was our heart with waiting, and*
> *the night-watch seemed so long,*
> *But His triumph-day is breaking, and*
> *we hail it with a song.*

There's a hush of expectation, and
  a quiet in the air;
And the breath of God is moving in
  the fervent breath of prayer;
For the suffering, dying Jesus is the
  Christ upon the throne,
And the travail of our spirit is the
  travail of His own.

Hark! we hear a distant music, and
  it comes with fuller swell;
'Tis the triumph song of Jesus, of
  our King Emmanuel;
Zion, go ye forth to meet Him,
  and my soul, be swift to bring
All thy sweetest and thy dearest for
  the triumph of our King.

So, as Peter Kreeft says, '"Have a nice day" or "Have a *new* day" – the choice is yours.'

RESOURCES

SELECTED RESOURCES FOR PART ONE – COSTLY GRACE FROM THE SERMON ON THE MOUNT

Apart from older and much valued material – especially by John Stott, Martyn Lloyd-Jones, and Don Carson – I am particularly indebted to the following:

Commentaries
Charles H. Talbert, *Reading the Sermon on the Mount: Character Formation and Ethical Decision Making in Matthew 5–7* (Grand Rapids: Baker, 2004) – extremely helpful especially in seeing the structure and patterns in the sermon.

Frederick Dale Bruner, *Matthew, A Commentary; volume 1. The Christbook, Matthew 1–12* (Grand Rapids: Eerdmans, revised edition 2004) – a rich and profound theological commentary, as indeed is volume 2, *The Churchbook, Matthew 13–28.*

Michael Wilkins, *Matthew, the NIV Application Commentary* (Grand Rapids: Zondervan, 2004) – another fine example of an up-to-date and accessible series.

Special studies
David Gill, *Becoming Good: Building Moral Character* (Downers Grove: IVP, 2000) – I have drawn so much from this insightful and stimulating study.

Glen Stassen and David Gushee, *Kingdom Ethics: Following Jesus in Contemporary*

Context (Downers Grove: IVP, 2003) – large, demanding and brilliant, and set to become a standard evangelical textbook on ethics.

Glen Stassen, *Living the Sermon on the Mount; A Practical Hope for Grace and Deliverance* (San Francisco: Jossey-Bass, 2006) – a very accessible and popular distillation of the above and very useful.

Dietrich Bonhoeffer, *The Cost of Discipleship* (London: SCM Press, 1959) – a classic and a deeply moving reflection by a great twentieth-century Christian martyr. A new edition with new translation is now available: *Discipleship* (Minneapolis: Fortress Press, 2001).

Audio tapes
Darrell Johnson, Associate Professor of Pastoral Theology at Regent College, Vancouver, is, for me, one of our finest biblical teachers now ministering, and Darrell's teaching on the sermon finally gave me the angles I sensed I needed to approach this particular 'mountain'. I am very grateful.

SELECTED RESOURCES FOR PART TWO – CRUCIAL WORDS FROM SKULL HILL

Commentaries
F.D. Bruner, *Matthew, A Commentary, Vol. 2, The Churchbook, Matthew 13–28*, revised edition (Grand Rapids: Eerdmans, 2004).

William Lane, *The Gospel of Mark, The New International Commentary of the New Testament* (Grand Rapids: Eerdmans, 1974).

Joel Green, *The Gospel of Luke, The New International Commentary on the New Testament* (Grand Rapids: Eerdmans, 1997).

Gary M. Burge, *John, NIV Application Commentary* (Grand Rapids: Zondervan, 2000).

Bruce Milne, *The Message of John, The Bible Speaks Today* series (Leicester: IVP, 1993) – the best accessible study available by a superb preacher–scholar.

Classic works on the doctrine of the atonement

James Denney, *The Death of Christ* (London: Hodder and Stoughton, 1911) – a foundational work on which I was weaned, forming convictions in me about the cross which haven't substantially changed.

Peter Taylor Forsyth, *The Cruciality of the Cross* (London: Independent Press, 1909/1957). *God the Holy Father* (London: Independent Press, 1897/1957). *The Work of Christ* (London: Independent Press, 1910/1958). I cut my theological teeth on these and many other of the extraordinary books by Britain's greatest theologian of the cross, and he remains my chief 'mentor' still in so many areas.

Recent fine works on the evangelical doctrine of the cross

John Stott, *The Cross of Christ* (Leicester: IVP, 1986).

Hans Boersma, *Violence, Hospitality and the Cross* (Grand Rapids: Baker, 2004) – an intriguing and demanding book but well worthwhile.

Paul Wells, *Cross Words: The Biblical Doctrine of the Atonement* (Ross-shire: Christian Focus, 2006) – a fine and readable restatement of the classic evangelical doctrine of penal substitution.

Stephen Clark (ed.), 'The Cry of Dereliction: The Beloved Son Cursed and Condemned' from *The Forgotten Christ: Exploring the Majesty and Mystery of God Incarnate* (Nottingham: Apollos, 2007) pp.93–139.

Both Boersma and Wells are especially helpful in providing rejoinders to recent reductionist attempts from within Evangelicalism to make the doctrine more 'user-friendly' to postmodern susceptibilities.

Studies of the Passion narratives

R.E. Brown, *The Death of the Messiah*, two volumes (New York: Doubleday, 1994) – monumental, exhaustive and occasionally exhausting.

Donald Senior, *The Passion of Jesus in the Gospel of Matthew/Mark/Luke/John*, *The Passion series*, four volumes (Wilmington: Michael Glazier, 1985–1991) – like Brown, a thorough study by an insightful Catholic scholar, but more accessible.

C.H. Spurgeon, *Spurgeon's Sermons on the Death and Resurrection of Jesus* (Peabody: Hendrickson, 2005) – a well-produced but inexpensive reprint of Spurgeon's incomparable sermons.

Richard Bauckham and Trevor Hart, *At the Cross* (London: Darton, Longman, and Todd, 1999) – fine reflections by two great scholars.

Studies of the seven words

Older works
Ronald Wallace, *Words of Triumph, The Words of Jesus from the Cross and Their Application to Today* (Richmond: John Knox Press, 1964).

Douglas Webster, *In Debt to Christ* (London: The Highway Press, 1957).

More recent studies of the seven words
Fleming Rutledge, *The Seven Last Words from The Cross* (Grand Rapids: Eerdmans, 2005).

Stanley Hauerwas, *Cross-Shattered Christ* (Grand Rapids: Brazos Press, 2004).

Christopher Seitz, *Seven Lasting Words* (Louisville: Westminster John Knox Press, 2001).

Other studies that I have drawn much from
Peter Bolt, *The Cross from a Distance, Atonement in Mark's Gospel* (Leicester: IVP, 2004).

Miroslav Volf, *Exclusion and Embrace, A Theological Exploration of Identity, Otherness and Reconciliation* (Nashville: Abingdon, 1996).

Charles Hill and Frank James, eds., *The Glory of the Atonement* (Downers Grove: IVP, 2004) – a splendid symposium.

James B. Nelson, *Thirst, God and the Alcoholic Experience* (Louisville: Westminster John Knox Press, 2004) – a remarkable interweaving of therapy and theology from a Presbyterian minister and reformed alcoholic.

NOTES

Preface
1. Dietrich Bonhoeffer, *Discipleship: Dietrich Bonhoeffer Works, Vol. 4* (Minneapolis: Fortress Press, 2001) pp.44–45.

Checkpoint – The Mountain of Testing
1. Simon Barnes, *The Times*, 4 January 2008.
2. Austen Farrer, *The Triple Victory: Christ's Temptation According to Matthew*, second edition (Cambridge, Massachusetts: Cowley Publications, 1990) p.73.
3. Ben Meyer, *The Aims of Jesus* (London: SCM, 1979) pp.240–241.
4. Christopher J.H. Wright, *Knowing Jesus through the Old Testament* (Marshal Pickering/Harper, 1992) p.124.

PART ONE – COSTLY GRACE FROM THE SERMON ON THE MOUNT

Introduction and Outline
1. E. Stanley Jones, *The Unshakeable Kingdom and the Unchanging Christ* (Nashville: Abingdon, 1972) p.149.
2. Craig Keener, *A Commentary on the Gospel of Matthew* (Grand Rapids: Eerdmans, 1999) p.161. See also in typically hard-hitting fashion, John Piper, *What Jesus Demands from the World* (Nottingham: IVP, 2007).
3. E. Stanley Jones, *The Unshakeable Kingdom and the Unchanging Christ*, op. cit. p.150.
4. Charles H. Talbert, *Reading the Sermon on the Mount: Character Formation and Ethical Decision Making in Matthew 5–7* (Grand Rapids: Baker, 2006) p.20.

5. Ibid., p.13.

Surprising Reversals – Beatitude People (Matt. 5:1–20)

1. Richard B. Hays, *The Moral Vision of the New Testament: A Contemporary Introduction to New Testament Ethics* (Edinburgh: T & T Clark, 1996) p.97.
2. Ibid., p.321.
3. Warren Carter, *Matthew and the Margins: A Socio-Political and Religious Reading* (Sheffield: JNTS, Sheffield Academic Press, 2000) p.131.
4. Ibid., p.131.
5. Craig Keener, *A Commentary on the Gospel of Matthew* (Grand Rapids: Eerdmans, 1999) p.169.
6. D.A. Carson, *The Sermon on the Mount: An Evangelical Exposition of Matthew 5–7* (Grand Rapids: Baker, 1978) p.17.
7. David W. Gill, *Becoming Good: Building Moral Character* (Downers Grove: IVP, 2000) p.128.
8. Ibid., p.131.
9. Dietrich Bonhoeffer, *Discipleship: Dietrich Bonhoeffer Works, Vol. 4* (Minneapolis: Fortress Press, 2001) pp.102–103.
10. David W. Gill, *Becoming Good*, op. cit. pp.132–133.
11. Frederick Dale Bruner, *The Christbook: Matthew 1–12*, revised edition (Grand Rapids: Eerdmans, 2004) p.161.
12. Warren Carter, *Matthew and the Margins*, op. cit. p.132.
13. Peter Berger, *A Rumour of Angels: Modern Society and the Rediscovery of the Supernatural* (Middlesex: Penguin Books, 1973) pp.70,89–96.
14. Os Guinness, *The Call: Finding and Fulfilling the Central Purpose of Your Life* (Nashville: Word, 1998) p.221.
15. The quotation here is from the earlier translation of Bonhoeffer's work, *The Cost of Discipleship* (London: SCM, 1959), pp.98–99. Used by permission.
16. Ibid., p.99. Used by permission.
17. Ibid., p.100.
18. Douglas Webster, *The Easy Yoke* (Colorado: NavPress, 1995) p.58.
19. Glen H. Stassen and David P. Gushee, *Kingdom Ethics; Following Jesus in Contemporary Context* (Downers Grove: IVP, 2003) p.42. The thrust of this brilliant and significant book is helpfully made more accessible by Glen Stassen in *Living the Sermon on the Mount: A Practical Hope for Grace and Deliverance* (San Francisco: Jossey-Bass, 2006).
20. Dale Bruner, *The Christbook, Matthew 1–12*, op. cit. p.169.

21. Ibid., p.172.

22. For stimulating reflections on this theme see Walter Brueggemann, *Inscribing the Text: Sermons and Prayers of Walter Brueggemann* (Minneapolis: Fortress Press, 2004) pp.79–84.

23. See Michael Wilkins, *Matthew, the NIV Application Commentary* (Grand Rapids: Zondervan, 2004), p.753.

24. David W. Gill, *Becoming Good*, op. cit. pp.163–164.

25. E. Stanley Jones, *The Unshakeable Kingdom and the Unchanging Christ* (Nashville: Abingdon, 1972) pp.21,159.

26. David W. Gill, *Becoming Good*, op. cit. pp.172–173.

27. Dietrich Bonhoeffer, *The Cost of Discipleship*, op. cit. p.102. Used by permission.

28. See most recently, Ronald Boyd-Macmillan, *Faith that Endures: The Essential Guide to the Persecuted Church* (Eastbourne: Sovereign World, 2006).

29. See N.T. Wright, *Jesus and the Victory of God* (London: SPCK, 1996) p.288.

30. David W. Gill, *Becoming Good*, op. cit. pp.199–200.

31. Richard B. Hays, *Moral Vision of the New Testament*, op. cit. p.321.

Surpassing Righteousness – The Law Fulfilled (Matt. 5:17–48)

1. John Piper, *What Jesus Demands from the World* (Nottingham: IVP, 2007) p.162.

2. Glen H. Stassen and David P. Gushee, *Kingdom Ethics; Following Jesus in Contemporary Context* (Downers Grove: IVP, 2003) p.142 and throughout their discussion.

3. David Instone-Brewer's research is set out fully in *Divorce and Remarriage in the Bible: The Social and Literary Context* (Grand Rapids: Eerdmans, 2002). He has helpfully summarised his findings in *Divorce and Remarriage in the Church: Biblical Solutions for Pastoral Realities* (Milton Keynes: Paternoster, 2003) and in even more abbreviated form in a Grove Booklet *Divorce and Remarriage in the 1st and 21st Centuries* (Cambridge: Grove Books Ltd, 2001).
   John Piper's stance can be accessed most directly in *What Jesus Demands of the World*, op. cit. pp.301–328.

4. Craig Keener, *A Commentary on the Gospel of Matthew* (Grand Rapids: Eerdmans, 1999) p.194.

5. Frederick Dale Bruner, *The Christbook: Matthew 1–12*, revised edition (Grand Rapids: Eerdmans, 2004) p.243.

6. Ibid., p.245.
7. I was much helped by Darrell Johnson's audio messages on this.
8. William Willimon and Stanley Hauerwas, *Lord, Teach Us: The Lord's Prayer and the Christian Life* (Nashville: Abingdon Press, 1996) p.46.
9. Dietrich Bonhoeffer, *The Cost of Discipleship* (London: SCM, 1959) p.134. Used by permission.
10. Martin Luther King, *Strength to Love* (Glasgow: Collins, 1964/1984) pp.54–55.
11. Marcus Borg established this firmly in *Conflict, Holiness, and Politics in the Teachings of Jesus* (Lampeter: The Edwin Mellon Press, 1984), chapter 7; and in his stimulating and more accessible book, *Jesus: A New Vision* (San Francisco: HarperCollins, 1987) pp.86–87,129–131.
12. Bonhoeffer, *The Cost of Discipleship*, op. cit. pp.136–137. Used by permission.
13. Frederick Dale Bruner, *The Christbook, Matthew 1–12*, op. cit. p.225.

Surpassing Righteousness – Spiritual Disciplines (Matt. 6:1–18)

1. Charles H. Talbert, *Reading the Sermon on the Mount: Character Formation and Ethical Decision Making in Matthew 5–7* (Grand Rapids: Baker, 2006) p.108.

The Lord's Prayer – The Heart of the Sermon (Matt. 6:9–15)

1. William Willimon and Stanley Hauerwas, *Lord, Teach Us: The Lord's Prayer and the Christian Life* (Nashville: Abingdon Press, 1996) p.16.
2. George Beasley-Murray, *The Book of Revelation, New Century Bible* (London: Oliphants, 1978) p.151.
3. See C. Clifton Black, 'The Education of Human Wanting: Formation by Pater Noster' in William P. Brown (ed.), *Character and Scripture: Moral Formation, Community, and Biblical Interpretation* (Grand Rapids: Eerdmans, 2002), pp.248–263.
4. Tom Wright, *The Lord and His Prayer* (London: Triangle, 1996) p.15.
5. Walter Luthi, *The Lord's Prayer: An Exposition* (Edinburgh: Oliver and Boyd, 1961) p.14.
6. George Eldon Ladd, *Jesus and the Kingdom: The Eschatology of Biblical Realism* (London: SPCK, 1966) p.57.
7. C. Clifton Black, 'The Education of Human Wanting', op. cit. p.250.
8. Piper's whole ministry is devoted to this truth. See especially *Desiring God* (Portland: Multnomah, 1986).

9. C. Clifton Black, 'The Education of Human Wanting', op. cit. p.237.

10. Ernst Lohmeyer, *The Lord's Prayer* (London: Collins, 1965) p.126.

11. Walter Luthi, *The Lord's Prayer*, op. cit. p.39.

12. Christopher Wright, *Deuteronomy: New Application Biblical Commentary* (Peabody: Hendrickson, 1996) pp.123–124.

13. Ibid., p.124.

14. Glen H. Stassen and David P. Gushee, *Kingdom Ethics; Following Jesus in Contemporary Context* (Downers Grove: IVP, 2003) p.462.

15. Joel Green, *The Gospel of Luke: The New International Commentary on the New Testament* (Grand Rapids: Eerdmans, 1997) p.443.

16. Stanley Hauerwas, *The Peaceable Kingdom* (London: SCM Press, 1983) p.89.

17. Gerald L. Sittser, *Loving Across Our Differences* (Downers Grove: IVP, 1994) pp. 94,101.

18. Glen H. Stassen and David P. Gushee, *Kingdom Ethics*, op. cit. p.462.

19. William Willimon and Stanley Hauerwas, *Lord Teach Us*, p.87.

20. Dallas Willard, *The Divine Conspiracy* (San Francisco: HarperCollins, 1998) p.291.

21. Peter Kreeft, *Fundamentals of the Faith* (San Francisco: Ignatius Press, 1988) p.233.

22. William Willimon and Stanley Hauerwas, *Lord Teach Us*, p.110.

Surpassing Righteousness: Priorities and Necessities (Matt. 6:19–34)

1. Frederick Dale Bruner, *The Christbook: Matthew 1–12*, revised edition (Grand Rapids: Eerdmans, 2004) p.321.

2. John Piper, *What Jesus Demands from the World* (Nottingham: IVP, 2007) p.280.

3. Frederick Dale Bruner, *The Christbook: Matthew 1–12*, op. cit. p.323.

4. Dietrich Bonhoeffer, *The Cost of Discipleship* (London: SCM, 1959) p.157. Used by permission.

5. Gerald Vann, *The Divine Pity; A Study in the Social Implications of the Beatitudes* (Glasgow: Fontana, 1974) p.26.

6. Glen H. Stassen and David P. Gushee, *Kingdom Ethics; Following Jesus in Contemporary Context* (Downers Grove: IVP, 2003) p.413.

Surpassing Righteousness – Relationships (Matt. 7:1–12)

1. Glen H. Stassen and David P. Gushee, *Kingdom Ethics; Following Jesus in Contemporary Context* (Downers Grove: IVP, 2003) p.178 citing W.D. Davies

and Dale Allison, *A Critical and Exegetical Commentary on the Gospel according to St. Matthew, Vol. 1* (Edinburgh: T & T Clark, 1988) p.673.

2. Charles H. Talbert, *Reading the Sermon on the Mount: Character Formation and Ethical Decision Making in Matthew 5–7* (Grand Rapids: Baker, 2006) p.137.

The Call for Commitment (Matt. 7:13–29)

1. Charles H. Talbert, *Reading the Sermon on the Mount: Character Formation and Ethical Decision Making in Matthew 5–7* (Grand Rapids: Baker, 2006) p.139.

2. Frederick Dale Bruner, *The Christbook: Matthew 1–12*, revised edition (Grand Rapids: Eerdmans, 2004) p.361.

3. Helmut Thielicke, *Life Can Begin Again: Sermons on the Sermon on the Mount* (London: James Clark, 1963) p.212.

4. P.T. Forsyth, *The Justification of God* (London: Independent Press, 1917/1948) p.152.

Focal Point – Mountain of Transfiguration

1. P.T. Forsyth, *The Person and Place of Jesus Christ* (London: Independent Press, 1909/1961) p.357.

PART TWO – CRUCIAL WORDS FROM SKULL HILL

Introduction and Outline

1. James Denney, *The Death of Christ* (London: Hodder and Stoughton, 1911) pp.235–236.

2. B.B. Warfield, *The Person and Work of Christ* (Philadelphia: The Presbyterian and Reformed Publishing Company, 1950) p.425. Warfield was writing in 1917.

3. P.T. Forsyth, *The Cruciality of the Cross* (London: Independent Press, 1909/1957) p.19.

4. Jurgen Moltmann, *The Crucified God* (London: SCM Press, 1974) p.7.

5. Martin Hengel, *The Cross of the Son of God* (London: SCM Press, 1986) p.179.

6. Dorothy L. Sayers, *The Man Born to be King*, p.23 cited by Douglas Webster *In Debt to Christ* (London: The Highway Press, 1957) p.16.

7. Luke T. Johnson, *The Real Jesus* (San Francisco: HarperSanFrancisco, 1996) pp.150–151.

8. James Denney, *The Death of Christ*, op. cit. p.67.

9. cf. Douglas Webster *In Debt to Christ*, p.70.

10 Derek Tidball, *The Message of the Cross* (Leicester: IVP, 2001) p.118.

11. Ibid., p.119.

12. P.T. Forsyth, *The Cruciality of the Cross*, op. cit. pp.81–82.

13. Kathleen Norris, 'Blood' in *Amazing Grace: A Vocabulary of Faith* (New York: Riverhead Books, 1998) p.114.

Moral Miracle – Word of Atonement

1. *Daily Telegraph*, Tuesday 7 March 2006.

2. Miroslav Volf, *Exclusion and Embrace: A Theological Exploration of Identity, Otherness and Reconciliation* (Nashville: Abingdon, 1996) p.125.

3. H.R. Macintosh, *The Christian Experience of Forgiveness* (London: Nisbet & Co., 1930) pp.190–191.

First One Home – Word of Acceptance

1. Karl Barth, *Deliverance to the Captives* (London: SCM Press, 1961) p.76.

2. Richard John Neuhaus, *Death on a Friday Afternoon* (New York: Basic Books, 2000) p.35.

3. R.E. Brown, *The Death of the Messiah, Vol. 2* (New York: Doubleday, 1994) p.1,005.

4. Tom Wright, *Surprised by Hope* (London: SPCK, 2007) pp.52,162–163.

5. Dietrich Bonhoeffer, *Meditations on the Cross* (Louisville: Westminster John Knox Press, 1996) p.30.

6. Ian Macpherson, *God's Middleman* (London: Epworth Press, 1965) pp.158–159.

7. From Elizabeth Clephane's hymn 'Beneath the Cross of Jesus', *Baptist Hymn Book*, 427.

8. Andrew Perriman, *The Coming of the Son of Man* (Milton Keynes: Paternoster, 2005) pp.86–87.

9. N.T. Wright, *The Crown and the Fire* (Grand Rapids: Eerdmans, 1995) p.21.

10. Miroslav Volf, *Exclusion and Embrace: A Theological Exploration of Identity, Otherness and Reconciliation* (Nashville: Abingdon, 1996) p.126.

11. Ibid., p.115.

12. Ibid., p.116.

13. Karl Barth, *Deliverance to the Captives*, op. cit. p.83.

Family Tree – Word of Affection

1. Richard Bauckham and Trevor Hart, *At The Cross, Meditations on People who were There* (London: Darton, Longman and Todd, 1999) p.123.
2. Beverley Roberts Gaventa, *Mary: Glimpses of the Mother of Jesus* (Edinburgh: T & T Clark, 1999) p.91. Roberts usefully summarises her earlier book in a helpful symposium edited by Cynthia Rigby and Roberts herself, *Blessed One: Protestant Perspectives on Mary* (Louisville: Westminster John Knox Press, 2002), chapter 4.
3. R.E. Brown, *The Death of the Messiah, Vol. 2* (New York: Doubleday, 1994) p.1,021.
4. Paul Wells, *Cross Words; The Biblical Doctrine of the Atonement* (Ross-shire: Christian Focus, 2006) pp.153–154.
5. Richard Bauckham and Trevor Hart, *At The Cross, Meditations on People who were There*, op. cit. p.122.
6. Ronald Wallace, *Words of Triumph: The Words from the Cross and Their Application Today* (Richmond: John Knox Press, 1964) p. 43.
7. Richard John Neuhaus, *Death on a Friday Afternoon* (New York: Basic Books, 2000), p.94.
8. John V. Taylor, *The Go-Between God: The Holy Spirit and the Christian Mission* (London: SCM Press, 1972), pp.127–128.
9. Christopher R. Seitz, *Seven Lasting Words: Jesus Speaks from the Cross* (Louisville: Westminster John Knox Press, 2001) p.25.
10. Richard John Neuhaus, *Death on a Friday Afternoon*, op. cit. p.95.
11. See Gary Burge, *John, The NIV Application Commentary* (Grand Rapids: Zondervan, 2000) p.534.
12. Dietrich Bonhoeffer, *Meditations on the Cross* (Louisville: Westminster John Knox Press, 1996) p.8.

Eclipse of the Son – Word of Abandonment

1. Frederick Dale Bruner, *Matthew, A Commentary: Vol. 2 The Churchbook, Matthew 13–28*, revised edition (Grand Rapids: Eerdmans, 2004) p.746.
2. C.H. Spurgeon, *Spurgeon's Sermons on the Death and Resurrection of Jesus* (Peabody: Hendrickson, 2005) p.369.
3. Peter G. Bolt, *The Cross at a Distance: Atonement in Mark's Gospel* (Leicester: IVP, 2004) p.144.
4. Corrie ten Boom with John and Elizabeth Sherill, *The Hiding Place* (London: Hodder and Stoughton, 1971) p.202.

5. Peter G. Bolt, *The Cross at a Distance: Atonement in Mark's Gospel* op. cit. p.137.

6. Bruce Milne, *Heaven and Hell: The Message of the Bible Series* (Leicester: IVP, 2002) p.174.

7. The phrases are Peter G. Bolt, *The Cross at a Distance: Atonement in Mark's Gospel* op. cit. p.132.

8. Tom Wright, *Mark for Everyone* (London: SPCK, 2001) p.216.

9. Cited by Peter G. Bolt, *The Cross at a Distance: Atonement in Mark's Gospel* op. cit. p.58.

10. See Hans Boersma, *Violence, Hospitality and the Cross* (Grand Rapids: Baker, 2004) pp.170–177.

11. Peter G. Bolt, *The Cross at a Distance: Atonement in Mark's Gospel* op. cit. p.58.

12. Douglas Webster, *In Debt to Christ* (London: The Highway Press, 1957) p.47.

13. Gordon Royce Gruenler, 'Atonement in the Synoptic Gospels' in Charles Hill and Frank James III (eds), *The Glory of the Atonement* (Downers Grove: IVP, 2004) p.104.

14. Thomas Weinandy, *Does God Suffer?* (Edinburgh: T & T Clark, 2000) p.217.

15. See Jurgen Moltmann, *The Crucified God* (London: SCM Press, 1974) p.149. 'It helps us to understand … what happened on the cross as something which took place between Jesus and his God, and between his Father and Jesus.'

16. Peter G. Bolt, *The Cross at a Distance: Atonement in Mark's Gospel* op. cit. p.135.

17. Colin E. Gunton, *Intellect and Action* (Edinburgh: T & T Clark, 2000) p.129.

18. Jurgen Moltmann, *The Spirit of Life* (London: SCM Press, 1992) p.137. Elsewhere Moltmann seems to speak somewhat inconsistently of a breakdown of the trinitarian relationship: see *The Trinity and the Kingdom of God*, p.80.

19. John V. Taylor, *The Go-Between God: The Holy Spirit and the Christian Mission* (London: SCM Press, 1972), p.102.

20. Jurgen Moltmann, *The Trinity and the Kingdom of God* (London: SCM Press, 1981) p.82.

21. Ibid., p.83.

22. See Ched Myers, *Binding the Strong Man: A Political Reading of Mark's Story of Jesus* (New York: Orbis Books, 1990) p. 391.

23. N.T. Wright, *The Crown and the Fire* (Grand Rapids: Eerdmans, 1995) p.45.

24. Peter G. Bolt, *The Cross at a Distance: Atonement in Mark's Gospel* op. cit. p.110.

25. Paul Wells, 'The Cry of Dereliction; The Beloved Son Cursed and Condemned' in Stephen Clark (ed.), *The Forgotten Christ* (Nottingham: Apollos, 2007) p.104.

26. Ibid., p.106.

27. Ibid., p.107.

28. Ibid., p.118.

29. Frederick Dale Bruner, *Matthew, A Commentary: Vol. 2 The Churchbook, Matthew 13–28*, op. cit. p.750.

30. Paul Wells, *Cross Words; The Biblical Doctrine of the Atonement* (Ross-shire: Christian Focus, 2006) p.163.

31. Frederick Dale Bruner, *Matthew, A Commentary: Vol. 2 The Churchbook, Matthew 13–28*, op. cit. p.750.

32. Frederick Beuchner, *Secrets in the Dark; A Life in Sermons* (San Francisco: HarperSanFrancisco, 2006) pp.101–102.

33. Ibid., p.103.

Stricken Deer – Word of Affliction

1. The details are summarised from Stephen Cottrell, *'I Thirst': The Cross – The Great Triumph of Love* (Grand Rapids: Zondervan, 2003) pp.112–114.

2. Luke T. Johnson, *The Real Jesus* (San Francisco: HarperSanFrancisco, 1996) pp.150–151.

3. Douglas John Hall, *The Cross in Our Context: Jesus and the Suffering World* (Minneapolis: Fortress Press, 2003) pp.124,127.

4. Hans Urs von Balthasar, *Mysterium Paschale* (Edinburgh: T & T Clark, 1990) p.126.

5. P.T. Forsyth, *God the Holy Father* (London: Independent Press, 1897/1957) p.58.

6. Hans Urs von Balthasar, *Mysterium Paschale*, op. cit. p.131.

7. Lesslie Newbigin, *The Light Has Come: An Exposition of the Fourth Gospel* (Grand Rapids: Eerdmans, 1982) p.256.

8. Donald Senior, *The Passion of Jesus in the Gospel of John* (Leominster: Gracewing, 1991) p.117.

9. Stephen Cottrell, *'I Thirst': The Cross – The Great Triumph of Love*, op. cit.

pp.83,86.

10. Paul Wells, *Cross Words; The Biblical Doctrine of the Atonement* (Ross-shire: Christian Focus, 2006) p.222.

11. James B. Nelson, *Thirst: God and the Alcoholic Experience* (Louisville: Westminster John Knox Press, 2004), p.23. I would not endorse all the doctrinal stances taken in this book but it remains a stimulating theological reflection that connects salvation, sin and suffering in a profoundly moving way. Other helpful Christian treatments of the subject include Gerald May's *Addiction and Grace* (San Fransisco: Harper and Row, 1988) and from a more evangelical perspective, William Lenters, *The Freedom We Crave: Addiction, the Human Condition* (Grand Rapids: Eerdmans, 1985). Lenters is especially good on addiction to religion!
A very helpful devotional study of longing for God is Margaret Magdalen's *Furnace of the Heart: Rekindling Our Longing for God* (London: Darton, Longman and Todd, 1998).

12. Ibid., p.24.

13. Ibid., p 23.

14. Donald Senior, *The Passion of Jesus in the Gospel of John*, op. cit. p.118.

15. John Stott, *The Cross of Christ* (Leicester: IVP, 1986) pp.335–336.

16. James B. Nelson, *Thirst: God and the Alcoholic Experience*, op. cit. p.146.

17. Richard John Neuhaus, *Death on a Friday Afternoon* (New York: Basic Books, 2000) p.146.

Mission Accomplished – Word of Achievement

1. I have sought to give popular expression to this in my book *A Passion for God's Story* (Milton Keynes: Paternoster, second edition 2006).

2. R.E. Brown, *The Death of the Messiah, Vol. 2* (New York: Doubleday, 1994) p.1,077.

3. P.T. Forsyth, *The Justification of God* (London: Independent Press, 1917/1948) p.221.

4. Ibid., p.223.

5. Don Carson, *The Gospel according to John* (Leicester: IVP, 1991) p.135, commenting on John 1:18.

6. P.T.Forsyth, *God the Holy Father* (London: Independent Press, 1897/1957) p.37.

7. P.T. Forsyth, *Positive Preaching and the Modern Mind* (London: Independent Press, 1907/1964) p.238.

8. For this insight I am indebted to Gary Burge, *The Anointed Community* (Grand Rapids: Eerdmans, 1987) pp.134–135 and *John: The NIV Application Commentary* (Grand Rapids: Zondervan, 2000) pp.529–530. This reading of the text goes back to Edwyn Hoskyns in Francis Noel Davey (ed.), *The Fourth Gospel* (London: Faber and Faber, 1947) p.532 and I was first made aware of it by Tom Smail, *Reflected Glory: The Spirit in Christ and Christians* (London: Hodder and Stoughton, 1975) p.108.

9. P.T. Forsyth, *Missions in State and Church* (London: Hodder and Stoughton, 1908) p.16.

Successful Handover – Word of Assurance

1. Karl Barth, *The Word of God and the Word of Man* (London: Hodder and Stoughton, 1928) p.188.

2. Luke T. Johnson, *The Gospel of Luke* (Minnesota: Liturgical Press, 1991) p.381.

3. Ronald Wallace, *Words of Triumph: The Words from the Cross and Their Application Today* (Richmond: John Knox Press, 1964) p.87.

4. C.H. Spurgeon, *Spurgeon's Sermons on the Death and Resurrection of Jesus* (Peabody: Hendrickson, 2005) p.386.

5. Paul Wells, *Cross Words; The Biblical Doctrine of the Atonement* (Ross-shire: Christian Focus, 2006) p.223.

6. Philip Yancey, *Soul Survivor* (London: Hodder and Stoughton, 2003) p.203.

Vantage Point – Mountain of Triumph

1. Mark Allan Powell, *Loving Jesus* (Minneapolis: Fortress Press, 2004) p.123.

2. For the notes struck here see especially Stephen G. Dempster, *Dominion and Dynasty: A Theology of the Hebrew Bible* (Leicester: Apollos, 2003) pp.232–233 and G.K. Beale, *The Temple, and the Church's Mission: A Biblical Theology of the Dwelling Place of God* (Leicester: Apollos, 2004) pp.175,198. See also Christopher J.H. Wright, *The Mission of God: Unlocking the Bible's Grand Narrative* (Nottingham: Inter-Varsity Press, 2006) cited from p.355. For a survey of the plot line of the Bible see my *A Passion for God's Story* (Milton Keynes: Paternoster, 2nd edition, 2006).

3. Richard Hays, 'Wisdom according to Paul' in Stephen C. Barton (ed.), *Where Shall Wisdom be Found? Wisdom in the Bible, the Church, and the Contemporary World* (Edinburgh: T & T Clark, 1999) p.123. For my own

reflections on allowing the right questions to be asked, see my *God's Questions* (Farnham: CWR, 2003).

4. Stanley Hauerwas, *Disrupting Times: Sermons and Prayers* (Eugene, Oregon: Cascade Books, 2004) p.5.

5. Charles H. Talbert, *Reading the Sermon on the Mount: Character Formation and Ethical Decision Making in Matthew 5–7* (Grand Rapids: Baker, 2006) pp.34–43. Talbert cites the earlier studies of W.C. Van Unnik and the biblical examples of the connections made (eg Joseph, Gen. 39:23/41:38; Moses, Exod. 3:12/Num. 11:17; Joshua, Josh. 3:7/Deut. 34:9; Gideon, Judg. 6:12/Judg. 6:34; David, 1 Sam. 10:7/1 Sam. 10:6; Israel, Hag. 2:4/Hag. 2:5 etc.

6. Ibid., p.34.

NATIONAL DISTRIBUTORS

UK: (and countries not listed below)
CWR, Waverley Abbey House, Waverley Lane, Farnham, Surrey GU9 8EP.
Tel: (01252) 784700 Outside UK (44) 1252 784700

AUSTRALIA: CMC Australasia, PO Box 519, Belmont, Victoria 3216.
Tel: (03) 5241 3288 Fax: (03) 5241 3290

CANADA: David C Cook Distribution Canada, PO Box 98,
55 Woodslee Avenue, Paris, Ontario N3L 3E5. Tel: 1800 263 2664

GHANA: Challenge Enterprises of Ghana, PO Box 5723, Accra.
Tel: (021) 222437/223249 Fax: (021) 226227

HONG KONG: Cross Communications Ltd, 1/F, 562A Nathan Road, Kowloon.
Tel: 2780 1188 Fax: 2770 6229

INDIA: Crystal Communications, 10-3-18/4/1, East Marredpalli, Secunderabad
– 500026, Andhra Pradesh. Tel/Fax: (040) 27737145

KENYA: Keswick Books and Gifts Ltd, PO Box 10242, Nairobi.
Tel: (02) 331692/226047 Fax: (02) 728557

MALAYSIA: Salvation Book Centre (M) Sdn Bhd, 23 Jalan SS 2/64, 47300
Petaling Jaya, Selangor. Tel: (03) 78766411/78766797 Fax: (03) 78757066/78756360

NEW ZEALAND: CMC Australasia, PO Box 303298, North Harbour,
Auckland 0751. Tel: 0800 449 408 Fax: 0800 449 049

NIGERIA: FBFM, Helen Baugh House, 96 St Finbarr's College Road,
Akoka, Lagos. Tel: (01) 7747429/4700218/825775/827264

PHILIPPINES: OMF Literature Inc, 776 Boni Avenue, Mandaluyong City.
Tel: (02) 531 2183 Fax: (02) 531 1960

SINGAPORE: Alby Commercial Enterprises Pte Ltd, 95 Kallang Avenue #04-00,
AIS Industrial Building, 339420. Tel: (65) 629 27238 Fax: (65) 629 27235

SOUTH AFRICA: Struik Christian Books, 80 MacKenzie Street, PO Box 1144,
Cape Town 8000. Tel: (021) 462 4360 Fax: (021) 461 3612

SRI LANKA: Christombu Publications (Pvt) Ltd, Bartleet House,
65 Braybrooke Place, Colombo 2. Tel: (9411) 2421073/2447665

TANZANIA: CLC Christian Book Centre, PO Box 1384, Mkwepu Street,
Dar es Salaam. Tel/Fax: (022) 2119439

USA: David C Cook Distribution Canada, PO Box 98, 55 Woodslee Avenue,
Paris, Ontario N3L 3E5, Canada. Tel: 1800 263 2664

ZIMBABWE: Word of Life Books (Pvt) Ltd, Christian Media Centre,
8 Aberdeen Road, Avondale, PO Box A480 Avondale, Harare.
Tel: (04) 333355 or 091301188

For email addresses, visit the CWR website: www.cwr.org.uk
CWR is a Registered Charity – Number 294387
CWR is a Limited Company registered in England – Registration Number
1990308

Day and Residential Courses
Counselling Training
Leadership Development
Biblical Study Courses
Regional Seminars
Ministry to Women
Daily Devotionals
Books and Videos
Conference Centre

Trusted all Over the World

CWR HAS GAINED A WORLDWIDE reputation as a centre of excellence for Bible-based training and resources. From our headquarters at Waverley Abbey House, Farnham, England, we have been serving God's people for over 40 years with a vision to help apply God's Word to everyday life and relationships. The daily devotional *Every Day with Jesus* is read by nearly a million readers an issue in more than 150 countries, and our unique courses in biblical studies and pastoral care are respected all over the world. Waverley Abbey House provides a conference centre in a tranquil setting.

For free brochures on our seminars and courses, conference facilities, or a catalogue of CWR resources, please contact us at the following address.
CWR, Waverley Abbey House, Waverley Lane, Farnham, Surrey GU9 8EP, UK

Telephone: **+44 (0)1252 784700**
Email: **mail@cwr.org.uk**
Website: **www.cwr.org.uk**